BREAKING FAITH

BREAKING FAITH

THE MULRONEY LEGACY OF DECEIT, DESTRUCTION AND DISUNITY

BROOKE JEFFREY

KEY PORTER BOOKS

Canadian Cataloguing in Publication Data

Jeffrey, Brooke
    Breaking Faith

Includes index.
ISBN 1-55013-373-X

1. Canada - Politics and government - 1984 -   .*   2. Progressive Conservative Party of Canada.   I. Title.

FC630.J44 1992   971.0647   C91-095625-1
F1034.2.J44   1992

Key Porter Books Limited
70 The Esplanade
Toronto, Ontario
Canada M5E 1R2

Typesetting: True to Type, Inc.

Printed and bound in Canada

92 93 94 95 96   6 5 4 3 2 1

Contents

For Jack and Mike

Acknowledgements

Seventeen years in the federal bureaucracy, during which time I was privileged to work with a number of outstanding public servants and ministers, contributed greatly to my practical education about the political system, and showed, by example, how it could and should work. This book has grown out of that accumulated knowledge.

Several individuals, bureaucrats and political insiders, provided information and advice or consented to interviews on the understanding they would remain anonymous; a number of chapters benefited from careful reading by others who also wished to remain unrecognized. They know how much I appreciate their assistance.

The staff of the Library of Parliament and Table Research provided invaluable documentary support in a consistently timely fashion. I am also deeply indebted to Loretta Craig Taylor and Douglas Tam, two somewhat masochistic individuals who cheerfully accommodated my incessant requests for additional material.

Considerable appreciation is also due to G.F. McCauley, a real writer whose generous assistance in eliminating the more convoluted turns of phrase in early drafts was invaluable; to my editor, Charis Wahl, whose incisive analysis and comments provided much-needed focus and greatly improved the final product; and to Key Porter, my publishers, for their willingness to support Canadian authors in such difficult economic times.

O.K. We've won. What do we do now?
— Brian Mulroney, September 4, 1984

The core responsibility of those who deal in public policy
is not simply to discover as objectively as possible what people
want for themselves and then determine and implement the
best means of satisfying these wants. It is also to provide
the public with alternative visions of what is desirable and
possible, to stimulate deliberation about them, provoke a
reexamination of premises and values, and thus broaden the
range of potential responses and deepen society's understanding of itself.
— Robert Reich, *The Resurgent Liberal*

Where there is no vision the people perish.
— *Proverbs* 29:18

Part I

BREAKING THE RULES

*How the Mulroney Government
Destroyed Our Faith
in the Political System*

1. Creating False Expectations
How the Mulroney Conservatives Set the Stage for Public Discontent

> The Liberals have dishonoured the system and it will never, never, happen again under a Conservative government. . . . I pledge to you here today that our appointments shall be of the highest quality. They shall represent the regions and bring honour to all of you and shall bring honour to this country.
>
> — Brian Mulroney, July 23, 1984

On January 7, 1991, the seventh annual *Maclean's*/Decima poll on the state of the nation confirmed what every casual observer of the Canadian political scene already knew: Canadians were angry — unhappy with their national government and politicians of all stripes. Actually, "angry" is an understatement. The poll results revealed that Canadians were outraged by the policies and behaviour of their elected representatives, from whom they felt increasingly alienated, and furious that there seemed to be nothing they could do about it. Their growing sense of "disempowerment" and belief that the institutions of government had failed them were leading growing numbers to lose faith in the political system itself.

With the country split by the constitutional debate, the economy in ruins, and the social fabric of the nation in tatters, Canada appeared to many of its citizens to be perilously close to the brink of destruction. Decima's president, Allan Gregg, said, "In the seven years we have been doing this research, we have never identified a blacker mood."

Canadians' dissatisfaction with their lot started close to home. One in three surveyed in the poll said he or she was unhappy with his or her personal economic situation; roughly the same number expected the recession, which had begun in April 1990, to be lengthy and "very severe." Yet, when asked whom they looked to first to protect their economic interests, only 27 percent of respondents chose "government," a dramatic decline from the 49 percent who did so in 1984.

This low level of confidence in the institutions of government was paralleled by attitudes towards politicians and political parties. A record 63 percent of Canadians said their opinion of politicians was "somewhat or significantly more unfavourable" than it had been five years earlier, and 61 percent considered governments to be "less effective in responding to people's needs." Seven in ten Canadians agreed that "all [three main political parties] would govern pretty much the same," which amply explains the creation and growing popularity of two new political parties — the Reform Party and the Bloc Québécois — in the two regions of the country upon which the Conservatives had depended to form their two successive majorities.

Even more worrisome than the massive rejection of politicians and governments of the day was the underlying lack of faith Canadians demonstrated in the political system as a whole. In the *Maclean's*/Decima poll, a wide variety of significant changes to the existing system were supported by an unprecedented and ever-increasing number of citizens. For example, 77 percent of respondents wanted to see governments "obliged" to participate in full public consultation processes before making "major" decisions, and 55 percent were in favour of removing elected representatives by petition before the expiry of their term of office — a sentiment reinforced by the results of referenda held in conjunction with provincial elections in Saskatchewan and British Columbia in the fall of 1991.

A third of those surveyed in the *Maclean's*/Decima poll said they were "somewhat or much less proud to be a Canadian than a few years ago." A Gallup survey conducted at roughly the same time found that the citizens of thirty-three of the thirty-seven countries polled were more optimistic than were Canadians about their future. Indeed, the 63 percent of Canadians who stated that they believed "1991 will be worse than 1990" was the highest level of negative expectation ever registered by Gallup.

Perhaps the most astonishing fact about this gloomy situation was the speed with which it developed. Barely six years earlier, Canadians were positively buoyant. The 1984 year-end *Maclean's* cover read: "A Confident Nation Speaks Up," and described that year's Decima poll results as "a snapshot of a nation in a state of grace."

In his introduction to the article on the 1984 poll, *Maclean's* senior contributing editor, Peter C. Newman, discussed the election of the Progressive Conservative party and Brian Mulroney, concluding that Canadians had not merely elected a new government on September 4, but had "deposited their hopes, dreams and expectations on Mulroney's unshrugging shoulders."

Six years later, the Mulroney government enjoyed the support of only 14 percent of the Canadian population. Of those who indicated in the 1991 poll that they were less proud to be Canadian, some 54 percent identified the federal government as the primary reason. A telephone hotline established in early 1991 by the Citizens' Forum reportedly logged so many calls suggesting Mulroney should be impeached that a special category had to be added to the Forum questionnaire. Chairman Keith Spicer noted in the foreword to his report that the importance of this emotional outpouring would be difficult to overestimate. In Spicer's words, "There is fury in the land against the Prime Minister."

A *Globe and Mail*/CBC poll published in November 1991 found little had changed. Despite a surprisingly high level of satisfaction with their personal quality of life, Canadians remained overwhelmingly "fearful about where the economy was going, pessimistic about the chances of reaching a constitutional agreement and cynical about their politicians and political institutions." Brian Mulroney continued to be viscerally disliked and distrusted by the great majority of Canadians, and his government remained as unpopular as ever.

What went wrong? A simplistic explanation of Canadians' massive discontent is their unrealistic expectations. The source of them? Brian Mulroney himself. By 1990, even some of his friends, supporters, and staff had admitted publicly that the personality of the prime minister was a significant factor in the dramatic decline of Tory fortunes and the bleak mood of the country. Mulroney had become the man Canadians loved to hate, a lightning rod for widespread disaffection.

An Environics poll in late 1990 reinforced this conclusion. It found that 31 percent of Canadians believed Mulroney to be the worst prime minister in Canadian history; another 27 percent considered him one of the worst. (Pierre Trudeau, by contrast, was considered "the best" or "one of the best" by 49 percent of those surveyed when he retired in 1984, at the height of his supposed unpopularity.)

Widely viewed as hypocritical, sanctimonious, shallow, and vain, Brian Mulroney has shown himself to be uninterested in policy matters or the public good; he is, however, obsessively concerned with pomp and circumstance, polls, the media, and the legacy of his predecessor, Pierre Trudeau. His inability to accept responsibility, which often leads him to lash out and blame others, as well as his opportunism and fierce partisanship, have frequently created major political crises out of minor resolvable problems. His tendency to equivocate, rewrite history and "embellish" stories has led many Canadians to conclude that their prime minister has great difficulty telling the truth. His much-touted loyalty to friends and his equally strong vengeance against enemies have cost him and his government further credibility. In short, he is a man whom Canadians do not merely dislike, but instinctively distrust.

Mulroney's background may also have contributed to his perceived failure to meet Canadians' expectations of how a prime minister should behave. Just as his excessive partisanship appears out of place in the leader of government, so his business experience as the former president of the American-owned Iron Ore Company seems to have left him with an undying admiration for Americans and an eye for the financial bottom line — attitudes that most Canadians do not share. Few Canadians believe government is a business like any other, and most have a deeply entrenched suspicion of Americans and Bay Street. Thus, Mulroney's focus, appropriate as it might be for a president of General Motors, is seen as skewed for a prime minister of Canada.

What, after all, can Canadians be expected to make of a leader whose principal criticism of their constitutional amending formula was "That's no way to do business"? Or of a man who declared triumphantly that his economic policy consisted primarily of ensuring that the country was "open for business"?

Mulroney's lack of experience in Parliament may be yet another facet of his unsuitability to govern. Having been elected leader of the Conservative party in 1983 without ever having run for elected office, he then sat in the House of Commons for less than a year before becoming prime minister. The result has evidently been a complete lack of understanding of or appreciation for parliamentary government, a failing he has never remedied. Two successive parliamentary majorities have allowed him to remain ignorant, and often disdainful of parliamentary practice, and his government has run roughshod over procedure and convention to a degree unimagined by his predecessors.

Mulroney's defence of his government's procedural strong-arming has been that it was essential, if the "overpowering" array of stalling tactics available to his opponents was to be overcome. He has completely ignored two facts. First, governments with bare majorities or in minority situations have coped with legitimate dissent in the past without resorting to such Draconian techniques. Second, the tactics of the opposition parties that so gall him were built into the parliamentary system to safeguard against just such overbearing behaviour on the part of the party in power.

Among the most devastating consequences of seven years of Mulroney government may well be the fact that many Canadians, so long exposed to the prime minister's intolerance of opposition, ruthless determination, and shameless attempts to avoid blame by pointing the finger at others, apparently have come to believe his self-serving rhetoric that Canada is a "difficult country to govern," and Canadians a "disputatious and fractious" lot.

Yet, a detailed analysis of the past seven years of Conservative rule demonstrates conclusively that much, if not all, of the blame for the country's current crisis of confidence rests squarely on the "unshrugging shoulders" of Brian Mulroney and his government, *not* with the political process or the other players in it.

It would be wrong to extend the blame for this crisis to the Conservative party or traditional Canadian conservatism. There is little evidence to suggest that all Conservatives are represented by Mulroney and his government, or that other Conservative governments would have implemented the same policies in the same way. On the contrary, the Mulroney era, as the following chapters demonstrate, is unique in our recent history, and the neoconservatism of his government has little in common with traditional Tory philosophy.

Neither the short-lived Clark interregnum nor the tumultuous Diefenbaker era offers any useful basis of comparison for the present government. Clark's tenure was too brief to allow serious conclusions to be made about the nature of his government. However, his identification with the "red Tory" element of the party and the quality of his cabinet appointments suggest an entirely different approach from Mulroney's.

Diefenbaker, although constrained for part of the time by his government's minority status, did implement initiatives without creating massive discontent. While some elements of his personality could be likened to those of Mulroney, his political philosophy was clearly very different. A strong nationalist and westerner who disliked Americans, central Canada, and "big business" with equal passion, Dief took a position on major issues that had little in common with those of Mulroney and his cabinet.

Historically, the only remotely possible comparison that can be drawn, it would seem, is of the present government with the Conservative government of R.B. Bennett during the Depression. Bennett's government was also wildly unpopular, and was in power during a period of serious economic upheaval. It, too, demonstrated a commitment to market forces and "tough" economic policies, and it, like Mulroney's government, came to be seen as dictatorial and unresponsive to electors.

Ironically, while Bennett's regime has often been described as ultra conservative, many of its actions belie that label. The Mulroney government, by contrast, has not yet been widely recognized for the truly neoconservative regime it is.

A pragmatic supporter of government interventionism, Bennett's government created the precursor to CBC Radio in 1932 and introduced legislation at the height of the Depression to establish social insurance, minimum wages, and marketing schemes. (He receives little credit in Canadian history books for these initiatives, as the legislation was struck down for jurisdictional reasons by the Judicial Committee of the Privy Council.) Clearly, then, Bennett and Mulroney are not cut from the same philosophical cloth.

Political philosophy is nevertheless an essential player in the fateful drama that has unfolded since 1984. The extent of the damage inflicted on this country over the past seven years can be explained *only* by the unlikely and unprecedented coming together in one government of two unique elements: a dogmatic commitment to a neoconservative agenda that falls outside acceptable policy limits in Canadian political culture, and a willingness to ignore the tenets of acceptable governmental behaviour and break, suspend, or neutralize all the traditional rules of the game to implement that agenda.

What Canadians so dislike about the Mulroney Conservatives, in other words, is not only what they have done, but how they have done it. Yet, many average citizens would be hard-pressed to say so because they lack knowledge of political institutions and procedure, media analysis has been poor, and modern issues complex. These three factors have contributed to a muddying of the waters. The many extraneous but prominently publicized issues highlighting the incompetence of the government, and the deliberate attempts by the prime minister and cabinet to obscure or conceal their policy intent behind liberal rhetoric, have also added considerably to the confusion.

As a result, there has been little recognition of the fact that the actions of the Mulroney government, taken together, constitute a consistent and deliberate pattern of undemocratic behaviour, and that their policy initiatives represent a dramatic shift to the right.

Canadians are acutely aware that something about the political system is not working the way it should, but, apart from obvious examples of patronage and incompetence, they are not sure what it is. The result has been increasing support for extreme and often unrealistic procedural remedies, in the vain and misguided hope that such changes will contain the damage. Yet, it is the players, not the system, that need replacing, as those who preferred the impeachment option recognized intuitively.

Canadians' equation of the Conservatives' mishandling of the processes and machinery of government with patronage and corruption should hardly be surprising. The focus was placed on them by Brian Mulroney himself during his successful 1984 election bid. For all intents and purposes, patronage was not a major issue before the 1984 campaign. Although public opinion was beginning to question some aspects of this process, the numerous appointments made by Pierre Trudeau immediately prior to his departure were resented, not so much because they were examples of patronage, but because the individuals involved were seen to be part of the tired Liberal dynasty the public desperately wanted to replace. It was not patronage per se, but the unacceptable calibre of the appointees that infuriated Canadians.

But Mulroney did not simply criticize these particular appointments, even though such criticism alone would have attracted many votes. Instead, he seemed compelled to broaden the issue to include the entire appointments process. Few Canadians had given much thought to the process; most were prepared to accept it as part of the way in which the political system functioned.

At his July 9 press conference to kick off his campaign, Mulroney specifically stated, "I commit myself to set up criteria for quality which will impress the Canadian people. I think what took place [the Trudeau appointments] is completely unacceptable in an open democratic society. We are going to reform this instrument in our national life." Later in his statement he declared, "I undertake today that all appointments will be of the highest unimpeachable quality. I'm going to send out a dramatic signal of renewal in this area of Canadian life."

In a Canadian Press interview a week later, he returned voluntarily to the issue, promising he would "remove these positions from automatic politics" and "bring a brand-new dimension of fairness and objectivity and representation for all Canadians."

Halfway through the campaign, during the televised leaders' debates, the issue of patronage appointments crystallized in dramatic fashion when Liberal leader John Turner, in response to a journalist's question, offered it to Mulroney on a silver platter. Turner declared that he had no choice but to comply with Trudeau's wishes, and, without hesitation, Mulroney told him, "You, sir, had an option" not to make the Trudeau-decreed appointments. In the decisive moment of the campaign, Turner, now on the defensive, replied once more that he had had no option but to comply. The significance of this exchange cannot be overemphasized. Overnight, the entire campaign changed tone. By the end of the week, and in every succeeding poll, the Tory lead increased dramatically.

Mulroney still takes enormous delight in reliving the moment, delivering both sides of the debate verbatim with colour commentary such as, "Then I hit him with it again!" Given Turner's over-whelming victory and vindication in the 1988 debates, it is perhaps not surprising that Mulroney continues to live in the past. It may also explain his inability to appreciate, to this day, the severity of the disappointment caused by the way in which he subsequently handled the issue he created.

As the next chapter outlines, the Mulroney government's blatant abuse of the patronage system and the appointments process rivals that of governments at the turn of the century, far outstripping any excesses on the part of his nearer predecessors. Most Canadians are unaware of the many other abuses of power and changes to the political process of which this government is guilty: the frequent revision of the rules of parliamentary procedure and of those guiding the legislative and committee system to benefit the government and stifle the opposition; the unequal relationships that have been created with interest groups, to benefit supporters, such as the business community, and to marginalize critics, such as social-action groups; the bypassing of the public service to favour partisan advice over expertise; and the neutralizing of watchdog and arm's-length agencies to limit debate and suppress alternative viewpoints. All of these developments represent serious departures from the traditional political process. Each of these insidious and deliberate changes has had profound consequences for the way in which the federal government operates vis-à-vis its citizens, and for the credibility of the government's highly unpopular policy agenda.

Although Canadians may not know what specific changes have been made to the process, they are only too well aware of some of the practical results. Canadians assume as a matter of course that their governments will behave fairly and equitably in their treatment of citizens and regions. Much of their dislike of the way Brian Mulroney's government has handled the reins of power is grounded in an intuitive sense that these basic values have not been respected. Whether their image is the CF-18 contract, the threats of blackmail over offshore oil made against Clyde Wells and Newfoundland during the Meech Lake débâcle, or the cavalier treatment of women's groups, environmentalists, and representatives of native peoples by cabinet ministers supposedly responsible for their concerns, Canadians sense that the Mulroney Conservatives do not believe every Canadian deserves equal treatment from his or her government. After witnessing massive bouts of patronage, influence-peddling, and lobbying by special-interest groups, most Canadians have come to the unpalatable conclusion that their national government listens only to the rich, strong, and powerful.

Similarly, since the implementation of a "modern" public administration in the 1960s, with its commitment to rational planning, impartiality, efficiency, and effectiveness, Canadians have taken for granted that their government will provide services in a timely and efficient fashion. Instead, during the past seven years, as a result of cutbacks, privatization, and downsizing, the public has been increasingly exposed to poor service and lengthy delays in the delivery of most governmental services, from the backlog in the processing of immigration, welfare, unemployment, and customs claims, to airport gridlock and massive decreases in transportation and postal services. For a growing number of Canadians, the federal government is rapidly disappearing as a provider of services.

The Mulroney Conservatives do not appear to believe the government is accountable to the electors for its actions, nor does the prime minister for his promises. Unlike Pierre Trudeau, whose forthright style would not be denied by even his most ardent enemy, Brian Mulroney and many of his ministers have made a career out of denying, correcting, clarifying, contradicting, or simply ignoring previous statements or commitments. Taking their cue from the front bench, much of the Conservative caucus has adopted an aversion to the truth and a refusal to accept responsibility, which has infuriated Canadians across the country.

The irony is that this behaviour has been counterproductive. It has scuttled more than one cherished project, the most obvious example being the Meech Lake Accord. While it is unclear how much public resistance the more extreme policy initiatives of his government would have encountered if the prime minister and his cabinet had presented them candidly, explained their rationale, and defended their merits, their automatic attempts to camouflage their objectives, denying any negative implications and limiting debate, have frequently prevented consensus and withheld legitimacy for the final outcome.

The unseemly haste with which they attempted, often successfully, to ram through many of their policy objectives — haste that ruthlessly subverted the democratic process — frequently led to the outcome being seen as lacking all legitimacy. Indeed, many of the Mulroney government's more moderate or otherwise uncontentious initiatives have been summarily rejected by the public because of the way in which they were presented.

All of these changes to the *way* in which the federal government "does business" are, of course, inextricably linked to the way in which Brian Mulroney and his team view the role of government and politicians. The prime minister's view of "politics as rewards" and his oft-recounted credo that you "dance with the one what brung you" have led him to approve or tolerate hitherto unacceptable activities on the part of his elected members. Moreover, his background in business has led him to view the role of prime minister as one of mere negotiator or deal-maker, and that of government as facilitator for the private sector.

Thus the objective of government is no longer to search for ways to ensure that the greatest number achieve the greatest good, or to arrive at a consensus that most of the disparate groups in our highly pluralist society can accept, but to distribute rewards and adjudicate among competing claims. The expressions "the common good" and "the national interest" are not part of Brian Mulroney's vocabulary. Negotiating with provincial governments is undertaken on the model of management–labour relations, and the content of a deal becomes secondary to reaching an agreement.

There can be little doubt that the damage Brian Mulroney has caused to the healthy operation of the political process is significant. From the integrity of Parliament and meetings of first ministers to an efficient, impartial public service, open government, and appointments based on merit, little remains of the high levels of legitimacy that the institutions and machinery of government enjoyed in Canada until recently.

Yet, abuse of the political process is only partially the source of Canadians' massive discontent. It is increasingly obvious that the anger and alienation of the general population today cannot be explained simply by the *number* of unpopular measures the federal government has introduced. It is the *degree* to which these measures and the motivating factors behind them represent an extremist, neoconservative viewpoint, running counter to the mainstream economic, social, and cultural values of the country, that lies at the root of the current malaise. It is difficult to overestimate the damage caused by this neoconservative agenda. Brian Mulroney and his government, when not engaged in pulling procedural chestnuts out of the fire, have had seven years of majority rule to impose their political agenda on the country.

The impact of many of their initiatives is only beginning to be felt or understood, and much of their agenda has been deliberately concealed behind liberal rhetoric. However, the real Tory agenda is finally being unmasked, and Canadians are horrified by what they see — primarily because it is not consistent with their views on policy matters and on the appropriate role of the state in managing them.

Certainly it is not what they thought they were opting for with their votes in 1984. Just as they believed they were supporting a commitment to even higher standards of government behaviour (an expectation the new Conservative government immediately destroyed), so, too, the voters in 1984 thought they were secure in the knowledge that *no* significant changes would occur in terms of policy direction. As virtually all analyses of that election have overwhelmingly concluded, voters wanted a change of personnel, not a change in course of the ship of state.

Scholars representing a range of perspectives, from Louis Hartz and Kenneth McRae to George Grant, have concluded that the Canadian political culture is essentially a classic "liberal" one.[1] Most Canadians value individual rights, tolerance, diversity, and equality of opportunity. The overwhelming support for the Charter of Rights and Freedoms entrenched in the Constitution in 1982, and the current heated debate over the possible subversion of those rights by elements of the latest constitutional proposals, can be seen as the quintessential expression of this liberalist tradition.

At the same time, Canadian history, geography, demography, and economics have produced some distinctive values in our political culture, which are generally viewed as having expanded this traditional liberal base to include certain elements of classic Toryism and socialism. Thus modern Canadian liberalism includes a strong commitment to social justice, an interventionist state, and regional equity. In addition, our proximity to the all-pervasive culture of the United States has ingrained a desire for independence in foreign policy and strong national symbols in our political culture.

What many Canadians are only now beginning to realize is that the Mulroney Conservatives simply do not share these values. They have no understanding of the importance of such concepts as fairness, equity, and equality of opportunity; no recognition of the importance of national symbols. They are determined to eliminate government intervention in the marketplace, reduce social justice, abandon regional equity — all because they see such policies as costly and inefficient.

Although Mulroney has often been described as a moderate Conservative, he was elected leader of the party because of the overwhelming support of the right wing — a fact he has never forgotten. His caucus, heavily weighted by extreme-right representation from western Canada and rural Ontario and Quebec, can be counted upon to remind him, as they have done with their lobbying on capital punishment, abortion, and gun-control legislation.

More important, however, is Mulroney's apparently tenuous grasp of political philosophy and his lack of commitment to *any* particular set of values. His proclivity for governing by polls betrays his obsessive desire to stay in power at all costs. In this vacuum, those ministers with a strong neoconservative bias have essentially been given free rein: Michael Wilson's relentless pursuit of deficit reduction and the unswerving commitment of several other ministers to privatization and reduced government involvement in the economy are prime examples, as is the great reluctance of other ministers to become involved in childcare, affirmative action, or housing and welfare reform, none of which they believe in.

Even more striking proof can be found in the numerous examples of internal conflict and confusion on policy matters to which Canadians have been treated over the years. Most have occurred when the prime minister, motivated by polls, has contradicted or overruled ministers driven by neoconservative theology. On several occasions, he initially approved their proposals, failing to understand their significance until public opinion demonstrated it. Mulroney himself has initiated little substantive policy. When he has, it has either been at odds with traditional Conservative party policy (free trade being the most obvious example) or ideologically, if not culturally, neutral (the Meech Lake Accord).

Another highly significant characteristic of the neoconservative agenda has been its negative nature. Given the philosophical underpinnings of "less government" and "non-intervention in the marketplace," it is hardly surprising that, with Canada's lengthy tradition of state intervention, almost all of their initiatives have involved tearing down rather than building. It is precisely because they wish to eliminate existing structures they despise that they see no need to offer constructive alternatives. The only alternative, for neoconservatives, is nothing.

Thus, in the area of economic policy, they have pursued privatization, deregulation, the elimination of tariff barriers with the United States, and the removal of restrictions on foreign investment. They have steadfastly avoided implementing any new social programs, such as a national childcare plan, and, contrary to the popularly held views of the sanctity of the social safety net, they have dismantled much of the framework for unemployment and family benefits, health care, post-secondary education, and regional-development programs.

Despite Canadians' view of their nation as a middle power and a peacemaker, the Mulroney Tories have cheerfully followed the lead of American presidents in almost all aspects of foreign policy, including eager participation in the Persian Gulf War.

The mindset of Brian Mulroney and his team remains so distant from that of the population they govern that they have no real understanding of why their government is so unpopular.

Seen in this light, the response of the Mulroney government to the calamitous situation in which they and the country now find themselves is entirely predictable. They continue to express astonishment at their unpopularity, to blame Canadians for being unwilling to swallow bitter but necessary medicine, to blame external forces beyond their control and, despite their seven years in power, the negative consequences of the Trudeau years. The truth is that the Mulroney government has *created* a series of crises where none needed to exist. Through ruthless determination and deliberate policy decisions, they have brought the country to the brink of economic and political chaos.

What has made this situation even less tenable for most Canadians is the fact that it has evolved against their wishes. They were promised, in two election campaigns, a different set of policies from those that have been delivered. In short, just as the Mulroney Conservatives promised improvements in the process of government and delivered regression, so they deceived Canadians with their election rhetoric about the sanctity of existing policies and programs.

The truism that parties do not win elections, governments defeat themselves, was nowhere proved with more clarity than in the results of the 1984 election. The Canadian public was determined to remove the Liberals from office. Brian Mulroney was in the right place at the right time. Despite misgivings about his personal credibility and judgment, Canadians decided to believe his promises because they wanted so badly to give someone other than the Liberals a chance to govern.

Following faithfully the strategy laid out by his polling experts, who strongly suggested Canadians wanted a change of players and an improved governmental *process*, but no changes in basic *policies*, Mulroney's 1984 campaign featured a vague "small towns, big dreams" vision of Canada. He attacked the Liberals on process issues, such as patronage, and talked in general terms about the need for change.

This position was summed up in two lines, frequently included in his standard speech, that journalists covering his tour eventually came to know by heart. "Canada is a splendid country," he would intone, "and I believe we can overcome the difficulties we face on many fronts with new vision, new direction and new hope for Canadians. It lies ahead of us to ensure that we provide both leadership and the programs to accomplish this."

In Quebec, he talked of a new era of conciliation, not confrontation, but gave few specifics. In Ontario, which most strongly opposed substantive change, he referred to "social justice" frequently but never spelled out specific objectives.

In the West, which was still reeling from the recession and the world oil crisis, he came closest to addressing concrete issues. The five-point plan announced in Prince Albert would, he said, produce "tens upon tens of thousands of new jobs," an early example of the inflated rhetoric that would cause him so much trouble in the future.

The break came with the televised leaders' debates, in which Mulroney delivered the knockout punch on patronage. The near-certain victory produced a change in the Big Blue strategy. From then on, Mulroney was to say even less and attempt to look prime-ministerial. The Liberals, desperate for a decisive blow, went on the attack about the true Tory agenda. Turner started to refer to Mulroney and the Conservatives as "Let's-pretend Liberals," claiming they were concealing a neoconservative ideology behind their classic liberal rhetoric.

The argument began to hit home, and Mulroney was obliged in the latter half of the campaign to deny that the principles of universality — medicare, in particular — were threatened. Social programs would not, he assured Canadians, be put on the block by a Conservative government. Attempting to stem the tide, he claimed, no doubt to his lasting regret, that universality was a "sacred trust."

Foreign policy, industrial strategy, regional development, cultural and linguistic policies were scarcely mentioned. Rather, the emphasis was on prosperity and job creation, the maintenance of existing social programs, and "positive" changes to the process of government, such as more conciliatory federal-provincial relations.

This is not to say that no concrete promises were made. On the contrary, the Tories were promising costly election goodies across the country. In a last-ditch effort to inject new blood into the race, both the New Democrats and the Liberals then tried to attack Mulroney on the cost of his campaign promises.

Earlier in the campaign, John Crosbie had inadvertently allowed reporters to see a document he admitted indicated the cost of the Tory promises. Mulroney denied its existence and refused to budge. When advisers pressed him hard to release a statement, any statement, on the costs, Mulroney replied, "Do you know what the polls are saying about how important the cost of our programs is to the average voter?" He then indicated a large zero and scornfully moved on to another topic.[2]

Six days before the end of the campaign, when no one was paying any attention and the election results were a foregone conclusion except for the magnitude of the Tory victory, he released the Conservative "estimated" costs at a speech to the Empire Club in Toronto. Apparently almost all his promises could be accommodated without increased government expenditures. This was, of course, a preposterous claim, given the enormity of the commitments, particularly since Michael Wilson was busily assuring voters that absolutely no tax increases were contemplated, as taxes were "already far too high."

Mulroney and Wilson knew that there were two options: either revenues, and hence taxes, would increase, or the promises would not be kept. In the end, both of these things came to pass, and no one was more surprised than Canadian voters.

The 1988 campaign was a replay of this scenario of raised expectations followed by dashed hopes. Despite their wariness of the prime minister and his government, many Canadians were finally convinced by Mulroney's promises — that social programs, regional-development programs, and cultural industries would not be affected by the Free Trade Agreement, that the economy would take off and many new jobs would be created. Although they represented somewhat less than 50 percent of the population, those who grudgingly gave Mulroney and his team a second chance were sufficient to return the Conservative government with a reduced majority.

Once again it took very little time for Canadians to be disappointed. With the government promptly introducing legislation to modify, reduce, or eliminate virtually all elements of the social safety net in the first year after their return to power, and with the economy in freefall and hundreds of thousands of jobs disappearing permanently, most Canadians, regardless of how they had voted in the 1988 election, believed that Mulroney and his team had once again badly misled them.

Then the Meech Lake fiasco crashed down upon their heads, despite Mulroney's promises of a more conciliatory approach to federal-provincial relations; and the implementation of the GST did even more damage than the previous thirty-two tax increases that Michael Wilson had assured them would never be necessary. Canadians by now were in no mood to tolerate any initiatives by any government. All but one of the six provincial governments forced to call elections in 1991 succumbed to anti-government sentiment. The map of Canada, once massively Tory blue, was redrawn, leaving only tiny pockets of Conservative support in Nova Scotia and Alberta, Liberals in control in the Maritimes, and the NDP holding three provinces that, together, make up 52 percent of the population.

Polls suggest that public opinion has so hardened and polarized on a range of issues, including those related to the constitutional dilemma, that compromise and consensus no longer seem possible. The electorate appears to nurture a bloody-minded determination to thwart the will of Mulroney and his government on all fronts, regardless of the merits of any proposal.

So it is, then, that Canada finds itself on the brink. Brian Mulroney and company have destroyed our faith in politicians and the political system and are now in the process of dismantling what is left of the country and our political culture. They have done so through a unique combination of intention, incompetence, and deceit, in an assault that has four distinct phases. The first, which took most of their first two years in power, resulted in all politicians being thoroughly discredited. The second phase, from late in 1986 to the collapse of Meech Lake, delegitimized the political system. Obviously neither of these results was consciously desired by the government. Indeed, the Mulroney government's ineptitude, ruthlessness, and deception have created a litany of unintended consequences.

Both the third and fourth phases involve the implementation of the neoconservative agenda. The third phase successfully brought down the country's economic infrastructure. Beginning with less-visible elements, such as the Canada Council and the National Research Council, they worked their way up, after four years in power, to the cornerstones of the modern Canadian state, such as Via Rail, Canada Post, Air Canada, and the CBC.

The Conservatives' determination to eliminate most if not all of these symbols of national unity produced an unprecedented outpouring of outrage and despair. Like the wildlife conservationists who warn that "extinction is forever," Canadians of all political stripes sensed that, once gone, the mechanisms that bound us together as a nation could never be replaced.

In the fourth stage, the one in which we currently find ourselves, the underlying values and beliefs of our political culture have been brought into question. Programs and policies that only a few years ago could have been taken for granted and were strongly supported by a majority of citizens are no longer certain. Just as they do not share most Canadians' attachment to national symbols, the Mulroney Conservatives have demonstrated little or no attachment to values ranging from tolerance, compassion, and respect for minority rights to the bedrock policies of social justice, such as universality, and the bilingual, multicultural nature of Canadian society preserved in a strong federal system.

To see how badly the Mulroney Conservatives have betrayed the trust Canadians placed in them one has only to examine the first phase of this four-part process, in which they discredited all politicians. Having promised "clean government," they returned to the practice of patronage politics on a level not seen since the prewar era, and then set about to convince citizens that this behaviour was no worse than that of earlier governments.

In the midst of their joyful deliberations on the spoils of power in September 1984, who could have predicted that, less than a year later, his government mired in scandals, Mulroney would moan that "no one ever wrote a manual saying how to be Prime Minister"?[3]

How Mulroney created "government as rewards," and how his new ministers struggled between partisan and governmental views of the world and the different ethical standards of the private and public sectors, is the subject of the next chapter. In it the man and his team emerge ill-equipped to govern, and the demoralizing effect of their deception and greed on the public's image of politicians becomes painfully evident.

NOTES

1. R. Jackson, N. Jackson, and N. Baxter-Moore, *Politics in Canada* (Scarborough, Ont.: Prentice-Hall, 1986), pp. 84–87.
2. M. Gratton, *So, What Are the Boys Saying?* (Toronto: McGraw-Hill Ryerson, 1987), p. 47.
3. Ibid., p. xvi.

2. Getting a Piece of the Action
How Conservative Patronage, Deceit, and Corruption Destroyed Our Faith in All Politicians

> I'm going to dance with the one who brung me. That means Tories. That's what this is all about.
> — Brian Mulroney, May 1983

> I was talking to Tories then, and that's what they wanted to hear. Talking to the Canadian public during an election campaign is something else.
> — Brian Mulroney, July 1984

In politics, so the saying goes, perception is everything. One perception, which is widespread, is that politicians speak for long periods of time without saying anything. Among journalists, the conventional wisdom suggests politicians never answer the question they are asked, only the one they want to hear. The obvious consequence is that, when a politician says something specific, people pay attention. And commitments made are not soon forgotten, either by the general public or by the media. Moreover, when journalists' questions are not merely answered but addressed at length and in copious detail, the responses are recorded for posterity.

These simple truths have been learned very slowly by Brian Mulroney, at great cost to himself and his government. The measure of this cost can readily be taken by examining public-opinion polls conducted during the past few years. Mulroney's popularity has plummeted to unheard-of depths for a prime minister. Since late 1990, his approval rating appears to have permanently settled at a rock-bottom 12 to 14 percent. His government, equally unpopular, did not even benefit perceptibly from the overwhelming public support for the Gulf War.

But these figures alone do not tell the whole tale, for leaders and governments often fall from grace. In politics, as Harold Wilson said, a week is a very long time.

What is of concern is that the profound public displeasure appears to have transferred itself from Mulroney to all those holding elected office, especially at the federal level. By early 1991, the Canadian people were telling the *Maclean's*/Decima annual poll, the Citizens' Forum, and anyone else who would listen, that they had lost confidence in all politicians.

Allan Gregg and Michael Posner's recent book, *The Big Picture*, provides a context for this phenomenon. In it, the authors point out that slightly more than 50 percent of Canadians in 1980 described their feelings towards politicians as "very or somewhat positive." Barely one in three felt this way by March 1990. At that time, a striking two-thirds of those polled agreed with the statement that "ethical and moral standards [of politicians] have really gone down in recent years."

Equally significant are the changes in the public perception of politicians' attributes. In 1984, those holding elected office were described by a majority as hardworking (70 percent), principled (63 percent), and competent (57 percent). In 1990, a minority continued to describe them as principled (43 percent) and competent (35 percent), while fully 81 percent agreed with the statement that politicians today "are more concerned with making money than with helping people."

How have these changes come to pass?

They do not stem from the public's unwillingness to swallow unpleasant but necessary medicine, as Mulroney and his followers would like to believe, but from the humiliation and outrage of having been deliberately deceived.

As the responses to the Citizens' Forum hotline demonstrated, by early 1991 Canadians perceived themselves to be the victims of a con artist who had nothing but contempt for their views.

This overwhelmingly negative perception resulted from three related factors that emerged at the very start of the Mulroney era: first, the inflated and unrealistic expectations created by Brian Mulroney during the 1984 election campaign with respect to public ethics and government standards; second, the rapid failure of his government to live up to those expectations, and its spectacular willingness to ignore them and indulge in far more blatant partisanship and unethical activities; and, third, Mulroney's subsequent successful attempts to rewrite history by tarring all politicians with the same brush.

As Stewart McLeod, a long-time journalist and member of the National Press Gallery, once remarked, "Just about everything can be traced back in one way or another to him talking too much. Too many promises. Everything comes back to haunt him. He didn't have to comment on everything, including patronage. . . . He could have got elected by saying a lot less. But there's so much on record. . . . It's right there, all these promises he couldn't possibly keep."[1]

Although Mulroney's initial failure to deliver on his promises conceivably could have been blamed on the inexperience of a party out of power for most of this century, that was simply not the case. His government's appalling performance was the direct result of his own attitudes, style of governing, and lack of integrity. Similarly, the prime minister's frequent attempts to rewrite history in defence of this dismal record can be accounted for only by his own almost pathological aversion to accepting responsibility and his apparent belief that you can fool all of the people all of the time.

It is almost as if he does not understand the reality of modern communications technology, which allows the media to compare a statement made today with an earlier one, and which allows people in all parts of the country to see a politician say one thing in one region and something totally different somewhere else.

After seven years, Mulroney has earned the dubious status of being the most deeply reviled political leader since R.B. Bennett, and the nickname "Lyin' Brian."

The source of Mulroney's troubles with credibility can be traced back to his formative years in the party's backrooms, striving for the leadership, and to his actions during the 1984 election campaign.

Mulroney's official biographer, L. Ian MacDonald, and former press secretary, Michel Gratton, have provided some useful insights into Mulroney's psychological makeup that help to explain why this should be so. Their accounts reveal an insecure individual whose need to be liked often overpowers his judgment. Jeffrey Simpson suggests that this need to be liked resulted in a desire to be friends with every faction in university politics and, then, within the Quebec Tory party. As fellow classmate, and later senator, Pierre De Bané told Simpson, "All through law school Mulroney made every group believe he supported its ideas. Almost every student fits into a pigeonhole; Mulroney fitted into them all, or so his classmates believed. It was an astonishing performance."[2]

Later, when he was ensconced in 24 Sussex Drive, the same need resulted in an overdeveloped interest in what others thought of him. As revealed by Gratton, his obsessive concern with the media and public-opinion polls led to unwise decisions and bizarre behaviour on many occasions.[3]

This need for approval may have been what drove Mulroney to politics in the first place, but it could not have played so great a part in his political evolution but for the supportive environment of the Conservative party in Quebec. The party was in total disarray and disfavour, and had been for a very long time. Numerous warring factions existed, apparently for the sole pleasure of destroying one another; intrigue and conspiracy were the principal activities of the membership. In short, the Conservative party in Quebec provided Brian Mulroney with an ideal opportunity. It was an easy target for a person of his outward confidence, conciliatory tone, and flexible views. But to be successful in that milieu also required a mastery of infighting techniques and a willingness to do what was expedient.

As Simpson recounts in *The Spoils of Power*, the "intrigue among Quebec Conservatives was never driven by ideology or intellectual conviction, but by personal rivalries and relationships sealed in telephone calls and secret meetings. In the politics of the shadows, networks of personal contacts counted for almost everything, and at this Mulroney excelled. . . . When Mulroney stepped onto the national stage he could not shake the habits of politics in the shadows. These habits perfectly suited the old-style politics of patronage, which depended upon a network of intense personal relationships, a commitment to personalities rather than ideas, and the need to expand political coalitions and mobilize participation by the expectation of rewards."[4]

Evidence of how Mulroney would behave in office was available long before the 1984 election. In 1983, Mulroney's campaign was heavily dependent on his extensive network of personal contacts. His promise of electoral victory under his leadership conjured visions of sugarplums — the spoils of power — in his faithful cronies.

In a meeting with potential supporters in Caraquet, New Brunswick, in May 1983, he outlined what would soon become a standard set of points. Beginning with "I look around this room and see half a dozen senators, maybe one or two judges," he then assured them he would not wait too long, as Clark had done, nor would he forget his friends. "There'll be jobs for Liberals and NDPers too," he would conclude, "but only after I've been prime minister for fifteen years and can't find a single living, breathing Tory to appoint."[5]

Having been present at one of these sermons on the spoils of power, veteran journalist Val Sears remarked that "it seemed to some people, especially in hindsight, to be a perfect indication of his approach to power, that power is a function of rewarding people, what he can do for his friends instead of for his country, and of what power can do for him."[6]

Once selected, the new leader of the official opposition wasted no time in making his intentions known. He had two objectives: appointing supporters, friends, and faithful Tories to positions of importance in the party and setting up a transition team to be ready for government after the election, which was expected within a year. Both objectives were to counter criticisms that the short-lived Clark government failed, in the eyes of the party, to do either.

Within two weeks of becoming leader, Brian Mulroney had appointed many of his key supporters to positions in his office and in the party. He then ran in a by-election created by the resignation of another supporter, MP Elmer MacKay. Having won handily on August 29 in the Tory stronghold in Central Nova, he appointed another ten friends and supporters to key party campaign and fundraising positions.

Once he had done all he could by way of appointments until seizing the reins of power, he ensured his second objective would be accomplished by appointing Senator Finlay MacDonald to head his transition team on government policies, procedures, and personnel. Reflecting the widespread Conservative mistrust of the public service, he said at the time, "If we gain power I am not going to deliver the Party to the civil servants and then ask them what to do and how to do it."

MacDonald recommended a four-part strategy, which involved looking at policy, machinery of government, staffing (of ministers' offices), and appointments (of faithful Tories). Members of the team included such senior caucus members as MacDonald, Michael Wilson, Sinclair Stevens, Harvie Andre, and Walter Baker (succeeded on his death by Don Mazankowski), as well as Peter White and Charles McMillan from the leader's office.

Given ongoing Tory concerns about the "loyalty" of public servants and the confidentiality of consultations with them, the group requested a series of briefings from the highly respected and scrupulously non-partisan parliamentary Research Branch.

The series of lengthy and comprehensive briefings on the range of issues outlined by the transition team was supplemented by written materials and responses to specific questions posed in advance by team members. The titles the team suggested for these papers, and the topics of the weekly briefing meetings, are particularly instructive, revealing much about the "real" Tory agenda: "Current Problems with Crown Corporations and Possible Remedies"; "The Canadian Cabinet System: Future Options"; "Senior Public Servants and the Neutrality Issue"; "The Growing Influence of Public Servants in Government"; "The Budgetary Cycle and Non-discretionary Spending"; "Organization and Operation of Ministers' Offices"; and "Governor-in-Council Appointments."

Lasting several hours at a time, the meetings were well attended by team members, but the leader put in a few cursory appearances, and rarely stayed long. At several of the briefing sessions, it became apparent that an internal debate about the advisability of a "witch hunt" in the public service was under way, but that consensus had already been achieved regarding the privatization of Crown corporations, the installation of a far more sophisticated and partisan appointments process, and the expansion of ministers' office staff to establish a partisan counterbalance, or parallel bureaucracy, to that of the formal public service.

Another important element in Mulroney's leadership campaign had been his willingness to support policies on the basis of their popularity and expediency rather than on any firm commitment to principles. As Patrick Martin, Allan Gregg, and George Perlin have noted in *Contenders: The Tory Quest for Power*, this opportunism tended to serve him well. He was never called to account for the many discrepancies and outright contradictions in the policy positions he had taken when wooing delegates in different parts of the country.

In the 1984 election, Mulroney was determined to wrest power from the governing Liberals and build a Conservative dynasty in Ottawa. In his zeal to ensure nothing prevented that victory, he repeated the tactics of his successful leadership campaign, committing his future government to campaign promises he could not hope to keep. (One count placed the total at 338 separate commitments.) He travelled the country, pledging to be all things to all people and regions. And, of course, he created a campaign issue — patronage — that proved wildly successful and delivered up a massive electoral victory.

Given the overwhelming public mood of unhappiness with the Liberals, and the near certainty of a Conservative victory, making a large number of promises seemed both unnecessary and ill advised. But it was his decision to make a major issue out of Pierre Trudeau's last round of patronage appointments — an issue that admittedly contributed greatly to the magnitude of the Liberal loss — that would prove not only unnecessary, but politically unwise. The problem was that Mulroney never took the issue seriously, but the public did.

On July 9, the very day he launched the election campaign with a commitment to "clean up" the patronage process, he was questioned on his frequent remarks during the leadership race about rewarding faithful Tories once he was in power. Mulroney replied, "I was talking to Tories then, and that's what they wanted to hear. Talking to the Canadian public during an election campaign is something else." A few days later, he was caught in his "no whore like an old whore" comments on Bryce Mackasey, which he thought were off the record. He was forced by his handlers to apologize quickly and categorically, but he could not limit himself to a simple statement of regret. On July 23 the *Globe and Mail* reported his remarks: "I pledge to you here today," he trumpeted, "that our appointments shall be of the highest order. They shall represent the regions and shall bring honour to all of you and shall bring honour to this country."

The hypocrisy of these contradictions was borne out by the elaborate plan his transition team had already prepared for implementing patronage appointments the minute the Conservatives took office. Mulroney had even admitted as much. In an interview with Allan Fotheringham in June, Fotheringham referred to the Conservative party's unhappiness with Joe Clark over his perceived failure to act on appointments when he had the chance. Asked the direct question "How fast are you going to get the ball rolling?," Mulroney replied, "It's already in train."

It was, indeed. A National Advisory Committee (NAC) on patronage had been appointed *before* the election began. During the campaign, while he lambasted Turner and Trudeau on the issue, Mulroney was quietly appointing the chairmen of the Provincial Advisory Committees (PACs) on patronage. The day before the swearing-in of the cabinet, the PAC chairmen met with Mulroney in Ottawa to receive their marching orders. Suitable committee members were appointed, the process moved into high gear, and the appointments began in earnest.

During his first mandate, the term "patronage" remained prominent, but for all the wrong reasons. It came to describe a wide range of activities and behaviour that the public found unacceptable, particularly from a man who promised he would bring new standards of "honour and integrity" to the operation of government.

At first there were ludicrous displays of petty partisanship: blue and multicoloured strings of lights replaced the predominantly red ones on Christmas trees on Parliament Hill; blue balloons were released along with red and white ones at Canada Day celebrations; and there was an aborted attempt to add blue lines and logos to Government of Canada stationery, already emblazoned with the red and white Canadian flag. Then came the expanded, streamlined, and more partisan appointments process that Mulroney's transition team had set in place — and with it, the introduction of blatant nepotism and cronyism. Worse still was the subversion of the bureaucratic process of government contracting so kickbacks and favouritism frequently replaced tendering and open competition, and the return to old-fashioned pork-barrelling on a scale not seen since the days of Duplessis, Pattullo, and Jimmy Gardiner.

Canadians watched, first in fascination, and then in disgust, as one after another Conservative cabinet minister was forced to resign in disgrace, and Tory backbenchers were arraigned and convicted on criminal charges related to abuses of their elected office. The odour of scandal and corruption attached itself irrevocably to Brian Mulroney and his regime.

Even more mesmerizing, however, was the increasing evidence that Brian Mulroney himself could not be counted upon to do the right thing. His spirited defence of several of his ministers, long after the rest of the country had seen enough evidence of their malfeasance to call for their resignations, led many to question his judgment. His failure to rein-in his more avaricious caucus members, or to condemn behaviour and demand apologies for misdemeanours, revealed a basic lack of understanding of the standards of behaviour expected of those in public life.

Yet, public disillusionment has taken a strange turn. Despite the fact that some 65 percent of Canadians believe "political corruption is increasing" in Ottawa, it is also the public's belief, as expressed in the 1991 *Maclean's*/Decima poll, that "all three [parties] would be pretty much the same." This distressing finding raises an obvious question: Why is it not simply Brian Mulroney and his Conservative government who are viewed as dishonest and corrupt?

Although Mulroney's personal popularity has suffered enormously because of credibility problems, he appears to have successfully shifted the responsibility for his government's ethical failures. He has done so, first, by blaming the system — "It was an institutionalized problem which we inherited" — then, by accusing other politicians of the same trespasses. His strategy, in effect, has been to defend his government's record by accusing previous governments of greater malfeasance.

The tragedy is that Brian Mulroney has successfully convinced many Canadians that his record is no worse than his predecessors'. In part, he merely says whatever is expedient, but he also has never been forced by the public, the media, or the opposition parties to address the overall numbers.

For the most part, he has been allowed to defuse a particular issue — such as the Sinclair Stevens fiasco — by referring to a well-known example from the recent past, as if this would even the score and justify Tory behaviour. No one has taken the trouble to point out that André Ouellet and Francis Fox are the examples used by Mulroney nearly every time one of his ministers is in difficulty, precisely because he has so few previous examples to choose from.

It is not only the sheer number of incidents that Mulroney has tried to downplay, but their range, diversity, and scope. Any examination of the various incidents and scandals that have plagued his government over the past seven years reveals a misuse of public office unprecedented in modern times. Not only the quantity but the quality of the wrongdoing — how many ministers have resigned, and for what reasons — puts the Mulroney government in a class by itself.

Brian Mulroney's defence of his government's record as better than that of past governments and other politicians is simply unjustified. Compared to the Trudeau era, in which four ministers resigned for cause in fifteen years, the departure in disgrace of eleven Mulroney ministers in seven years can hardly be defended as exemplary. The fact that this "best defence is a good offence" strategy has, in large measure, succeeded, despite the evidence refuting it, is both remarkable and disturbing in a modern democratic society in which access to information and freedom of the press should presumably provide a counterbalance to government propaganda.

The inescapable conclusion is that the Mulroney Conservatives' failure to bring about positive change is the least of their failings. Rather, having raised the issue and promised change, they then expanded and revelled in the existing practice of patronage, without concern for appearance or public opinion. It is this flagrant flouting of their campaign pledges on patronage, and the nonchalant attitude of the prime minister to wrongdoing, that have provoked such public wrath and disillusionment.

The appointments process is merely the first and most visible example of the Mulroney government's real attitude towards public ethics. In theory, the PAC process established by Mulroney's transition team was to be a "scientific" approach to patronage. Some three thousand order-in-council appointments had been identified on computer, along with the expiry dates of their incumbents' terms, so that replacements would be automatic. In reality, appointments would not only be made more often on a partisan basis, but be implemented more quickly. The names of thousands of "deserving" Tories were to be provided by the PACs and cross-matched in the computer with upcoming vacancies so that potential appointees could be available immediately.

The existence of this detailed system was consistently denied by Mulroney, as was the Tory "hit list" for the immediate replacement of 350 high-profile Liberal appointees. However, a member of his transition team, Harvie Andre, was more candid. Months before the election, while Mulroney was assuring the media he had no knowledge of such nasty matters, Andre was quoted in the *Ottawa Citizen* as saying, "A PC government will gradually replace every one of the 3,300 Liberal appointees with 'our people.'"

By December 1984, the PAC system was fully operational, and the appointments began. In an effort to counter the possibility of negative public reaction, Mulroney boasted to his advisers that he was deliberately beginning with two highly visible non-partisan appointments: Stephen Lewis (NDP) to the United Nations and Lloyd Francis (former Liberal Speaker) to Portugal.

Needless to say, these two appointments fooled no one. On December 4, twenty of Mulroney's personal friends and party organizers received appointments. Two weeks later, on the Friday before Christmas, when no one was supposed to be paying attention, another long list of the faithful received their rewards, including eleven Conservatives who replaced the entire board of Petro-Canada. By December 31, some 150 Tories had new positions. By mid-March 1985, a further 146 appointments had been made. And so it went.

To use Mulroney's words for the Trudeau appointments, the public were indeed witnessing an "orgy" of patronage unlike anything they had seen since the Second World War. While the Trudeau administration had replaced individuals infrequently, and only as their terms expired, over sixteen years, the Tories were attempting to accomplish massive turnovers in months. Doing so "necessitated" removing several high-profile appointees before their terms expired. In some cases, sizable settlements had to be paid to avoid lawsuits that the government could not win. (Years later, one of these appointees who refused to go quietly, Joel Bell of Petro-Canada, won a huge settlement for wrongful dismissal.) None of this was lost on either the media or the public.

Even more offensive to the public was the fact that so many of the new appointees were obviously not qualified. Certainly many Liberal appointees had a connection with the Liberal party, but it was commonly accepted that the vast majority of these appointees possessed legitimate qualifications for their positions. Many of the Tory appointees, however, not only lacked credentials, but felt no need to pretend they had any.

A former municipal Toronto politician and party worker, Gayle Christie, responded to questions about her ability to function on the board of Air Canada by saying she knew how to drive a car. A journalist who obtained access to Tory application forms in the PAC system and Privy Council profiles of appointees found that virtually all of the successful candidates included several pages listing their contributions to the party.

No areas were sacrosanct. Even appointments to positions that traditionally had been among the most non-partisan were subject to massive influxes of unqualified party workers. Fourteen of the forty-one appointees in July 1987 to the National Parole Board listed party ties as relevant work experience. When a third of the members of the federal Human Rights Tribunal were replaced with appointees who listed no experience in the human-rights field but had made extensive party contributions, former B.C. Human Rights commissioner Kathleen Ruff declared, "These appointments have the potential for perverting the whole course of federal human rights."

Among the most contentious of Mulroney's appointments were those to the foreign service and the judiciary. Personal friend Lucien Bouchard was given the plum position of ambassador to France, former Ontario Conservative attorney general Roy McMurtry became high commissioner to Britain, future press secretary and journalist Bruce Phillips was posted to the embassy in Washington, and former Conservative Environment minister Tom McMillan became the consul in Boston. Yet, Mulroney continued to counter all criticism of partisan interference by citing the Lewis and Francis appointments.

Mulroney had missed the point: the issue was not only that the foreign-service appointees were Tories, but that they were politicians rather than career diplomats. As the president of the Professional Association of Foreign Service Officers, Jean-Louis Delisle, wrote in a letter to the prime minister in January 1986, Mulroney had made more political appointments to the service in seventeen months than Pierre Trudeau had made in eleven years. Delisle continued, "The apparently accelerated rate of such appointments calls into question your personal commitment, as well as that of your government, to the continuation of a professional career foreign service."

By September 1989, after five years in office, Mulroney had made twenty-four appointments of non-diplomats to key foreign-service postings, more than any other prime minister. By contrast Pierre Trudeau made seventeen such appointments in 15 years, and Mackenzie King eighteen during his twenty-two-year tenure in office. Yet, Mulroney continued to avoid the issue and declare that "no prime minister has appointed so many non-party members to such high decision-making functions in such numbers." This, in turn, was a moot point, given Trudeau appointments such as Ed Lawson and Eugene Forsey to the Senate and Ed Schreyer as governor general.

A similar tale was unfolding on the judicial side. Mulroney repeatedly referred to his non-partisan appointment of a woman to the Supreme Court, yet a study released by York University professors Peter Russell and Jacob Ziegel in June 1989 revealed that patronage was a determining factor in at least 50 percent of the 224 judicial appointments made by the Mulroney government in its first term of office. This fact did little to inspire public confidence in the administration of justice.

In short, within months of his coming to power, there was overwhelming evidence that Brian Mulroney had no intention of changing the patronage-appointments process, except to appoint Tories in place of Liberals. His system worked so effectively to accomplish that end that journalist Stevie Cameron wrote in January 1987: "If Brian Mulroney has a single friend who hasn't been appointed to a board, commission or agency or hasn't been awarded the title Queen's Counsel or hasn't been given a fat contract or Senate appointment, that friend deserves to be annoyed."[7]

As Cameron noted, many of the appointments were not simply of faithful Tories. Many of the first and most visible appointees were long-time friends of the prime minister and relatives of several of his ministers. This return to the days of cronyism and nepotism was both unexpected and embarrassing to most Canadians.

In April 1985, for example, it was revealed that Finance minister Michael Wilson's brother-in-law had been awarded a $234,000 contract through his advertising firm. One month later, the public learned that External Affairs minister Joe Clark's brother Peter, a Calgary lawyer, had been made the official agent for Central Mortgage and Housing Corporation and had been awarded all legal work of the government's office for the Olympics. Clark's sister-in-law, Marcia, had been appointed to the National Parole Board.

Not to be outdone, Justice minister John Crosbie had ensured that his sons, Michael and Chesley, were appointed federal agents for fisheries, income tax, and pollution-related prosecutions via their law firms. Despite their considerable youth and lack of experience, to say nothing of the fact their appointments came from the very department for which their father was responsible, the prime minister continued to defend these and other appointments.

By June 1985, the permissive attitude of the government was so all-pervasive that John McMillan, brother of Tourism minister Tom McMillan and PMO policy adviser Charles McMillan, was complaining publicly that he had not yet made any money from his appointment as a legal agent of the government. Another of the prime minister's close friends, Sam Wakim, was allegedly approaching a number of Toronto law firms for employment by promising them government contracts if he was hired. Shortly after he was engaged by the firm of Weir and Foulds, they received some $200,000 in government contracts that had previously gone to another firm.

The attitude of the government was even more clearly revealed in a letter written by Youth minister Andrée Champagne in March 1986 suggesting that government funds should be used for propaganda to recruit Canadian youth to the Tory party. When it was leaked to the media, she initially denied responsibility for the letter by suggesting her signature had been forged, and then claimed it was only a staff proposal. Although she was demoted from the cabinet in the next shuffle, most observers believed the way in which Champagne had bungled the publicity, not the letter's content, had sealed her fate. This premise received further support when it was learned that backbench Conservative MP Marcel Tremblay had written letters to Conservative supporters in Quebec, suggesting that $1 billion in untendered contracts would be awarded to Quebec companies that contributed to the PC party.

Indeed, the formalized process of government bids and tenders, which had been firmly established decades earlier in order to eliminate favouritism and pork-barrelling, was soon politicized by the Mulroney government. Awards were often made to high bidders with Tory connections; increasingly tenders were not even put out. Incidents too numerous to list gained the spotlight for a short time — incidents such as a $3.4 million DRIE grant to a company on which Public Works minister Stewart McInnes had just resigned his directorship, a $4.9 million advertising contract to (Dalton) Camp Associates, and a $5 million grant ordered by deputy prime minister Mazankowski to the wealthy Ghermazian family from his home province of Alberta.

Once again the total picture is more significant than the sum of the parts. By 1988, the opposition parties were claiming that Public Works contracts, large and small, were being routinely awarded without competition. Intervention by political staff in ministers' offices in the awarding of departmental grants and contracts had become commonplace. Public servants no longer expected guidelines or standard procedures to be automatically followed.

Worse still, the accusations had continued to swirl around the prime minister and his cabinet since early 1985 about the existence of a massive kickback scheme on government contracts. These accusations focused on the Department of Public Works and its minister, Roch LaSalle. Outraged businessmen were alleging that those receiving government contracts were routinely forced to pay a fixed percentage of that contract directly to the Conservative party in Quebec, in order to be considered for further work. Inadvertent confirmation of this system had come from none other than Mulroney's Quebec communications adviser from Blue Thunder, Roger Nantel. Explaining to the media that a $2 million advertising contract he and his Ontario partner, Peter Simpson, had just received was not really all that big, Nantel supported his statement by pointing out that a significant portion would be passed directly to the Conservative party organization in Quebec for "educational purposes." Peter Swain, an advertising guru who had handled the Conservative account since 1972, had refused to accept the contract later given to Nantel because "the terms and conditions were unacceptable."

Allegations were also continuing to surface that several Tory MPs had benefited personally from this system. In May 1986, fifty charges of bribery and influence-peddling were laid against backbench MP Michel Gravel, LaSalle's regional lieutenant. Thereafter, the scandal grew so large it led to LaSalle's resignation under a cloud in early 1987, and the laying of charges against a number of party workers. The sordid matter climaxed in the allegations of widespread corruption by former Environment minister Suzanne Blais-Grenier before the 1988 election. Miraculously the trials of Gravel and fellow Tory MP Richard Grisé, charged with similar offences, were delayed until after the election.

Within days of the Conservatives' return to power, Gravel pleaded guilty, preventing Blais-Grenier and others from testifying, and the Crown from making its case in detail.

The convictions of Gravel and Grisé did not mark the end of the tales of graft and corruption, however. In early 1990, RCMP commissioner Norman Inkster confirmed that the Force was investigating several other members of Parliament. Criminal charges were subsequently laid against Tory MPs Jean-Luc Joncas, Gabriel Fontaine, and Edouard Desrosiers; investigations continued into the activities of Gilles Bernier, Bob Hicks, Terry Clifford, Maurice Tremblay, and Roch LaSalle.

The facts speak for themselves. In less than seven years, Brian Mulroney had seen five of his backbenchers and several more Conservative organizers charged and/or convicted of criminal offences directly related to their office. More were in the offing. These offences ranged from breach of trust and influence-peddling, to theft and fraud. By contrast, no member of Parliament had been charged or convicted of such an offence in the previous sixteen years.[8]

Those concerned with the overall credibility of politicians might possibly have dismissed the malfeasance of a few, or even several, backbench members of caucus as unfortunate but inconsequential in the grand scheme of things. However, the forced departure of eleven cabinet ministers in less than seven years, for reasons ranging from blatant conflict of interest to misuse of public funds, could not be so dismissed. Nor could the initially tolerant attitude of the prime minister and his partisan defence of such an abysmal record. His efforts to put the best possible light on it eventually cast a shadow on all elected officials.

The first minister to resign, Robert Coates, had served only six months in the Defence portfolio when he was forced to step down in February 1985 over allegations of impropriety and breach of security involving a visit to a strip club during an official tour of NATO facilities in Germany.

The prime minister was visibly reluctant to accept his resignation, referring to Coates as an "honourable man" who had served his country with "probity and distinction." Although Coates resigned promptly when his escapades were made public by the *Ottawa Citizen*, it later became known that the prime minister had been aware of the situation for two weeks prior to the appearance of the article. He had done nothing and, presumably, would have continued to do nothing if the matter had not been made public. Indeed, questions about the prime minister's judgment were raised when he implied that he had asked for Coates's resignation as soon as the matter became known.

These questions grew more forceful during the next ministerial fiasco, only a few months later. The "Tunagate" scandal, as it came to be known, was remarkable not so much for the lapse of judgment shown by the popular Fisheries minister, John Fraser, as for the outright contradictions that developed between Fraser's and Mulroney's accounts of what had happened. Although Mulroney had initially defended his minister, he demanded Fraser's resignation instantly upon learning that the minister had contradicted his claim that he had had no knowledge of several aspects of the issue.

To Mulroney's lasting chagrin, it was soon obvious that both the opposition in the House of Commons and the general public believed Fraser's account of events. (Fraser later became the first elected Speaker of the House of Commons, and many believe his support from members came partly out of a desire to right a perceived wrong.)

Mulroney himself appears never to have forgotten this incident, or at least one of his versions of it. Nearly five months later, interviewed by a *New York Times* reporter in Washington, D.C., Mulroney volunteered that "when it was brought to my attention, bang! Immediately the minister's resignation was secured." Unfortunately this contradicted Mulroney's own official version of events, a point the Canadian press was delighted to raise upon his return home.

The Fraser scandal was followed almost immediately by the resignation of Communications minister Marcel Masse, who informed the House that he was being investigated for election-campaign irregularities. (In the end, members of Masse's riding association were charged with these crimes, but he was not, and he eventually returned to the cabinet.)

The image that Mulroney was developing was becoming evident in the comments of many observers, who pointed out that Masse had not informed the prime minister in advance of his decision to resign immediately, rather than waiting for the results of the investigation to become public. Many implied Mulroney would not have behaved so straightforwardly.

Undoubtedly the most infamous and damaging of these scandals, however, was that involving Sinclair Stevens. The Industry minister was initially accused of a conflict of interest in April 1986 with regard to a loan negotiated by his wife from clients of his department. The affair soon expanded to include all his personal financial dealings and the administration of his "blind" trust. Despite almost daily revelations in the press of the most damaging kind, Stevens refused to admit any wrongdoing and indicated he had no intention of resigning. His decision was fully supported by the prime minister.

After several weeks of stonewalling by Stevens, deputy prime minister Erik Nielsen, and Mulroney, Stevens finally resigned on May 11. On accepting Stevens's resignation, Mulroney referred to the departing minister as a "great Canadian" who had served with "distinction" and whom he expected to be "fully vindicated." He then went on to accuse the media of "McCarthyism and slander."

When reminded in the wake of the resignation that concerns had been raised about Stevens's financial dealings as early as December 1984, and that he had personally promised to review conflict-of-interest guidelines "at an early opportunity," Mulroney resorted to the partisan defence that was to become his trademark. He retorted that his ministers were resigning as soon as improprieties were alleged, whereas "the Liberal policy was never, never under any circumstances, submit a resignation unless you were just one step ahead of the sheriff." Asked which former Liberal ministers he had in mind, he refused to answer.

When the royal commission on the Stevens affair finally reported more than a year later, in December 1987, it found that Stevens had violated the government's conflict-of-interest guidelines fourteen times during his tenure as minister. The inquiry cost the public $2.7 million, in addition to the $500,000 in legal fees for Stevens, which the government agreed to pay.

In the interim, André Bissonnette, the junior Transport minister, was fired by Mulroney for alleged involvement in the Oerlikon affair, a scandal that had been rocking the government for months. The matter focused on a number of questionable land flips from which Bissonnette and a number of his friends and relatives had benefited financially. He was charged with several counts of fraud, conspiracy, and breach of trust, but was acquitted by a jury in February 1988. His close friend and political organizer, Normand Ouellette, was convicted on a number of similar charges related to the Oerlikon affair.

Roch LaSalle finally resigned shortly thereafter. Although he had been under fire over his role in the Gravel affair, he had managed to remain in the cabinet with the prime minister's blessing until it was learned that several members of his ministerial staff had criminal records, and that he was on very close terms with a number of known criminals. Although LaSalle denied all knowledge of their records, the publicity was apparently too much even for Mulroney, who finally accepted the minister's resignation.

As late as the summer of 1991, the RCMP were still investigating the ramifications of the Oerlikon affair, the apparently related and unsolved murder of Montreal contractor Marcel Taddeo, and LaSalle's alleged involvement in the complex financial operations related to the Gravel charges.

After the Sinclair Stevens findings were made public, the pressure on the Mulroney government to "clean up their act" and live up to the conflict-of-interest guidelines led directly to the resignation, in February 1988, of Michel Côté, minister of Supply and Services, over an unreported loan of $256,000 from a personal friend who was also a government contractor.

Since then, four more ministers have resigned, three of them under a cloud (Lucien Bouchard having resigned over a political disagreement with the prime minister).

This total of eleven ministers stepping down in disgrace in seven years is higher than under virtually every administration since that of Diefenbaker. In particular, it stacks up badly against the four ministerial resignations for cause during fifteen years of Trudeau's government, none of which was for misuse of public funds or personal gain.[9]

A major portion of the blame must be allocated to Brian Mulroney himself. His failure to act quickly on the early incidents, his apparent willingness to tolerate impropriety unless and until it became a matter of public knowledge, led inevitably to the conclusion that honesty and integrity in government were not a high priority for the new prime minister.

This image was not improved by the new conflict-of-interest code tabled by the prime minister at the height of the scandals in fall 1985. Not only did the new code, which came into effect January 1, 1986, not prevent further scandals (more of them unfolded over the following year and a half), but it hardly differed from the existing rules introduced years earlier by the Trudeau government with respect to ministerial conflict of interest.

Perhaps one of the most misleading aspects of the code was the fact that enforcement allegedly lay with the prime minister. Indeed, when tabling the document on September 5, 1985, Mulroney stated categorically that "we have taken great pains to ensure that the new Code leaves no doubt that the ultimate responsibility for the ethical standards of government rests with Cabinet and, more particularly, with me."

If Canadians were expecting to see a change in Mulroney's attitude after this announcement, they were sadly mistaken. Two and a half years, and several scandals later, the prime minister was chiding the media for making "a big national drama" out of the resignation of Michel Côté. Moreover, while attending a local carnival in his riding, Mulroney also rejected the notion that he was personally responsible for Côté's conduct. Apparently he had forgotten his statement in the Commons. Rather than rereading it in *Hansard*, he went on the offensive, referring to a "spate" of ministerial resignations in the Trudeau cabinets of the 1970s and the more recent resignations of ministers in provinces not held by Conservatives. "I don't think anybody has said that Mr. Peterson was to blame. I don't think anybody has said Mr. Bourassa was morally deficient," he declared defiantly.

When asked whether he believed his government was being hurt by all the scandals and resignations, he replied that "resignations aren't necessarily a bad thing of themselves in the parliamentary system." He pointed out that some of his former ministers had merely had trouble with the "nuances" of government conflict-of-interest requirements, and concluded his denial of responsibility with a nod to human nature. "As long as there are imperfections in people — and we're all imperfect the last time I looked — as long as imperfect people are involved in the professions, from politics to the media, mistakes will be made."

The prime minister's adroit shifting of blame to others was as remarkable as his difficulty with the truth. There was, for example, the ridiculous episode of the nanny for the Mulroney children. Despite the presence of such an employee on the public payroll since October 1983, Mulroney denied that the public paid for such an expense. When confronted with the public records, he first denied such an individual's existence, and then had his press office issue a "clarification" in which it was explained that the individual was not a nanny but a person "who interfaces regularly with the children."

Throughout the following years, equally ludicrous denials caused journalists and the general public to question Mulroney's veracity. From the remarkable "You never heard me say that" denial of his well-known leadership pledge to reduce the deficit to $3 billion by 1990, to his confrontation with the *Vancouver Sun* in 1987 over his interview on the "drug epidemic" in Canada, which the newspaper had taped to counter just such a denial, Mulroney did not come across as a man in whom Canadians could place their trust.

When he defended his deputy prime minister, Erik Nielsen, in light of revelations that the veteran Tory had repeatedly taken advantage of electronic-technology malfunctions to listen in on Liberal caucus meetings in the Diefenbaker era, one could not but conclude that Brian Mulroney simply could not distinguish between acceptable and intolerable behaviour on the part of public officials.

He was also personally involved in a number of issues over the years in which his show of poor judgment further damaged his moral leadership in government. Among the more spectacular were the revelations by the *Globe and Mail* in 1987 that more than $350,000 from the PC party Canada Fund, a fund allegedly for the exclusive use of the party during election campaigns, had been used to pay for interior decoration, furnishings, and renovations to the two official residences of the prime minister. When it was revealed that this sum was over and above the $100,000 that had been paid by the National Capital Commission when the Mulroneys took up occupancy, even lifelong Tories were forced to question what kind of person was in charge. Although not illegal, such abuses clearly violated the spirit of the Elections Act. Neither the framers of the act nor the individuals who made the donations had envisaged such a use of political contributions.

Nor was Mulroney immune to the temptations of pork-barrelling. On his instructions, Transport Canada spent $6.1 million upgrading the airport at Baie-Comeau, while much larger airports were forced to make do with less-sophisticated technology. His decision to overrule the public-service recommendation and relocate a new federal penitentiary from Drummondville to Port Cartier in his riding, at an additional expense of $3 million and considerable hardship to inmates and their families, caused even seasoned observers to gasp at his audacity.

Ultimately, however, it was his efforts to escape responsibility for the actions of others and for the bad record of his government that caused the public to lose faith in him and, eventually, in all politicians. With each year it became more difficult for Canadians to remember what responsible government was like, and thus harder for them to dispute his claims that his predecessors were worse.

Other politicians recognized this problem and attempted to distance themselves from him. In 1987, Liberal leader John Turner gave a major address on the subject of ethics in government, arguing that Mulroney had single-handedly placed the issue on the public agenda and created a crisis of confidence in the political system. Turner argued that, "by confusing personal, party and public interest, the Mulroney government has undermined the very foundation of the State. There is a clear distinction to be made between the State, the prime minister and the party with the majority. The State exists for the common good, not the personal interests of the few and the powerful."

NDP leader Ed Broadbent attacked Mulroney in the House of Commons on a number of occasions. He and members of his caucus often made the point that the new prison in Port Cartier might need to be used to accommodate all of the former ministers and MPs who were being charged. On one occasion, an exasperated Broadbent asked Mulroney rhetorically in "Question Period": "What does a minister have to do to be forced to resign from [your] cabinet?"

Yet, when the 1988 election arrived, Mulroney was essentially unrepentant. Although admitting that he had not done as well as he would have liked on the appointments issue, he responded to a question on patronage by David Halton during the televised debate by listing the percentage of women and ethnic Canadians appointed to various boards and agencies, concluding that "significant progress" had been made. Not only did the answer have nothing to do with the question, but many women's groups, including Conservative ones, had questioned the "progress" he had made.

After the election, he continued his partisan appointments with a vengeance, notably during the GST debate when an additional eight Tory senators were named to break a possible deadlock. His former schoolmate and principal secretary, Bernard Roy, was given a highly lucrative contract to negotiate land claims and related issues flowing from the Oka crisis, despite the fact he had no known expertise in this area.

When Bruce Phillips, after a time in PMO on returning from Washington, was appointed Privacy commissioner, even thoroughly jaded opposition MPs were astonished by this placement of an openly partisan individual in a highly sensitive, impartial position.

Brian Mulroney had clearly not been reformed by his past misadventures. Although incidents were handled with more dispatch as time went on, the lingering impression was that Mulroney had learned only to be more discreet and to react more quickly when an issue became public, not to attempt to prevent such incidents from occurring in the first place. More importantly, his betrayal of this fundamental element of public trust set the stage for his approach to the structures of government and the political process. Having successfully put the levers of power in the hands of his supporters, he attempted to turn the tools of government to his purposes.

Displaying the same callous contempt for parliamentary tradition and the fundamentals of the federal system as he had for the appointments process and the ethical standards of politicians, Mulroney ignored his campaign promises of a more conciliatory approach to governing in his determination to impose the neo-conservative game plan on an unsuspecting nation. The disastrous consequence of this approach is the overwhelming public perception that major reform of virtually all elements of the system is necessary to prevent collapse. Yet, it is Mulroney's attempts to alter and pervert the processes of government, not the malfunctioning of the system itself, which have led to the current decline in legitimacy of the entire political machine. How he set about to achieve these ends, and the ways in which he dealt with obstacles in his path, are the subject of the next chapter.

NOTES

1. C. Hoy, *Friends in High Places* (Toronto: Key Porter Books, 1987), p. 77
2. J. Simpson, *Spoils of Power: The Politics of Patronage* (Toronto: Collins, 1988), pp. 355–78.
3. M. Gratton, *So, What Are the Boys Saying?*, pp. 59–65.
4. Simpson, *Spoils of Power.*
5. *Globe and Mail*, May 24, 1983.
6. Hoy, *Friends in High Places*, p. 72.
7. *Globe and Mail*, January 31, 1987.
8. Library of Parliament, Information and Technical Services Branch, "Vacancies in the House of Commons Caused by Death or Resignation since June 25, 1966," Doc. No. 63e.
9. Library of Parliament, Information and Technical Services Branch, "20th Ministry. 20.04.68–3.06.79" and "21st Ministry 20.01.80–24.06.84."

3. Neutralizing the Opposition
How the Mulroney Conservatives Destroyed Our Faith in the Political Process

When we come to Ottawa there's going to be a new game in town.
— Brian Mulroney, June 1983

When the many callers on the Citizens' Forum hotline during the winter of 1991 who were certain they had the answer to Canada's problems were told that impeachment of the prime minister does not exist as an option in the parliamentary system, a number of them angrily suggested it should become one and that this lack was just one more inadequacy of our system of government.

Across the country, there was growing evidence of widespread disillusionment with the institutions of government. An Angus Reid/Southam poll in March 1991 found that a majority of Canadians believed "Canada's political institutions are fundamentally flawed and must be reformed to keep the country together." The "actions of political leaders" were blamed by 51 percent of those surveyed for the weakening of national unity, but 57 percent believed that a "change in the system of government" would be necessary to reduce the threat to national unity posed by the ongoing constitutional debate.

While the initial focus of this perceived need for change was the Senate, since the failure of the Meech Lake process an expanded list of proposals has emerged — proposals related to the constitutional amending formula, the electoral system, and the distribution of powers between the federal and provincial levels of government. The very foundations of our political system appear to have lost their credibility. Parliament, the federal public service, the system of federal-provincial meetings of first ministers, known as executive federalism — all are being called into question.

This widespread discontent is being expressed in the classic populist language of the evangelist. Virtually all of the suggestions for institutional reform have placed an emphasis on the concept of "empowerment" — that is, on greater direct control of the political system by citizens through enhanced public-consultation processes, such as constituent assemblies, referenda, an elected Senate, and the ability to remove sitting members during their term of office.

Through this concern with the machinery of government the Canadian public appears to be demonstrating not only the after-effects of the Meech Lake débâcle, but also their loss of faith in politicians generally. As the Reid poll and others have shown, it is largely because Canadians are unwilling to put their trust in those holding elected office that they have turned to structural solutions they believe will allow them greater control.

The most disturbing part of this unfolding trend is that it need not have developed. It is not the institutions of government but the individuals running them that are the primary source of our present troubles. Just as even the strictest conflict-of-interest legislation cannot prevent individuals from breaking the rules, so no political system is immune to deliberate manipulation when the party in power is prepared to ignore or change the rules of the game. Indeed, the institution of Parliament has not failed to represent Canadians; the governing Conservatives have. From their first day in office, Brian Mulroney and his colleagues exhibited both ignorance and contempt for parliamentary procedures and traditions. As they began to learn the ropes, they were forced to face the fact that even having a massive majority does not allow a government to run roughshod over the opposition in a parliamentary system. Indeed, it became clear to them that the system was designed to allow the opposition every legitimate opportunity to express the views of the citizens they represent, and to point out the flaws and weaknesses in the government's program.

This opportunity for opposition criticism and delay was not well received. Mulroney and his new cabinet, having waited so long to take control, did not expect governing to be such a difficult and demanding process. Demonstrating the same contempt for parliamentary conventions and tradition he had shown for the appointments process, Mulroney paid lip-service to the sanctity of parliamentary procedure while quickly and ruthlessly ensuring opposition criticism and "distractions" would be kept to a minimum. As a result, standard parliamentary practices and rules of procedure were soon altered to suit the convenience of the government. Closure and time allocation, traditionally considered Draconian measures to limit debate, became the rule. Procedures of parliamentary committees were blatantly disregarded to limit critical opposition or interest-group input. Many of the conventions of parliamentary behaviour were flouted as well. As time passed and difficulties persisted, the government decided the best way to beat the heat was indeed to leave the kitchen; the actual number of parliamentary sitting days decreased considerably.

But Parliament was not the only institution to be "modified." The operation and structure of the executive level of government, the federal bureaucracy and arm's-length agencies, the relations between the government and interest groups, as well as its interactions with the provinces — all experienced significant changes.

Within the executive level of government, the cabinet, changes were put in place immediately. The increased importance and authority of the Prime Minister's Office, and the creation of a formal role for a deputy prime minister, had the effect of both centralizing and bifurcating the decision-making process to a remarkable degree that, in retrospect, proved both impractical and unwise.

The elimination of many central coordinating agencies and the increased power of ministers of line departments, for example, were changes initially applauded by many experts as a move towards greater accountability and efficiency. Unfortunately, these changes were accompanied by a reorganization of the cabinet committee system to reflect the neoconservative commitment to less government and the prime minister's brokerage-style politics, moves that eliminated most of the potential benefits and left the Mulroney government adrift and vulnerable to one embarrassing incident after another in the early years.

It soon became apparent that, in Mulroney's view of the role of government, special interests were to be accommodated rather than national needs being identified and met. This brokerage approach to decision making, more akin to American-style party politics, had a number of consequences. It led to the rise of a powerful and well-connected class of lobbyists and consultants. It also resulted in a more aggressive and confrontational approach by interest groups, and particularly those unable to afford the expensive lobbyists. Ultimately, the effect was to marginalize the legislative process, reduce the role of the bureaucracy, and enhance the role of special interests in Canadian society.

Meanwhile, in the public service, for which most Mulroney Conservatives harboured both contempt and pathological distrust, the appointment of partisan supporters to senior civil-service positions and public servants to the Prime Minister's Office were accompanied by witch hunts in several departments and the creation of a new "parallel bureaucracy" in ministers' offices, headed by powerful and highly paid chiefs of staff.

This politicization of the federal bureaucracy reflected the government's determination to confine officials to a reactive role. The confusion that resulted as the government itself became reactive, as well as the ongoing demoralization of the public service, are the result of an approach that values party loyalty and partisan considerations over competence and experience.

The neoconservative commitment to less government, met by decreasing the size of the federal public service, produced the worst possible result. The elimination on paper of many full-time public-service positions was accompanied by increased hiring of contract staff who did not appear on the public records as employees, but nevertheless ended up costing the government more. More significant still was the government's determination to use such staff reductions to eliminate program support for interest groups critical of the government, such as women and native peoples.

As a result of the temporary relief attained in personnel reductions in areas such as air-traffic control, immigration, and unemployment-insurance processing, Canadians are now unable to obtain a modicum of service from the demoralized remaining staff, many of whom have been assigned the workloads of three former employees. Yet, the "savings" obtained by these personnel reductions have made little or no impact on the size of the federal deficit, and failed to impress the influential members of the business community whom the government was attempting to accommodate.

The public service was further demoralized by the Mulroney government's contempt for the parliamentary concept of ministerial responsibility. As one minister after another landed in difficulty, civil servants were publicly blamed for administrative, and even political, decisions. The climax was the very public castigation of the most senior public servant, the Clerk of the Privy Council, during the Conservatives' attempts to save Michael Wilson over the budget leaks. This unpalatable and irresponsible scenario was repeated two years later, when several senior public servants were sacrificed in a convoluted and hopelessly contrived attempt to save Barbara McDougall and Joe Clark in the infamous Al-Mashat immigration case.

The Conservatives had not fared much better at the federal-provincial level. The brief honeymoon in first ministers' relations quickly deteriorated in the face of federal intimidation and threats against "recalcitrant" provinces. Long before the Meech débâcle, the federal government had begun to alter long-standing arrangements on federal-provincial agreements and threatened to impose both the Free Trade Agreement and the GST without provincial consent.

In short, within months of coming to power the goodwill built up by the Mulroney Conservatives on the campaign trail had been dissipated. By displaying a dictatorial style and a callous disregard for parliamentary procedure, political conventions, the impartiality of a merit-based professional public service, and the long-established canons of federal-provincial relations, Brian Mulroney set the negative tone for political discourse in the country for the next seven years.

Although they did not know it at the time, the friends and relatives of Brian Mulroney who shared his stunning electoral victory with him at Manoir Comeau on the evening of September 4, 1984, were celebrating the delivery of a Trojan Horse.

Of the 282 seats in the House of Commons, they had taken an unprecedented 211. They had built a winning coalition of the West and Quebec. In addition, they had outdone even the Diefenbaker sweep; they had won a majority of the votes in every region and province.

With such an overwhelming majority, they reasoned, a Conservative government would be able to write its own ticket. The new Mulroney administration would be able to implement its agenda in record time, unhindered by any significant opposition.

It did not take them long to learn how wrong they were. They soon came to understand that an overwhelming parliamentary majority is a mixed blessing at the best of times. Theirs was a disaster waiting to happen. Of their 211 members, 128 (60 percent) had been elected for the first time. After appointments to the cabinet, there would still be 171 to keep occupied and out of trouble. As the previous chapter demonstrated, they were frequently unsuccessful.

Moreover, as Robert Fleming has noted in his annual reviews of Canadian legislatures, the caucus produced by the 1984 election represented a significant change from the past. It included many more individuals with business and entrepreneurial experience, and far fewer with previous political involvement. This overall lack of parliamentary experience on the part of the Conservatives was, of course, compounded by the fact that their leader had barely a year's time in the House under his belt. Given his perceived need for regional representation in his cabinet appointments, many of his new ministers would have no parliamentary experience at all.

Of course, not even the Tory organizers anticipated the overwhelming mandate they received. Nor could they have any control over the "raw material" they were given to work with. But it was

clear from the earliest days of the new administration that little
if any thought had been given to the operation and administration
of the House of Commons or to a legislative agenda.

What the Mulroney team *had* spent much of the previous year
planning, in addition to an electoral strategy, was the takeover
of power. Unfortunately, as noted in Chapter 1, Mulroney's transition
team was successful in taking over the patronage-appointments
process and little else. Initial proposals for the organization of
cabinet and the PMO had bogged down in dissent, as had the initiative
to take control of a "hostile" public service.

In addition to having a lack of consensus on structural plans,
the Conservatives had no proactive agenda ready. Having been
elected on the basis of a largely "negative" platform that rejected
the Liberals but failed to provide positive alternative initiatives,
it was difficult to determine what system could best accommodate
the objectives they had not yet identified.

There were also practical political problems. Mulroney obtained
the leadership with the support of 75 percent of the far-right
wing of the party. He was therefore indebted to representatives
of this element in caucus, most notably Erik Nielsen, whom he
had appointed acting leader of the opposition and House leader
in the year before the election. What was to be done with the
Diefenbaker-era veteran? What was to be done with the large
number of Clark supporters? He had appointed them to the "shadow
cabinet" to ensure party solidarity after the bitterly fought leadership
campaign, but he did not trust them. What was to be done to
accommodate the expectations of Westerners and Quebeckers, upon
whom he had built his winning coalition?

All of these considerations, in turn, would have to be meshed
with the view of the role of government that Brian Mulroney
brought to the job of prime minister. As his actions so clearly
demonstrated, this view differed dramatically from that of his
predecessors. Unlike Pierre Trudeau, who was the archetypal
proponent of the "rational management" theory of government,
Brian Mulroney perceived the prime function of the federal
government to be that of horse trader.

In an article on recent developments in the machinery of
government in Canada, Peter Aucoin sums up the difference

between these two models. "Whereas Trudeau was most concerned with the role of knowledge and analysis in the pursuit of comprehensive planning and rational decision-making," he writes, "Mulroney has a much more political conception of ideal government, namely, the pursuit of compromise among competing interests."[1]

Mulroney's "brokerage" theory of government demanded a decision-making process based on negotiation and bargaining, not on the development and evaluation of objective policies. Mulroney's personal style of management, which is transactional rather than collegial, reinforced this need. As both Aucoin and Colin Campbell[2] have noted, Mulroney's preference for one-on-one dealings flows directly from his goal of appeasement rather than consensus in resolving conflicts at any cost. The imposition of this view of government on the existing system produced unanticipated and undesirable results. When coupled with the changes made to satisfy the political considerations identified above, it led to a worst-case scenario, described by Campbell as "politicized incompetence."

Electors had not expected dramatic changes in the direction of the ship of state, but they had expected a competent crew to keep it on an even keel. Instead, they quickly discovered that, despite his confidence during the campaign, Brian Mulroney and his team had no idea what they were doing. This image was reinforced every time the Conservatives attempted to launch an initiative, as they were foiled repeatedly by the centralized decision-making process that meant only Brian Mulroney knew what the game plan was at any given time.

Evidence of Mulroney's difficulties emerged in the early days. Having berated the previous government throughout the election campaign for its "outrageous" extravagance, profligate spending, and oversized administration, the prime minister swore in the largest cabinet in Canadian history. His forty-member team was a flagrant attempt to accommodate regional representation and internal political factions of the party. There were a large number of Clark supporters in key positions, and Clark himself was named minister of External Affairs. Quebec and the West were overrepresented, in several cases by individuals with no previous political experience; Erik Nielsen was appointed deputy prime minister and vice-chairman of cabinet.

Mulroney then introduced a new version of the "Inner Cabinet" concept that had been so strongly rejected during Joe Clark's brief term of office. His version of the Priorities and Planning Committee, the real inner cabinet, was an attempt to counterbalance his overblown neophyte cabinet by limiting those with strategic decision-making powers to a manageable and experienced group, but it was also a reflection of Mulroney's need to interact with individuals directly to achieve his objectives and maintain control.

Not surprisingly this reorientation of decision making created a greatly increased role for the Prime Minister's Office (PMO). Under previous regimes, it had been essentially a political and strategic adviser; most policy development and the coordination of substantive government initiatives lay with the senior bureaucrats of the Privy Council Office (PCO). Under Mulroney, the staff of the PMO increased immediately by one-third, the budget by 50 percent, and the policy component from four to fourteen individuals. These increases were well publicized at the time, and led to considerable consternation on the part of a public that had expected a more modest operational style, not an expanded and more "presidential" one.

The troubles with the new clout assigned to the PMO increased as inexperienced ministers lurched from one scandal to another. Because their central point of reference was not cabinet but the PMO, the prime minister found himself and his personnel drawn directly into virtually every incident.

It wasn't long before several key individuals in the original Mulroney PMO, all long-standing friends and loyal supporters, were identified as part of the problem by the media, the general public, and even the Tory caucus. Mulroney was forced to make some adjustments. Virtually all of the original team disappeared in late 1986/early 1987, and Mulroney brought in two new players who were neither personal friends nor known Tories. This step should have been viewed as positive (and, indeed, from the perspective of improved efficiency in the office, it proved to be so), but a new problem was created: two key positions were to be filled by "seconded" career public servants, Derek Burney and Marc Lortie. This American-style "politicization" of the civil service was heightened when long-time Tory strategist Dalton Camp was appointed to the newly created public-service position of "senior adviser to the cabinet" in the PCO, publicly funded at assistant-deputy-minister level.

This blurring of the distinction between political and bureaucratic staff had begun much earlier, but the appointment of Camp was the last straw. The *Globe and Mail*, well known for its Conservative leanings, published a scathing editorial on August 27, 1986, criticizing this attempt to re-create the machinery of government in the Conservatives' image. Its editorial decried the fact that "Mr. Camp, given regular access to cabinet meetings and an unmistakable invitation to help the Conservatives win the next election, has been made a very powerful man. And to do it, Mr. Mulroney has sanctioned the flagrant politicization of the Canadian civil service."

The editorial contrasted the appointment with Mulroney's well-known promises of less-partisan influence in the operation of government, and with Camp's own words when, as a young politician in New Brunswick, he had declared that the political machine created by the ruling party in that province was unacceptable. In his memoirs, Camp had attacked the "wealthy, highly skilled patronage machine" and had declared in a radio interview that "the masters of this machine do not sit in the Legislature. We do not elect them. They do not seek office, but the spoils of office. The greatest task at hand is to crush that machine." Nearly thirty years later, Camp was put in charge of an even more powerful machine, and many Canadians were outraged.

Such appointments were consistent with Mulroney's belief in the need to maintain centralized control, and his party's belief that the public service could not be trusted. Indeed, one of Mulroney's first acts after the appointment of a forty-member cabinet was the creation of a new position in the office of each minister, that of chief of staff. These positions, intended to provide each minister with a partisan counterbalance to the departmental bureaucracy, were funded by the taxpayer at the level of assistant-deputy-minister. Had they been staffed as the transition team originally intended, with competent and experienced individuals, the plan might have had some merit. However, as Campbell notes, "Too many of the 1984 appointments went to party operatives more interested in political organization than policy." In many cases, the blind were leading the blind; both novice ministers and chiefs of staff lacked experience with the bureaucracy and the legislative process, and on-the-job training was not provided.

The results predictably were disastrous. From Tunagate and the Commercial/Northlands bank failures to the toxic-mussel crisis and the CF-18 fiasco, the Mulroney ministry gave the Canadian public no reason to believe they were in control of the day-to-day operation of government.

Nor did Erik Nielsen's attempts to "re-evaluate" the entire federal bureaucracy. Nielsen, a junior minister in the brief Clark interregnum, was totally out of his depth; moreover, his extreme and well-known negative views on the public service and "overgovernment" were leading his task force to consider options that were unacceptable even to the mainstream of his own party. The infamous "Buffalo Jump" proposal on Indian Affairs was a classic example of this mindset. When its recommendations for an "integrationist" approach and massive decreases in federal funding and responsibility became public knowledge, it not only set back the clock on federal relations with native peoples by twenty years, but caused the government considerable unnecessary negative publicity.

Indeed, when word of this and other options began to leak out — an inevitability given the involvement of more than one hundred private-sector "volunteers" during eighteen months — Mulroney was forced either to deny that serious consideration was being given to these options (thereby undermining Neilsen's credibility) or to express ignorance of the task force's deliberations (thereby undermining his own).

Neilsen's stonewalling over the Sinclair Stevens affair (Mulroney was on a tour of the Far East) and his grudging apology for the twenty-year-old eavesdropping revelations finally provided Mulroney with sufficient reason to demote him.

However, he did not take this opportunity to eliminate the position of deputy prime minister as well. Instead, he continued with the concept of a split leadership, handing the reins of what he liked to call the position of "Chief Operating Officer" over to another Westerner and former Clark supporter, Don Mazankowski. Under "Maz," a more competent and personable manager, the position increased in importance and became further entrenched. An entire bureaucracy grew inside the PMO to service it.

The subsequent decreases in ministerial bungling may partly be attributable to this development, but members of the cabinet and the caucus remained in the dark as to the game plan, if any, of the prime minister, who spent less and less time in cabinet meetings. When he did attend, he reportedly devoted much of his time to reading favourable press clippings aloud, giving pep talks, and delivering long monologues on the importance of an improved image.

Mulroney conducted the "real" business of government as chairman of the board, on the phone and in private meetings with individuals. Some analysts have argued that this deliberate split in the management of the executive branch was a positive move, which allowed Mulroney to practise a "strategic" prime-ministership in the face of deepening national crises; others would argue that the crises evolved in large measure as a result of his failure to get a handle on the machinery of government in the first place.

By allowing his ministers to make many little decisions, while keeping the big ones to himself, and by permitting his surrogates to supervise the day-to-day operations, Mulroney balkanized the executive branch. Ministers had little or no incentive to coordinate their activities, and no one inspiring them with an overall set of objectives or vision. Rudderless, many quickly drifted into the purview of special interests and others, ironically, into that of officials within their own departments. On several occasions, legislative and other initiatives with directly conflicting objectives were advanced simultaneously by different ministers. Ministers regularly, if inadvertently, contradicted each other on a range of issues. Without guidance on the "Big Picture," several offered their own assumptions as policy, forcing Mulroney to intervene after the fact to attempt damage control. In short, the decision-making process of the Mulroney government was a two-tiered one in which neither level was aware of the other's thoughts or activities.

Not surprisingly, there were plenty of opportunities for special interests to influence the decision-making process. Given the prime minister's conviction that the primary role of government was to broker competing claims, such intervention was actually encouraged. Given Mulroney and his colleagues' belief that power should be used to reward friends and followers, it was inevitable that professional lobbying became a growth industry.

Unfortunately for the Conservatives' image, the Canadian public did not see things the same way. The frequent revelations in the first two years of Mulroney's mandate that friends, party workers, and former advisers were being paid handsome sums to influence the outcome of public-policy deliberations did not sit well with the average voter. Particularly irksome was the fact these lobbyists appeared to be selling their privileged access, rather than expertise and information. Invariably, they represented the interests of big business.

One such lobbying firm alone, Government Consultants International (GCI), was advocating at least six different questionable deals in less than two years. Owned by close friends of Mulroney — former Newfoundland premier Conservative Frank Moores and Gerald Doucet, the brother of Mulroney's senior PMO staffer Fred Doucet — the firm was involved with offshore oil firms, fisheries, and defence and transportation interests. The latter caused a particular furore, given Moores's patronage appointment as a director of the board of Air Canada, a position that he eventually resigned to avoid further media "harassment."

Mulroney responded to questions in the House with his usual lack of sensitivity on the issue, dismissing concerns as "unfounded" and accusing the opposition once again of "McCarthyism." Although he had promised legislation in 1985 to regulate lobbyists, it was not until 1987 that a bill was actually tabled, and it was never passed, having died on the order paper with the 1988 election. A reintroduced version after that election was so watered down that it required direct lobbyists — those paid by a third party to lobby the government on a specific issue or issues — merely to register, providing the names of their client(s) and the issue(s) on which they were working. They were not required to divulge with whom they had dealings in the government.

Needless to say, the lobbying business did not suffer. In 1991, cases were still coming to light on a regular basis that involved the friends and associates of the prime minister. In one well-publicized incident, Mulroney's former press secretary Bill Fox (let go in the PMO overhaul of 1987); former PC Party president Bill Jarvis; and two former chiefs of staff, Harry Near and Elizabeth Roscoe, were hired by Telesat Canada to lobby the government on their appeal of a CRTC ruling on a rate increase. In another, former PMO chief of staff Fred Doucet (brother of Gerald) was reported to be representing the interests of the Italian-French aircraft consortium attempting to purchase Boeing/de Havilland, an acquisition that required approval from Investment Canada.

From the public's perspective, it was business as usual for the Mulroney government, and business was certainly perceived to be calling the shots — from the amendments to the Patent Act on pharmaceuticals and the dismantling of the Foreign Investment Review Agency and the National Energy Program, to the introduction of the $500,000 capital-gains exemption and the awarding of the Oerlikon contract, many of the early policy decisions of the government were clearly seen to be an effort to accommodate the interests of the business community.

Had their changes to the political process been restricted to the executive branch, the Mulroney Conservatives might have limited the perception of incompetence and inefficacy to themselves rather than the system. The public was not happy with the way decisions appeared to be made, but they could see in the early days that the blame lay squarely with the individuals and party in power, not with the machinery of government itself.

But this clarity did not last long. Once the cabinet's decisions had been made, however disjointedly and lacking in direction, they had to be implemented. Legislation had to be introduced and passed through Parliament. And it was here, of course, that the Mulroney government was completely out of its depth. Lacking both experience and expertise, it found itself humiliated on a number of occasions in the early days, bested by the opposition on procedural points, presenting business in a haphazard manner or having no business at all for the House to consider. Rather than learn from such experiences that mastering the system was essential, however, the Mulroney team relied almost exclusively on its huge majority to force its will on the opposition. When this did not work as smoothly or quickly as they hoped, they decided to alter the rules of the game itself. This had the effect of discrediting Parliament as well, since ordinary Canadians, largely unaware of these changes, were forced to conclude that either the system did not work or their elected representatives were not defending their interests.

Behind the rule changes was the Mulroney team's assumption that Parliament is not a very important part of the political process. In their view of the world, special interests — whether sectoral or regional — are to be accommodated in policies to ensure re-election. Governments with such a massive majority should not be forced to consider the concerns of politicians representing a minority of citizens.

This majoritarian view of democracy is innately incompatible with and non-comprehending of the parliamentary system. It explains the direct correlation between their early difficulties in the House and their pursuit of increasingly repressive and Draconian measures, which were needed to limit the damage the system could inflict on their agenda.

As scandal after scandal landed one minister after another in hot water, the Tories quite rightly perceived that the daily "Question Period" was an unending source of media and opposition ammunition. Speeches on bills and Opposition Days provided further opportunities for criticism of the government's behaviour and its agenda. The Tories were so unprepared for the complexities of the legislative agenda and the parliamentary calendar that, for much of their first year in office, they were obliged to introduce recycled Liberal legislation that had died on the order paper with the calling of the election. Not only did they have no specific agenda of their own, but they were inept at the process by which their own proposals might be turned into legislation.

The choice of a House Leader — the organizer and shepherd of the government's legislative agenda and chief liaison with the opposition parties — is particularly instructive from this point of view. First, they chose the extremely amiable but inept Ray Hnatyshyn. In reasonably short order, he was replaced by the less amiable, but only slightly more adept, Doug Lewis. They then moved with greater speed to the superficially civil, but highly partisan and far more organized, Don Mazankowski, and, finally, to the high-handed, ruthless, and always combative Harvie Andre. Each successive appointment represented an escalation of their "war" against the opposition and the traditional rules of procedure.

Mulroney's claims to the contrary, it is an irrefutable fact that the most repressive techniques available to the government to limit debate — namely time allocation and closure — have been used far more often by his government than its predecessors. Although Mulroney argues that the Trudeau regime resorted frequently to these tactics, the reality is quite different. In fifteen years in office, the Trudeau government resorted to closure three times. In its first four-year mandate, the Mulroney government invoked closure five times, and time allocation (a slightly less repressive measure) eighteen times.[3] Moreover, the Conservatives' use of these mechanisms has actually been *increasing*. In only the first half of its second mandate, between 1988 and April 1991, the Mulroney government resorted to closure fourteen times.

Many of the practices of Parliament are less formally defined. While not rules per se, several conventions and traditions of parliamentary procedure are well known to practitioners, but difficult to explain or defend in the face of government determination to ignore them, as the opposition soon found when they attempted to rouse public or media interest in some of the early chicanery of the Mulroney government.

Some of these practices might be described as common courtesies — consulting with opposition House leaders on the agenda for the coming week; providing advance copies of major ministerial statements to opposition critics well in advance of their delivery in the House, in order to allow these critics time to prepare the replies they must give immediately after the minister completes his or her remarks; notifying opposition leaders of important statements by the prime minister, and of invitations to state events or meetings with visiting dignitaries. Others involve administrative matters, such as the assignment of office space or seating in the House. Sometimes things became simply ludicrous, as in the early attempts by several Conservative MPs and frontbenchers to substantially alter their statements in the draft *Hansard*, the record of the proceedings of the House. On several occasions, veterans were left speechless at the Tory ignorance or audacity.

While each "lapse" may not seem significant, the cumulative effect was substantial. Opposition members, far more experienced and knowledgeable, were first shocked and then outraged when it became apparent the actions of the government were not accidental but deliberate, and that matters would therefore be unlikely to improve. Indeed, despite their massive majority, the government appeared to be determined to deprive the opposition of the few advantages remaining to it, no matter how small.

Nowhere was this more evident than in the operation of the committee system. Committee clerks, the professional House staff whose role is to advise the committee chairs on appropriate procedure, were often ignored. The new Tory chairs apparently took their cue from Mulroney and the front benches, and began to impose their own view of the world on the workings of the committees. Quorums were redefined in some committees to permit the exclusion of opposition members, documents were routinely provided only to government members, government members were allowed to question witnesses first, and the *de facto* time allowed for questioning witnesses was often extended for government members and reduced for the opposition.

One chair attempted to prevent opposition members from obtaining an advance copy of the committee's report, on which they had all worked for some time, when it was learned that they would also be submitting a dissenting opinion in a minority report. Another attempted to have guards forcibly remove opposition members if they disagreed with his rulings.

Worse still, witnesses were treated in a highly adversarial and partisan fashion, unheard of in previous regimes. Attempts were made to charge or subpoena "uncooperative" witnesses (usually public servants); government members often refused to hear witnesses deemed "hostile" to the government and its policies. (Sadly, this practice continues unabated. One recent example is the deliberate and widely publicized refusal of the Dobbie-Castonguay Committee to hear many nationally known expert witnesses believed by the committee to be critical of the government's constitutional proposals. Manitoba opposition leader and

Meech Lake critic Sharon Carstairs was repeatedly refused a hearing; Professors Jack London and Anne Bayevsky were alledgedly "uninvited" by the committee shortly after making public comments critical of the package; and another expert, Sheldon Godfrey, was castigated by irate committee members throughout his presentation critical of the distinct-society clause.)

Needless to say, in light of such behaviour, the mood of the House deteriorated very quickly. Speaker John Bosley was unable to control the increasing hostility and aggression of MPs on both sides of the House, attitudes learned from the bad example set by Mulroney and his cabinet. Characteristically, all of this ill will and deliberate subversion was taking place behind a smokescreen of conciliatory rhetoric. The Throne Speech of November 5, 1984, had actually made a specific reference to the positive reform of the House and the importance of parliamentary procedure. It stated, in part: "Members of the House of Commons will be asked to approve the appointment of a parliamentary task force on the reform of that House. The central focus of this task force will be the enhancement of the private member. From that perspective the task force will examine and make recommendations concerning the powers, practices, organization and resources of the Commons."

Mulroney was fond of pointing to this task force in defence of his government's record, as if to suggest that, because he had established this group, no one could seriously question the sincerity of his commitment to Parliament. Typically, however, things were not what they seemed. In fact, the task force was not a new initiative. It was actually an extension of the work of an existing special committee (which had already tabled eight reports) established by the Trudeau Liberals after the bell-ringing incident in 1982. Chaired after 1984 by veteran Tory MP Jim McGrath (who was subsequently rewarded with the lieutenant-governorship of Newfoundland), the committee had already achieved a considerable degree of credibility, which Mulroney would have been foolish to ignore. At the same time, he and his advisers were intent on finding new ways of keeping their overabundance of backbenchers occupied. The recommendation to create "legislative committees" to examine government legislation was seen as an ideal way to keep idle hands busy, and it was enthusiastically adopted.

Of course, every innovation risks unanticipated consequences. The possibility that both standing and legislative committees might actually become as "independent" as their rhetoric and the McGrath recommendations had suggested was not something the Mulroney team had seriously considered. When some committees began to show such independence, the front bench interpreted it as impertinence or the result of cooptation by the opposition members.

A case in point was the report tabled in April 1985 by the Special Committee on Equality Rights, chaired by the moderate Tory MP from Toronto, Patrick Boyer, a lawyer and author of several books on electoral matters. As the wide-ranging recommendations in the report were the result of what Boyer and his members considered compelling factual evidence, it was a surprise to discover that they were not well received by the government, or indeed by the majority of their fellow caucus members.

The government was unhappy because the recommendations would have meant significant amendments to existing legislation and the restructuring of several government programs; moreover, the issue was sufficiently topical that it received considerable publicity, forcing some response to public demands. Meanwhile, the caucus, dominated by the extreme right, found many of the recommendations, such as the inclusion of sexual preference in the Charter and the introduction of women into the combat units of the armed forces, to be morally repugnant and incompatible with "Conservative" philosophy.

Few of the committee's recommendations were implemented, and Boyer, an early pick for promotion to the cabinet, continues to languish in the back benches. Since that time, committee chairs, appointed by the House leader, have been chosen with increasing attention to their voting records and willingness to "toe the party line" — a phenomenon that the Conservatives had criticized in the past and that the McGrath report expressly sought to eliminate.

This was not sufficient for the Mulroney team, however. In the wake of their 1988 electoral victory, which delivered a reduced majority, they felt obliged to alter the committee system again — this time without recourse to any task force or consultative process. Part of their problem was that their reduced numbers meant they would find it difficult to staff all the committees they had created. As well, having been returned to power, they believed they should ensure their next four years would provide smoother sailing.

They eliminated, on the pretext of efficiency and cost-cutting, seven standing parliamentary committees. Needless to say, these were committees that could potentially embarrass the government or had a history of doing so. They then moved to take control of the remaining twenty-one committees by neutralizing the chairs. Many of the individuals appointed had no previous experience chairing a committee; half had not previously been members of the committee in question or shown an interest in the area. This was the well-known Felix Holtmann phenomenon, in which a Manitoba pig farmer from the Agriculture Committee came to chair the Committee on Communications and Culture.

Next the government became determined to neutralize the opposition to its policies that had emanated from the Liberal-dominated Senate in the first four years of its mandate. Anxious to avoid another showdown with the Senate, which had stalled and threatened to refuse consent on the Free Trade Agreement in 1988 until the government sought a new mandate, the Mulroney government moved shortly after that election to curtail their powers by installing an aggressive and more partisan leadership in the traditionally low-key, non-partisan Upper Chamber.

While the merits of the actions of the Liberal senators, who for years had been delaying, amending, or defeating government legislation, are a moot point, the legality of their moves under the existing rules of procedure could not be questioned. This time the government, determined to push through its unpopular GST with no resistance, relied on its equivalent of the House Leader in the Senate, Lowell Murray, to ensure no procedural "shenanigans" by the opposition prevented them from doing so. As time progressed, however, it became clear that Murray, never having bothered to master the Senate rules of procedure, was being outwitted at every turn by the Liberals' wily warhorse, Allan MacEachen. Murray's inflexibility and combative tone only encouraged the Liberals.

As the deadline drew closer and things were not progressing quickly enough, the government was once again forced to resort to Draconian tactics. With no recourse to closure, Mulroney's team then decided to abandon the rule book and use the Speaker, an allegedly impartial position, to impose their will. The uproar that followed, as the opposition protested the Speaker's behaviour by engaging in attention-getting tactics with bells, whistles, and filibusters, is well known to most Canadians, and provided free entertainment during much of November and December 1990. Quite apart from the lack of decorum displayed by individuals on both sides, however, the fundamental issue of the government's and the Speaker's rule violations remained, although they were downplayed or addressed only superficially by the media and dismissed as frivolous by Mulroney himself.

In the end, when it began to look as if even the rewriting of the Senate rule book by the Speaker and Conservative House leader might not do the trick, the government took the unprecedented step of invoking an obscure provision of the Constitution to appoint eight additional (Tory) senators, thereby ensuring the Liberals were outnumbered, and a Conservative majority in the Senate would pass the GST.

Public outcry followed this latest round of patronage appointments, heightened by the inappropriateness of most of the individuals chosen, such as Nova Scotia premier John Buchanan, former PC Party president Michael Meighen, former federal Tory cabinet minister Pat Carney, and two former Tory provincial ministers. With the passage of the GST the Upper Chamber, which had been temporarily "legitimated" by its resistance to unpopular government measures, lost all credibility. Captured by the Mulroney government, it now appeared to be merely one additional level of the system that did not represent the wishes of the people.

By the end of December 1990, the government was totally exhausted and discredited over the lengthy GST battle in the Senate. Unable to end the session before final passage of a number of bills, which would die automatically on prorogation, Parliament rose for the Christmas recess and was not scheduled to return until late January.

In early 1991, the government introduced a new set of proposals for procedural change in the House of Commons, proposals that had evidently been formulated by the executive without any prior consultation. Although House Leader Harvie Andre attempted to present them as changes designed to improve efficiency and responsiveness, they were decried on all sides as further constraints on the ability of Canadians to hold the government to account.

Critics argued that the unofficial disregard for parliamentary practices, such as the obligatory tabling of estimates and government responses to committee reports, was likely to become entrenched procedure if this package were adopted. However the sweeping changes were passed April 12, 1991, over strong opposition protest, after the government invoked closure. The changes essentially had two effects: limiting the time spent in the House and in committees debating government initiatives, and shutting the House down entirely for longer periods of time.

While the House was in session, the rule changes would, among other things, reduce the length of speeches; limit the number of committees meeting at any given time; facilitate the use of closure and time allocation; redefine refusal to give unanimous consent to require twenty-five rather than one dissenting member; and cut by one-third the time allotted for debating the Throne Speech, opposition motions, and bills authorizing the raising of money (budget borrowing bills).

In addition, a series of changes were introduced that severely curtailed the independent operation of committees, including strict limitations on the number of witnesses permitted before legislative committees. An all-powerful fourteen-member Tory-dominated House Management Committee was also established to determine which measures would be referred to which committees.

Both opposition parties attacked the changes vigorously. Liberal House Leader David Dingwall declared: "The government forgets the only source of its legitimacy is the House of Commons" and accused the government of "further efforts to denigrate the institution." NDP House Leader Nelson Riis accused the government of forgetting the dictum of its Tory predecessor, John Diefenbaker, who rejected calls to streamline parliamentary procedure by insisting that "Parliament is not a sausage factory."

The overall effect of these measures was viewed by the *Toronto Star* editorial of March 27 as a "muzzle for MPs, not reform." A spokesperson for the Canadian Bar Association stated that the changes to committee procedure would mean that "committees, which are the only forum for public input on an issue, will be stacked in favour of the government." Other advocacy groups publicly expressed their concerns that the new rules would discriminate against small, poor, and citizen-oriented lobby groups whose only point of access is committees, while "powerful well-funded lobbies can play an influential role in the development of legislation before it is ever introduced in the House."

The second half of the government's package was equally badly received. The government argued that reducing the sitting time of the House to three weeks of every four would allow members, particularly those with long distances to travel, to spend more time with their constituents. Opponents argued that, in the days of fax machines, telephones and jet service, this extra time was totally unnecessary. They also pointed out that the result would be to reduce the parliamentary calendar from 175 days to 134, "Question Period" by 25 percent (41 fewer), and Opposition Days by five — a boon to government endurance.

The move to reduce the sitting time of the House was merely the formalization of an ongoing trend. During their first four-year mandate, the Conservatives had consistently extended the length of scheduled breaks. At the beginning of their second mandate, after meeting for a few days in December 1988 to ensure passage of the Free Trade Agreement, the Mulroney government adjourned Parliament until April 1989, rather than January, as had been scheduled in the calendar. By cutting the sitting by several more days in June 1989, they reduced the time the House was in session for the previous 52 weeks to a mere 84 days, barely half the 166 sitting days originally scheduled in the calendar.

Speaking in the limited debate allowed on the proposals, veteran Liberal member and former Environment minister Charles Caccia summed up the sentiments of Canadians when he noted that, while debates on rule changes in the parliamentary system are always difficult "under the best political circumstances in normal political times," the debate that was taking place was made more difficult by the desperate situation in which the government found itself and its lack of public credibility.

"In asking that a new package of rules be adopted at this time the government is really asking the impossible," he declared. "The credibility of the government is at the present extremely low. The credibility of the leader of this government is even worse. . . . Therefore I submit to you that this government lacks the moral authority that accompanies credibility. It is requesting the acceptance of a package whose substance is very controversial and it lacks the needed authority to assert its viewpoint. It only has the numbers when it comes to a vote. That is the use of force, rather than the use of reason, in parliamentary terms."

Such devastating criticism, however, did not deter the Mulroney government. Having forced passage of their package by using closure yet again, they promptly adjourned the parliamentary session for a month.

Like the parliamentary rules of procedure, the traditional concept of ministerial responsibility has always appeared to be virtually meaningless to the Mulroney team. True to form, in April 1989, Michael Wilson disclaimed responsibility for the most massive budgetary leak in Canadian history and, although examples abound of ministers of Finance in other parliamentary systems resigning over far less significant revelations, he was urged by the prime minister to remain in his post.

After nearly five years, still the only Finance minister the Mulroney government had known, Wilson was one of the few members of cabinet with any public credibility left in terms of the "honesty and integrity" factor, but this credibility was to dissipate almost immediately in the wake of the budget scandal. Typically it was Wilson's handling of events, and not the scandal itself, that caused further irreparable damage to the image of the Mulroney cabinet.

The crisis came on the eve of Wilson's budget speech in late April, when Global News journalist Doug Small broadcast details of the budget on national news, confirming there had been a budget leak of unparalleled gravity. After a hurried consultation with the Prime Minister's Office, Wilson responded by calling an extraordinary press conference the same evening at which he read details of the budget documents aloud.

As several conflicting versions of the leak scenario emerged in the following weeks, it became clear that the overwhelming consideration in the government's response had been to protect Michael Wilson. Unfortunately, their strategy of throwing civil servants to the wolves in an unprecedented display of public identification and blame had not been sufficient to deter an opposition that smelled blood; the Tories were then forced to adopt a second line of defence, bringing the RCMP into a dubious "criminal" investigation that eventually resulted in charges being laid against two individuals in addition to the hapless Small. (These charges were later dismissed by the presiding judge when the case eventually came to court, but only after he delivered a scathing diatribe about the incompetence of the prosecution and misuse of the judicial system.)

The leak alone should have been sufficient reason for Wilson to step aside, but, incredibly, he continued to receive the unflinching support of the prime minister, even after it was revealed that a second breach of budget security had taken place, in which officials of a life insurance company obtained a complete copy of the budget on April 25, and had so informed the minister's office.

Indeed, the existence of the second leak became publicly known only in late May, when an executive of the insurance company issued a press release indicating he had informed the Finance department of the issue a month earlier. The following day, eleven editorials in major newspapers across the country called in vain for the resignation of the Finance minister as the only way to preserve the credibility of the budgetary process.

Wilson's refusal to leave, aided and abetted by encouragement from the prime minister, was then buttressed by the government's attacks on senior civil servants who, it was implied, had been slow and inefficient in apprising the minister of events. Given that the prime directive of senior officials is to keep their minister fully informed at all times, few Ottawa insiders believed the government's version of events.

This unpalatable and irresponsible scenario, which sent a message throughout the public service that no action at all would be the wise course if one were to avoid blame, was to be repeated less than two years later with the sacrificing of several senior officials in the Department of External Affairs in order to save Joe Clark and Barbara McDougall from the fallout over the Al-Mashat affair. This latter case, arguably the most outstanding example of deception and incompetence during their entire seven-year tenure in office, saw the Mulroney government succumbing to an unprecedented level of public-service bashing. It began when Canadians first learned that a former Iraqi ambassador to the United States had been given the red-carpet treatment, and processed on a fast track that allowed him to enter the country as an immigrant only weeks after his application was received.

Canadians' desire to know how this could have happened and their outrage that it occurred during the height of armed hostilities was predictable. What could not have been predicted was the degree of panic, confusion, and backstabbing that ensued as several cabinet ministers were implicated in the decision and a complex cover-up was launched in which senior public servants and a political aide were scapegoated.

By early June 1991, over 70 percent of Canadians indicated they did not believe the government's story. The obvious duplicity and attempts to avoid blame only made matters worse, and the affair was the subject of daily questioning by the opposition in the House of Commons until its recess in late June.

The fallout from the débâcle seriously damaged the other remaining pillar of the front bench, Joe Clark, despite the fact that concern for Clark was apparently the driving force behind the complex web the Mulroney government attempted to weave, much as the desire to "save" Michael Wilson had fuelled the government's efforts during the budget leak. On both occasions, however, the damage to the goodwill and professionalism of the public service was inflicted without any significant benefit to the government, which again appeared unable to learn from past mistakes.

As noted political scientist Kenneth Kernaghan wrote in a letter to the *Globe and Mail* in mid-June 1991, the tradition of anonymity and neutrality of public servants has always been considered essential to the effective functioning of the bureaucracy. "It is startling and depressing to see," he stated, "that even long-serving politicians either don't understand or don't care about what is proper conduct between elected officials and public servants."

The failure on the part of Mulroney's ministers to accept formal responsibility for the actions of their departments and officials led to the public's growing sense that their national government simply could not be held accountable for its actions, a dangerous perception that inevitably decreased the legitimacy of parliamentary democracy as a whole.

As columnist John Hay noted in an *Ottawa Citizen* article of June 19, 1991, "The real harm is the disruption of the responsibility that governors owe the governed. . . . Operating a democracy assumes that all the scoundrels with government power are in the House of Commons, from which we can remove them at the next election. If the elected rascals cannot be held accountable, nobody can be."

Avoiding responsibility, public scrutiny, and criticism had actually been an important objective of Mulroney and his team for several years. After their first two scandal-plagued sessions of Parliament, Brian Mulroney's former press secretary, Michel Gratton, has recounted at length the development of a deliberate "communi-cations" strategy in the PMO to keep the prime minister out of the public eye and, most importantly, away from the national media.

As Gratton pointed out, the irony of this strategy was, first, that it did not succeed precisely because Mulroney could not stop himself from responding to questions, and, second, that such a strategy was deemed necessary for a man obsessed with being liked by the media. His arch-enemy, Pierre Trudeau, a man whose disdain for journalists was well known, rarely hesitated to encounter them. In March 1989, the *Ottawa Citizen* noted that Trudeau had held weekly press conferences for most of his tenure and that Mulroney had not held a formal press conference since January 19, 1987.

The ill-fated effort to keep Mulroney away from the media was eventually modified to ensure that, when he did encounter them, he maintained control of the situation. Planned announcements with no follow-up questions, and informal scrums, replaced formal press conferences in which he would have had to respond to questions journalists had prepared. Although unhappy with this situation, there was little the media could do other than reflect their frustration and lack of access to information in their coverage.

While the weekly press conference is clearly not a formal element of the political process, this deliberate alteration of the traditional relationship between the prime minister and the media did contribute to the overall decline of the system.

The frequent and deliberate attempts by the Mulroney team to limit other sources of public knowledge also heightened the public's distrust. Although it has long since been lost among the host of more serious breaches of faith, the initial furore over the Conservatives' early paranoid reaction to legitimate requests for information from the bureaucracy was considerable. As incidents multiplied in which officials were intimidated by their political masters and, in effect, muzzled, while the political staff to whom requests were now being referred routinely refused to release the most innocuous information, journalistic hostility and public scepticism grew.

In short order, the government extended its concern to the Access to Information Act, a measure that had been widely applauded when introduced in 1983. A well-used mechanism of public access, it became an essential tool of the media as normal channels of information dried up. It was through this legislation, for example, that details of lavish ministerial spending and use of government jets became known. In light of these revelations, and in order to avoid further embarrassment, the government began to intervene regularly, restraining Commissioner Inger Hansen's authority and refusing legitimate requests.

In the 1984 campaign, the Conservatives promised to ensure "parliamentary review and revision" of the Access to Information Act, after which it would be "implemented in spirit and in fact." Instead, the Mulroney government proceeded to ignore the report of its parliamentary committee recommending improvements. Hansen's annual report to Parliament in June 1988 was a ringing indictment. It accused the government of lacking "any genuine commitment to the principles of the Act." It charged that "by inadvertence or design [the government] has undermined both the letter and the spirit of the Act. . . . The parliamentary committee laid out the route to an even better Act. The government has blocked the road." In November 1991, following a five-year investigation, Hansen's successor, John Grace, issued a report calling for tightening of the rules of procedure and a clarification that "potential embarrassment to the prime minister or the government is not a valid reason for denying or delaying access to requested records."

Such damning accusations flew in the face of Mulroney's own campaign rhetoric about open, accessible, and conciliatory government, and hammered one more nail in the coffin of the political system, which was becoming thoroughly discredited.

On April 21, 1991, Parliament was once again recessed so the government could avoid meeting the opposition and ignore growing public criticism. A sure sign of the government's desperation was the fact the House had sat only five days in each of January, February, and April. Nonetheless, by the end of April, the Mulroney team was finally ready to announce their solution to their "image" problems — a long-awaited cabinet shuffle, to be followed by the unveiling of a new Conservative agenda in a Speech from the Throne.

The shuffle was deemed necessary largely because the entire image of the cabinet was suffering from its numerous difficulties with credibility and responsibility over the past two years. Unfortunately the shuffle was not the success Mulroney & Company had hoped for. To begin with, it resembled a game of musical chairs, with very few new players added to the team. The same old faces reappeared at the swearing-in ceremony, and few Canadians cared what their new responsibilities were.

Mulroney's inability to make appointments on merit rather than political calculation seemed to know no bounds. In difficulty in the West, he appointed a car dealer from Vegreville, Alberta, to the prestigious Finance portfolio; in difficulty with women voters, he appointed Barbara McDougall to External, knowing full well that he himself would run the show on foreign policy in any event. The cynicism of these plays for public sympathy was not lost on most Canadians.

Meanwhile Joe Clark, kicking and screaming all the way, was finally "persuaded" to leave External and accept the new position of minister responsible for National Unity. Michael Wilson, fresh from his dazzling successes in Finance, was appointed to a new superministry of Industry, Trade, Commerce, Science and Technology, otherwise known as the Ministry of Competitiveness and Prosperity.

The irony of these two last appointments can hardly be overlooked. Having lost almost all of his original supporters, friends, and nationalist recruits through scandals and resignations, Brian Mulroney found himself dependent on two one-time adversaries for the leadership of the party. Wilson, who had placed third in the leadership and refused to drop out to support either Clark or Mulroney, and Clark, whom Mulroney had not only schemed long and hard to replace, but had publicly ridiculed for his "community of communities" approach to federalism, were now the only two ministers with any public credibility left on whom he could depend. Their job would be to bail out both him and the government.

The subject matter of Clark's and Wilson's portfolios was, of course, no accident. A bilingual Westerner with credentials in Quebec and largely untainted by the Meech process, Clark was clearly the best bet to carry the can for the government on the new National Unity initiative, particularly as Mulroney had little intention of giving him a very long leash. Indeed, the subsequent announcement that Mulroney's favourite mandarin, Paul Tellier, would remain in charge of the file and report to both men suggested that Clark would have little clout in the process.

Wilson meanwhile was still viewed by the business community as reasonably credible, despite his "failings" on the deficit and the debt, which most were prepared to attribute to lack of political will on the part of his cabinet colleagues. Thus he was the logical choice for the ministry that was to champion private enterprise and free trade.

For Mulroney, fiercely partisan even within the party, and never one to forget alliances and enemies, the realization that his own people had not been up to the job must have been painful. To be forced to accept his own unpopularity and work through former rivals must have been a bitter pill indeed.

As if to counter this effect, his few appointments from the back benches were noteworthy for loyalty if not ability. Despite promising and credible backbenchers from the Toronto area, such as Patrick Boyer, David MacDonald, and Alan Redway, Mulroney once again revealed the degree to which partisanship and loyalty were preferred to competence or intelligence with the appointment of Pauline Browes, an obscure but fiercely partisan member who resembled in many ways Shirley Martin, another modest talent whose performance after being appointed to cabinet in an earlier shuffle had also been undistinguished.

The message to backbenchers and the general public was crystal clear — duffers could succeed in Brian Mulroney's government if they toed the line. Independent thoughts and proactive policy development were bad career choices.

When Parliament returned to hear the new Speech from the Throne on May 13, Brian Mulroney and his government obviously believed they had matters well in hand. The Throne Speech spent considerable time lamenting overly partisan behaviour in the House of Commons, implying that the opposition was responsible for this disgraceful state of affairs. The solution, after much pontification, was to address "the way in which the government is questioned, grievances are raised and legislation is examined." Given the events of the previous five years, few could doubt the government had in mind here less, not greater, freedom of expression.

Canadians now believed not merely that politicians had failed them, but that no elements of the decision-making process of national government were functioning well. The executive, the bureaucracy, and the legislature were variously seen as incompetent, impotent, self-serving, and unrepresentative.

The final blow came when the improved relationship between the federal government and its provincial counterparts, a vital element of the political process in any federal state, and a cornerstone of the Mulroney campaign platform, crumbled. The public, which had clearly wanted a more conciliatory approach to intergovernmental relations after the last few years of the Trudeau regime, were dismayed to see the brief honeymoon between Mulroney and his counterparts deteriorate rapidly into a level of acrimony, mistrust, and ill will equal to or surpassing anything seen in the final years of the Trudeau government.

Indeed, long before the national-unity debate and the Meech Lake failure, the operation of federal-provincial relations had deteriorated into an expanded version of Mulroney's brokerage politics, an approach totally unsuited to the operation of a country with the political culture and regional, linguistic, and other cleavages of Canada.

After a successful first ministers' conference in Regina in February 1985, Mulroney apparently thought he had tamed the beast. Future issues with regional or provincial complications would simply mean a phone call or two to his newly won cronies. When he was quickly disabused of this notion by ongoing requests for greater financial and program assistance by the provinces, he decided he should ignore the formal consultation mechanism in favour of redoubled efforts at one-on-one negotiation.

He also believed, as Gratton and several former premiers have often recounted, that "politics as rewards for friends" could successfully apply to provincial relations. Hence he went to bat twice for fellow Conservative Grant Devine with a timely announcement of emergency agricultural relief just as Devine was on the verge of losing provincial elections to the NDP. He did the same for Tory John Buchanan of Nova Scotia in similar circumstances, to the tune of $508 million in federal aid for offshore oil and gas development.

Former Ontario premier Frank Miller, another Tory, publicly described Mulroney's early approach as a well-intentioned but ill-conceived attempt to "buy" friendship and harmony. According to Miller, the abolition of the National Energy Program and the Atlantic Accord were seen as simplistic attempts by Mulroney to resolve conflict by acceding to special interests, rather than considering policy initiatives in the light of actual needs and the national interest.

The other side of the coin was Mulroney's personal penchant for vengeance against political enemies. Chagrined at Liberal Frank McKenna's initial resistance to both free trade and Meech Lake, Mulroney made it known that lucrative federal contracts for navy frigates would not go to New Brunswick if the premier's position did not change. McKenna supported the FTA, and the frigate contract stayed in New Brunswick.

Similarly, when the offshore-fisheries disputes arose with France, the federal position shifted, depending on the views on federal initiatives taken by the Newfoundland government. When Meech appeared to be failing, partly because of premier Clyde Wells's resistance, Mulroney, as well as ministers John Crosbie and Lowell Murray, publicly blackmailed the Newfoundland government concerning transfer payments and the future of the Hibernia oil development in an effort to force Wells to capitulate.

With Liberals in power in three of the four provinces in Atlantic Canada, which gave early evidence of regretting its increased support for the Mulroney Conservatives in 1984 and returned massively to the Liberals in 1988, that region was frequently on the receiving end of negative government initiatives, both economic and social. The creation of the Atlantic Canada Opportunities Agency, originally presented as a positive move to devolve authority, eventually came to be seen as a clever attempt by the federal government to shed its financial obligations to the region. Subsequent unilateral moves by Michael Wilson to "adjust" transfer payments in federal budgets also hurt the Atlantic provinces most severely.

Similar punishment was meted out to the Ottawa area after it returned Liberals in twelve of the thirteen local ridings in the 1988 election. Shortly thereafter, Don Blenkarn, a colourful and outspoken Ontario Tory backbencher known for his blunt opinions but usually factual statements, indicated that the nation's capital would surely pay the price for its stunning rejection of the Conservatives. Although Mulroney and his remaining regional minister, Paul Dick, were quick to deny the statements, the subsequent cuts and disruptions to the public service and increasingly strained relations with the municipal government belied their words of reassurance.

But the most blatant example of Mulroney's vengeance and "spoils of power" approach was reserved for Manitoba. NDP premier Howard Pawley, who had never warmed to Mulroney, even in Regina, quickly became an arch-enemy when Mulroney announced in October 1986 that a $1.4 billion contract for the maintenance of the CF-18s would go not to Bristol Aerospace of Manitoba, but to Canadair in Quebec, although Bristol's bid was lower than Canadair's by more than $3.5 million, and a panel of experts had recommended it.

When Mulroney, unrepentant, ignored the premier's concerns, a furious Pawley told reporters he considered the action to be treacherous and dishonest, and threatened to boycott further constitutional talks. Mulroney, for his part, told his officials that "henceforth all federal business in Manitoba would be done over Pawley's head; he should have none of the credit and be kept in the dark as much as possible."[4]

Completely underestimating the fallout, Mulroney defended the obviously political motivations by stressing that the Quebec aerospace industry needed assistance. This explanation landed him in further hot water when reports emerged shortly thereafter that the government had awarded 45 percent or $421 million of federal contracts to Quebec between September 1984 and March 31, 1986, compared to $10 million for Newfoundland and $257 million for Ontario.

A Reid poll in early November 1986 indicated that 56 percent of Canadians believed the decision was "unfair, unjust, unacceptable and politically motivated," a sentiment that continued to mount and translate itself into a perception of the government as pro-Quebec and anti-West.

Two years later, during the next federal election, many Tory MPs in western Canada were to pay the price for the CF-18 decision. In the longer term, as Chapter 4 demonstrates, it was instrumental in the creation of the Reform Party.

Thus by the time the Meech Lake process was in full swing, the ill will and mistrust among premiers and the federal government was already considerable. Coupled with Mulroney's subsequent attempts to "buy" a constitutional package by manipulating the players, and perverting the negotiating process by excluding officials, relevant interest groups, and, ultimately, the Canadian public, it is no surprise that the concept of "executive federalism," which the first ministers' conferences came to symbolize, has suffered irrevocable damage and is now viewed as an essential part of the institutional problem.

Clearly, Mulroney did not learn, as Frank Miller put it, that "you can't buy, no matter what you give away from the store, peace for long in the Canadian federation."[5]

Certainly, Brian Mulroney's approach to the institutions of government and the political process has had profound consequences for the country. There has, indeed, been a "new game in town," and most Canadians find it severely wanting.

NOTES

1. P. Aucoin, "The Machinery of Government and Mulroney's Brokerage Politics," in Pal and Taras, eds., *Prime Ministers and Premiers: Political Leadership and Public Policy in Canada* (Toronto: Prentice-Hall, 1988), pp. 50–59.

2. C. Campbell, "Mulroney's Brokerage Politics: The Ultimate in Politicized Incompetence," in A. Gollner and D. Salée, eds., *Canada Under Mulroney: An End of Term Report* (Hull: Les Editions Marquis, 1988), pp. 309–35.

3. Library of Parliament, Information and Technical Services, "Closure Use in the Canadian House of Commons," Doc. No. 31e, 10/4/91.

4. M. Gratton, *So, What Are the Boys Saying?*, p. 195.

5. C. Hoy, *Friends in High Places* p. 84.

4. Making Deals
How the Mulroney Conservatives Destroyed Our
Faith in the Political Consensus

I, for one, have learned that nothing is cast in concrete! . . .
Those who refuse to negotiate in good faith in such circumstances and in the face of such high stakes, ultimately will
have to pay the price on the occasion of the next election
or referendum.
  The debate would be entirely open to the public at all
times. There would be no sessions behind closed doors.
— Brian Mulroney, *Where I Stand*

After a century and a quarter of defying economic, demographic,
and geographic odds, and bringing citizens together in common
cause to build one of the most prosperous and stable countries
in the world, Canada today appears to be coming apart at the
seams. The sense of national unity and purpose that once existed
has been replaced by a cacophony of disparate voices. Tensions
among regions, and ethnic and linguistic groups have never been
greater. Native peoples are on the verge of insurrection. Racially
motivated incidents, particularly involving new immigrants, are on
the rise. And all this in a country that has always prided itself
on its tolerance.

As a nation, we appear to have lost our way. The political
consensus on which this country has operated — the collective
agreement on an underlying set of values and beliefs that unites
us — appears to be slipping away, undermined by a government
with no national vision and no commitment to those values.

Evidence of the uncertainty this lack of leadership has caused
can be found, first and foremost, in the declining credibility of

mainstream political parties, whose traditional role has been to aggregate the interests of these various groups and regions in our society. In their place, Canadians are increasingly turning to "fringe" parties to register their protests and their frustration. A survey of voting intentions by Gallup near the end of 1990 suggested that *no* political party at the federal level would receive enough support to form a government, while support for the two old-time political parties combined was at the lowest level ever recorded.

Although Canada has a long history of protest movements and third parties, there is something qualitatively different about the two major recipients of today's protest votes. In Quebec, where the appeal of sovereignty-association is at an all-time high, the newly formed Bloc Québécois led by former Mulroney cabinet minister Lucien Bouchard has received increasing support in public-opinion polls and appears poised to elect several candidates in the next federal election. An Environics poll conducted at the end of 1990 for CTV put support for the Bloc at 37 percent, ahead of the second-place Liberals at 28 percent, with the Conservatives and NDP trailing far behind. A year later the gap had widened; a Gallup poll of November 21, 1991, placed the Bloc's support in Quebec at 42 percent, compared to the Liberals' second-place standing at 25 percent.

In some areas of the West, the reactionary policies of the Reform Party receive more support than both mainstream national parties put together. Its leader, Preston Manning, has so galvanized widespread anti-Conservative sentiment that few Conservative MPs in Alberta, including Joe Clark and Don Mazankowski, are given even a fighting chance of retaining their seats. Preaching the gospel of the ultra-right, Manning toured the nation in 1991 in an apparently successful attempt to expand his membership base from western Canada to Tory bastions in southwestern and rural areas of Ontario.

Attempts by the Mulroney government to blame this situation on the failure of the Meech Lake Accord, and more specifically on the bad faith or intransigence of Elijah Harper, Clyde Wells, and Pierre Trudeau, have met with limited success.

The blatant clutching at straws that produced, first, the Citizens' Forum and then a wide-ranging set of federal proposals flogged by the Dobbie-Castonguay Committee after its near collapse and resurrection, have met with cynicism, disapproval, and virtually no expectation of success. In November 1991, fully 75 percent of Canadians in Quebec and in the rest of Canada indicated they did not believe there would be a successful resolution to the impasse in 1992, despite the fact the committee was to table its report in February and a referendum was to be held in Quebec by June 1992.

Yet, only seven years earlier, Peter C. Newman, reflecting on the results of the annual *Maclean's*/Decima poll, announced that "an astounding three-quarters of Canadians surveyed pronounced themselves satisfied or very satisfied with their economic lot and an even higher proportion optimistic or very optimistic about the future."

According to Newman, a prime source of this optimism was the newly elected prime minister, Brian Mulroney, whose victory he described "as welcome as the rebirth of green at the end of winter." After sixteen years of Pierre Trudeau, Canadians believed they had found a conciliator whose objective, as outlined in his 1984 Throne Speech, was to "breathe a new spirit into federalism and restore the faith and trust of all Canadians in the effectiveness of our system of government."

By 1991, Brian Mulroney's personal popularity, at 12 percent, was the lowest ever recorded for a Canadian prime minister. Profoundly unhappy with his government's corruption, bungling, and mishandling of the economy, Canadians became furious at Mulroney's outrageous treatment of regions, interest groups, and individual Canadians during the final months of the failed Meech Lake process. Instead of a conciliator, Canadians discovered they were saddled with a deal-maker who wanted a solution at all costs.

Given his repeated commitments in 1984 to a new kind of cooperative federalism, Mulroney's approval rating of only 9 percent in the Environics poll of November 1990 as to "who best represents your view of Canada" is even more telling. By contrast Pierre Trudeau was mentioned by 28 percent of respondents, and Clyde Wells, a Trudeau disciple, by 13 percent.

A root cause of this deep-seated national malaise is Mulroney and his government's failure to understand the Canadian political culture. Indeed, the concept of "political culture" is virtually meaningless to them. As we have seen in earlier chapters, the Mulroney Conservatives simply do not share many of the values that Canadians hold dear. Nowhere has this been a greater problem for them than in the third "pillar" of their 1984 platform, National Reconciliation. Brian Mulroney may occasionally talk a good game on national unity, but neither he nor most of his ministers have any understanding of how to achieve it.

This lack of understanding was inadvertently demonstrated by one of Mulroney's most nationalist Quebec ministers, Marcel Masse, long before the Meech Lake débâcle. Put in charge of Culture and Communications, Masse wasted no time taking on a perceived arch-enemy of Quebec nationalists, the CBC. Under the guise of a long-awaited review of the Communications Act, the CBC mandate was changed by Masse to eliminate its directive "to promote national unity." Challenged by opponents to justify what was perceived to be an outrageous lack of sensitivity to the underpinnings of Canadian culture, Masse described the old mandate as a blatant and unacceptable propaganda tool for strong federalists.

On January 31, 1990, in an appearance before the parliamentary committee examining the new legislation, Masse stated, "I have removed [the obligation to promote national unity] because it is, first, maintaining this political value artificially and, second, it was a constraint on freedom of expression. This obligation also opened the door to intolerable political interference."

During the past seven years, Canadians have been dismayed by the lack of leadership on Mulroney's part. They reject his apparent willingness to "give away the store" to special-interest groups, big business, and, on the constitutional front, the provinces, in order to avoid confrontation. They also reject his tendency to become doctrinaire, devious, or belligerent when negotiations are not going his way.

Neither attitude is consistent with the "Canadian" tradition of compromise. Indeed, much of the criticism of Trudeau in the last four years of his tenure focused on his apparent abandonment of compromise and negotiation for a more confrontational and sometimes unilateral approach to federal-provincial relations. Trudeau, however, seemed to have taken these actions deliberately, in full knowledge of their deviation from the norm. During the

1980–81 constitutional negotiations, and again during the debate over the Canada Health Act in 1984, he made specific attempts to communicate with the public his view that compromise would no longer work on these particular issues, which needed strong leadership on the part of the national government. By contrast, Brian Mulroney's brokerage politics appear to exist in complete ignorance that they represent a departure from the accepted norms of the political culture.

Of course, compromise is only one of several elements of the Canadian political culture, a culture most experts believe has evolved in opposition to its American counterpart. Historians point to the strikingly different patterns of settlement and development — the so-called revolutionary and counter-revolutionary models — that gave rise to very different attitudes concerning government, authority, and community. The underlying elements of the Canadian national identity have resulted largely from these initial differences, reinforced by an ongoing desire to avoid cultural domination by their next-door neighbour.

As American political sociologist Seymour Martin Lipset has demonstrated in his book *Continental Divide: The Values and Institutions of the U.S. and Canada*, Canadians continue to define themselves and their values in contradistinction to their American neighbours. We describe ourselves as less confrontational, less violent, less ruggedly individualistic, and less litigious, or as more tolerant, more charitable, more democratic, and more egalitarian — the words "than Americans" are commonly understood to complete these thoughts.

In the postwar era, Canadians came to place a high value on national symbols that accomplished this objective. More recently, less concrete but uniquely Canadian elements of government policy have been described by many students of Canadian political culture as heightening and reinforcing these cultural differences.[1] As a result, bilingualism, the multicultural "mosaic" (as opposed to the American melting pot), the preservation of regional identities, and a supportive approach to state intervention, notably with respect to social policies such as medicare, came to be appreciated partly for the way in which they served to differentiate Canada from the United States.

Confirmation of these views comes from empirical data provided by Allan Gregg and Michael Posner in *The Big Picture*. They write: "What made Canadians distinct in the 1980's was that we weren't Americans — and we were proud of it. We genuinely believed we treated our poor and disadvantaged better, that our health-care system was superior, that our laws protecting the environment were tougher."

Canadians were disillusioned and dismayed by 1990 because this self-perception no longer appeared to be valid. "As we enter the 1990's, that moral edge is eroding. We view the quality of our life, which underpins our superiority complex, as increasingly threatened. . . ."

Their analysis begs the question as to why this should be so. Although many of the data compiled in their study are useful, the book's conclusions, and particularly those drawn by Gregg, are often unconvincing. Given Gregg's close association with the Mulroney government, for whom he and the company he founded, Decima Research, have been the official pollster for most of the past seven years, this is perhaps not surprising.

Nowhere does Gregg refer to the federal government's role in bringing about this decline. Yet, critics would argue it is precisely the Mulroney government's policies in dismantling the welfare system, eroding the universality of medicare, and loosening the constraints on environmental protection (particularly regarding the Rafferty-Alameda and James Bay II projects in 1990–91) that brought about this decline and caused Canadians to lose their sense of satisfaction.

If there was ever any doubt as to the size of the gulf that separates the values and beliefs of Mulroney Tories from ordinary Canadians, it was removed once and for all during the two years of the free-trade debate. Asked to defend the deal, Mulroney and his ministers spoke always in economic terms. They referred to industries and businesses that would benefit, to prosperity and an increase in jobs. Rarely did they mention benefits for Canada as a whole, and they never developed a vocabulary to place the Free Trade Agreement in the context of a national vision with which Canadians could positively identify.

The depth of opposition to the deal therefore surprised Mulroney and company not only because of its intensity, but also because it was based as much, if not more, on the "non-economic" issues of social and cultural policy. Both John Turner and Ed Broadbent used these issues to their advantage, and were able to capture elements of the national vision with their criticisms of the deal. Turner's talk of the natural north-south pull and the deliberate attempts by previous Canadian governments to overcome it by constructing an east-west infrastructure, and separate cultural identity, struck a responsive chord. Neither Mulroney nor Michael Wilson, nor John Crosbie, was well equipped to respond to these attacks, and their Quebec colleagues even less so.

The mobilization of the cultural community in opposition to the deal left them largely nonplussed. The same mentality that saw no particular value in the CBC also saw no problem with increased American influence, as long as it resulted in greater economic benefits.

There was, of course, no hint of what was to come in the Tory platform in 1984. Indeed, the programs underpinning our cultural values were rarely referred to during the campaign. Mulroney's book *Where I Stand* contained almost no references to social policy, immigration, bilingualism, or multiculturalism. In its treatment of federalism, the emphasis was almost exclusively on process rather than content or substance.

The Throne Speech, however, did address these matters as part of reconciliation and national unity, mouthing appropriate liberal rhetoric on almost every aspect of Canadian political culture. There were "commitments" to "ensuring the equality of the two official languages. . . . Fostering the rich multicultural character of Canada . . . honouring the commitment to Canada's aboriginal peoples . . . [and] Achieving a national consensus [that] reflects the diverse regional identities."

Since no precise initiatives were proposed, it is difficult to know whether this vocabulary found its way into the Throne Speech as a result of interventions by veteran public servants, or whether it was a deliberate attempt by the Mulroney Conservatives to conceal their true intentions behind platitudes. For the speech was a mélange of ideas with no apparent philosophical framework. The section on national unity addressed a number of other concerns that appeared to be out of place, but likely reflected Mulroney's real modus operandi. It was almost as if, unable to arrive at a consensus, he decided to throw everything into the pot to please as many people as possible.

Hence, the national-unity section contained unexpected references to the need to make the taxation system "simpler and fairer," the need to "harmonize policies of the two orders of government," and the creation of a committee of deputy ministers headed by the deputy prime minister to review all government programs.

The most significant lines were clearly found at the end of this section: "Nowhere is the need for national reconciliation more urgent than in Canada's economic life. . . . My ministers will embark on the long, complex and painstaking road of building a national economic consensus."

This economic theme was reinforced even in the brief reference to the need to obtain Quebec's acceptance of the 1982 constitutional amendment. Given that this issue was to become the cornerstone of Mulroney's legacy, it is amazing to examine the vocabulary used here. Stating that "it is obvious that the constitutional agreement is incomplete as long as Quebec is not part of an accord," he went on to demonstrate that his commitment to building consensus was far from absolute: "While their principal obligations are to achieve economic renewal, my Ministers will work to create the conditions that will make possible the achievement of this essential accord."

The issue of national unity was also discussed in broader if somewhat self-congratulatory terms: "For the first time in many years, all regions of the country are represented in a national government. The mandate received by my Ministers is a magnificent opportunity to build a renewed national consensus."

It was indeed a magnificent opportunity, but one that Mulroney and his colleagues threw away in short order. How they came to do this is once again a highly instructive example of the unique combination of deliberate policies and abuses of the democratic process that have come to characterize this regime.

An added factor in this case, however, is the unnatural political coalition Mulroney built to achieve power in the first place. In *Where I Stand*, he stated that the Conservatives could not win without Quebec and that a Quebec–western Canada alliance would be a winning combination. But it is not so much the geography of this ill-fated coalition as the unrepresentative nature of those who supported him that caused all the trouble — nationalists and separatists from Quebec, and ultra right-wing Conservatives from the West.

Mulroney's Quebec roots and the party's inability to win without Quebec were hammered home in the run up to the Convention. Quoting from *Where I Stand*, he reminded delegates that, "with few if any exceptions, the Conservative Party has been consigned to the Opposition benches for one reason alone — its failure to win seats in French-speaking areas of the nation." In one-on-one discussions with delegates, he was particularly fond of pointing out that, of 102 ridings with a francophone population of more than 10 percent, the Liberals had won 100 in the last election. "You give Pierre Trudeau a head start of 100 seats and he's going to beat you 10 times out of 10."

In his focus on winning, he seems to have missed the importance of having a set of positions on the issues. Indeed, Mulroney's lack of particular vision for Quebec and its role in Confederation was called into question when one journalist revealed that the leadership hopeful's ten-point constitutional "plan" had been drawn up on a paper bag during a campaign flight, to counter persistent requests for details from the media. However, as "electability" was the number-one issue with delegates to the Conservative convention, as Martin, Gregg and Perlin demonstrated, Mulroney managed to keep the focus off both his lack of policies and the many contradictory statements he made to the two sides of his coalition during the leadership campaign.

In Calgary, to cement his right-wing western support, Mulroney spoke on April 28 to more than six hundred people. First, he directly attacked Joe Clark's position on full compensation to Quebec when opting out of federal-provincial agreements. Then he stated, "To try to curry the favour of the Parti Québécois organization during a leadership campaign is dangerous to the candidate who does it, it's dangerous to the future of the party he seeks to lead, and it's dangerous to the united country he seeks to govern." Luckily for Mulroney, this statement does not appear to have been reported in Quebec, where he was relying on just such support. The following year, he accepted a number of declared separatists both as candidates and as party workers during the election campaign.

In short, during the leadership campaign and the 1984 election, he built a coalition of two extremes, based on promises and positions for each that were rarely compatible and often contradictory. The practical consequences of this strategy were enormous. The need to maintain and foster this coalition has coloured virtually all of the Mulroney government's actions in the area of nation-building. Part of the problem was that Mulroney became enslaved to his success in carrying out this exercise in doubletalk and deception.

In Quebec, where the Conservatives were still viewed as the underdog going into the 1984 campaign, Mulroney and the Conservatives were forced to accept whomever they could find to stand for them in many ridings. Apparently the fact that many of their candidates and local workers had been supporters of the "Yes" vote in the referendum was not considered relevant. Either they believed they had no choice but to accept them or they simply did not care. As a result, when Blue Thunder swept the Conservatives to victory across the province, taking an astonishing fifty-eight of the seventy-five seats, a number of these *indépendantistes* became members of his caucus.

Many of these new members spoke little English, few had been outside of Quebec, and almost all of them represented an anti-federal (and anti-Trudeau) nationalist perspective, which would come to haunt Mulroney on several occasions over the next seven years. As incumbents, they were difficult, if not impossible, to challenge in the 1988 election, where they were almost certain to be returned. In fact, the second Conservative sweep produced sixty-three seats in Mulroney's "home" province.

As if that were not serious enough, however, Mulroney promptly made things more difficult for himself by appointing at least three, and possibly four, separatists to his cabinet. Benoît Bouchard and Monique Vézina stated publicly that they were active supporters of the "Yes" side in the Quebec referendum, as did a later addition to the cabinet, Lucien Bouchard, who was personally recruited by his old friend Brian Mulroney. Marcel Masse did not publicly disclose his position at that time, but few would disagree that Masse was also an ardent supporter of Quebec nationalism.

In the West, meanwhile, Mulroney had different problems. As usual, the region had delivered for the Tories; in 1984, they took fifty-eight of seventy-seven seats, a number that declined somewhat, to forty-eight seats, in 1988. Their predominantly right-wing and rural agenda did not fit well with the more moderate social views and emphasis on economic priorities he was hoping to convey as the new Conservative image. Instead, he was forced to deal with such issues as pornography, capital punishment, prostitution, gun control, and abortion — issues he would have preferred to avoid — in an attempt to keep them pacified.

Moreover, many of the western members of his coalition and caucus were hostile to bilingualism and what they perceived to be the undue influence of Quebec on the federal government. Caucus members from Quebec were horrified to discover many of their colleagues could not and would not speak French and had no understanding of or sympathy for Quebec's aspirations.

That Mulroney was able to maintain caucus solidarity and keep these two groups from each other's throats for as long as he did lends credence to the claims of his backbenchers that he is a consummate salesman behind closed doors. Nevertheless, the coalition was doomed to eventual failure, another victim of Mulroney's deal-making approach and catering to vested interests rather than trying to achieve consensus.

In many ways, the Meech Lake Accord can be described as Mulroney's chickens coming home to roost. But the demise of the accord, which was the culmination of Mulroney's ill-fated national reconciliation efforts, should be viewed as only the last in a long line of mistakes and misguided actions that have come perilously close to destroying the political consensus in this country.

Indeed, for many, Meech Lake was merely the last straw. Mulroney and his government repeatedly demonstrated their lack of commitment to or understanding of key political values and beliefs that have traditionally united Canadians, thereby setting the stage for the crisis of confidence that followed the collapse of the accord.

An obvious example of this lack of commitment is his treatment of official bilingualism. While Leader of the Opposition, he had gone to Manitoba and faced down his provincial counterparts on the question of official languages. Who could have been prepared for his subsequent lack of support for this fundamental concept once in office?

By August 1984, his coalition was already giving him trouble on the Manitoba issue, but agreed to tolerate his support for bilingualism for pragmatic reasons. As *Saturday Night* related, "Mulroney knows some members of his caucus have given in . . . because they have bought his strategy that it is essential for winning power in Ottawa. They support the strategy rather than the fundamental principle behind it." In short, they recognized they needed Quebec to win.

Once in power, Mulroney was faced with a possible revolt of his western "dinosaurs" on the proposed legislation to update and reinforce the twenty-year-old Official Languages Act. Although it was alluded to in the 1984 Throne Speech, it took him until 1987 to even introduce the legislation, which, although adequate, had no effect as it languished without being implemented.

He was also mindful of the other base of his electoral support, namely, Quebec. He refused to criticize his secretary of state, Lucien Bouchard, when the latter assured Quebec minister Gil Rémillard that Ottawa would not enact a new Official Languages Act without consulting Quebec. Nor would it "impose" bilingualism on Quebec.

Although these hardly sounded like the words of a federal minister responsible for the promotion of official-languages policy, Bouchard had even more remarkable musings shortly before and during the 1988 election campaign. Minority language rights, Bouchard claimed, could be asymmetrical rather than uniform across the country, as French was obviously more endangered outside Quebec than English was within that province. Bouchard also repeatedly defended the notwithstanding clause, which he viewed as "essential" for Quebec's survival, although even Mulroney was on record as saying it should be removed from the constitution. The concept of cabinet solidarity, like the tradition of ministerial responsibility, obviously held little meaning for Mulroney and Bouchard, who could not see that the public's image of their government and its objectives was becoming more confused every day.

Later, when two western provinces — Saskatchewan and Alberta — lost court cases concerning their non-performance on official languages and then introduced legislation to counteract the effect of these rulings, Mulroney could not bring himself to criticize them. Given that the Quebec government was actually taking the side of these provinces for its own ulterior motives, he clearly could see that his best political move was to avoid alienating either side of his "coalition."

Bilingualism, by contrast, received faint praise from Mulroney, and almost no concrete support. Indeed, the Commissioner of Official Languages had to beg in 1989 that the new Official Languages Act be implemented, and guidelines drawn up. Similarly, the use of the notwithstanding clause by Premier Bourassa in 1989 to counteract an averse court ruling with respect to his province's language legislation was barely addressed by Mulroney, despite calls from the opposition parties for a solid denunciation. Ironically, Bourassa's use of this clause, and his subsequent introduction of the infamous "inside-outside" signage legislation (Bill 178), so provoked the rest of the country that it became critical to the public's negative perception of the Meech Lake Accord.

Official language policy was not the only victim of the Quebec-West coalition and the neoconservative failure to appreciate the values of the political culture. Multiculturalism posed another classic problem for Mulroney and his team.

Like bilingualism, multiculturalism has lost much of its meaning during the Mulroney years. From their earliest days the emphasis of the Conservatives was placed not on cultural activities or improved race relations, but on doing business, and on the conversion of the "ethnic vote" to the Conservative cause. A revealing comment from Mulroney himself was quoted in the *Ottawa Citizen* of June 6, 1984. Mulroney said that visible minorities "should have a piece of the action in a very real way." He then pledged that he would recruit a number of Canadians of neither English nor French ancestry to run for his party in the upcoming election.

However, in their official campaign literature, the Mulroney Conservatives promised to "promote public awareness of Canada's diversity; promote programs designed to instill a greater appreciation of the unique racial, cultural and religious values which are held by Canadians of different origins." They committed themselves to "affirm the policy of multiculturalism as a policy for all Canadians; enact appropriate legislation to ensure stronger representation in Cabinet through an appropriate ministerial base."

Their campaign promises also included specific pledges to strengthen legislation on hate literature, to improve the representation of minorities in the media, and to "give appropriate consideration to the implementation of the recommendations of the Parliamentary Task Force on Visible Minorities" and "acknowledge the moral necessity for redress of past injustices to ethnocultural communities."

Yet, once they were in power, the gap between their rhetoric and their subsequent actions was cause for considerable frustration on the part of the groups affected, as well as the electorate in general. It took more than three years and three ministers of Multiculturalism before legislation to establish a Multiculturalism Act was introduced on December 1, 1987, even though similar legislation had already been tabled by the Trudeau government in 1984. When it finally appeared, it fell far short of the expectations of the ethnocultural community.

As sociologist Daiva Stasiulis of Carleton University concluded in a 1988 analysis of the Tory record on multiculturalism, the legislation was consistent with their attempt to maintain a superficial symbolic commitment to the concept while ensuring their measures were "modest in scope and expenditure of resources."[2] They were prepared to create a parliamentary committee on multiculturalism, to introduce legislation on hate literature, and to "upgrade" an existing program from a "directorate" to a "sector." They were not, however, prepared to allocate significantly greater resources to race-relations efforts or immigrant settlement and language-training programs. Indeed, even some minimal increases in the early years of their mandate were eliminated during the across-the-board expenditure cuts of later years.

Perhaps most revealing of the neoconservative approach, however, was the emphasis on appealing to successful business-oriented members of the ethnocultural community, at the expense of everyone else. In April 1986, the minister responsible sponsored a glossy "Multiculturalism Means Business" conference in Toronto, at which Brian Mulroney was the keynote speaker.

As the *Globe and Mail* reported on April 11, in the aftermath of the conference, many multicultural groups felt threatened by the new approach. Minister Otto Jelinek's "attempts to explicitly wed multiculturalism to capitalist morality, combined with his threat to fund only those groups who showed an 'investment' in Canada, upset immigrant service and community groups, already struggling on shoestring budgets and facing increased demands for their services."

In short, the new Tory approach abandoned multiculturalism as a vehicle for promoting national unity in favour of one that viewed cultural diversity as good for business and a means of reducing internal ethnic inequalities. As Stasiulis put it, "Proposals to turn language and culture into a commodity for foreign markets and investment could be successful with the profit-minded, yet fail to mobilize the sort of sentiments that have traditionally sustained support for multiculturalism policy."

A consequence of this approach was a lack of emphasis on race relations at a time when the increasing number of visible-minority immigrants was leading to strain in the cultural fabric of the nation. The analysis by Stasiulis concluded: "The new positive nexus between ethnicity and profit [which] favours the material interests of more privileged class segments of ethnic communities sits uneasily beside . . . efforts to reduce ethnic inequality and racism. Concerned minorities might legitimately inquire whether [the government] will be willing to jettison the policy's role in combatting racism . . . in order to win the support of business."[3]

This concern proved well founded. One of the few areas of agreement by the coalition of Quebec nationalists and right-wing Westerners was that neither particularly cared for the multicultural theme to begin with. The neoconservatives used this consensus to withdraw the federal government financially from the race-relations fray by placing greater emphasis on the private sector and other levels of government. Thus, the Conservative version of employment-equity legislation, introduced in 1986, had virtually no enforcement mechanisms. It simply required employers to "report their progress." Not surprisingly, the result, as demonstrated by the reports for 1988 through to 1990, are unimpressive.

Similarly, human-rights issues generally have met with little support from the Mulroney government. Perceived as unimportant politically and marginal in financial terms, the groups supporting these causes have been basically ignored. Having established a parliamentary committee, only of necessity, to examine the implications of the coming into force of section 15 of the Charter in spring 1985, the government then rejected almost all of the contentious recommendations of that committee's report — notably those relating to women in the armed forces and issues involving sexual preference — most of which were vehemently opposed by the right-wing element of the caucus.

At the same time, the parliamentary committee reviewing appointments to human-rights boards and tribunals came in for considerable publicity over the nature of the government's appointments. Many of its nominees had no experience in the area, some expressed patently racist opinions, and a handful were discovered to have unsavoury connections with discredited regimes or organizations in other countries.

What all the nominees did have, of course, were strong ties to the Conservative Party. Leading human-rights experts and ordinary Canadians were forced to conclude that the issue was seen to have very little importance by the government, except as an opportunity for patronage appointments.

Their attempts to use multiculturalism and human rights for partisan purposes culminated in a blatant vote-getting ploy shortly before the 1988 election campaign. Having promised in 1984 to provide redress to Japanese Canadians and others in similar situations, the Mulroney government delayed negotiations for four years. Suddenly, just weeks before the writ was dropped, a deal was announced.

By 1990, so low in public-opinion polls as to be almost off the scale, especially with voters in urban, "ethnic" Ontario, Mulroney personally launched another blatant public-relations exercise, offering redress to Chinese and Ukrainian Canadians. This time, however, his motives were well understood by most Canadians, and his hypocritical efforts produced no outpouring of positive reinforcement.

One other "ethnic" issue caused widespread divisiveness; yet, it was a simple matter that probably could not have developed in the pre-Mulroney era. It involved the right of Canadians practising the Sikh religion to wear turbans while serving in the RCMP. It was, therefore, essentially a western Canadian issue, since the Mounties serve as the provincial police force in the Prairie provinces and B.C. Under pressure from the right-wing and western element within his own caucus, the prime minister allowed an essentially straightforward matter to become an issue of national scope, blown out of all proportion as it gained momentum over the course of a year and more of inaction. The public, who already knew by now that the Mulroney government did not really believe in either bilingualism or multiculturalism, were subjected to the spectacle of their nation's leader agonizing over his response to a thinly disguised appeal to racism.

A similar bias also emerged in the case of immigration and refugee policy. In spite of its appropriate liberal rhetoric on the campaign trail, the same government that later refused to recall Parliament over constitutional or native crises of nationwide importance showed its true colours in the summer of 1986, when it did not hesitate to reconvene Parliament in light of the national "emergency" created by a handful of Tamil refugees in a leaky raft drifting ashore on the coast of Newfoundland. The vocabulary used by Mulroney and several of his ministers at the time, and especially Secretary of State Benoît Bouchard, who once mused about the "racial purity" of the Lac St. Jean region, appeared to many experts to be designed to increase anxiety and heighten racism, despite its stated purpose of "cooling tensions."

The Tory "crackdown" on immigration and refugee policy continued unabated through their first mandate, and well into their second. Having decreased the "family class" category of immigrants, the cornerstone of Liberal immigration policy, the Mulroney government then moved on to introduce a new category of immigrant: the "business/investor class" — foreign entrepreneurs willing to invest large sums of money upon arrival, who were given VIP treatment.

To add insult to injury, the allotment for the family-class category was readjusted upwards shortly before the 1988 election and has since been reduced once more.

At the same time, the refugee situation was rapidly becoming untenable, largely because of Tory cutbacks in staff and programs. The government ignored three independent studies and the recommendations of a parliamentary committee, introducing bills to limit access and expedite processing of refugees. These were immediately declared to be in violation of our U.N. obligations and unanimously criticized by service groups and agencies working in the field, including the Canadian Council of Churches.

To no avail. Since then, the refugee backlog has increased exponentially, and the plight of individuals caught in the process, often for years, is regularly reported by the media. Yet, the government has gone on the offensive. The belligerent tone taken by former Immigration minister Barbara McDougall has been echoed by the current minister responsible, Pierre Cadieux, who announced in fall 1991 that legislation would be introduced to tighten up the screening process for new arrivals and facilitate the deportation of those who fail to meet the more stringent criteria.

The phenomenon of "economic" refugees has undoubtedly increased in recent years, causing justifiable concerns over "queue-jumping" and abuses of the system. But the government's aggressive, dogmatic approach to the situation has led to the creation of a less fair system, and quite possibly to increased attempts by desperate people to circumvent it.

Despite mounting evidence that Canada's new return practices have put legitimate refugees in jeopardy, and criticism of such practices by human-rights groups, Canadians have been led to believe by their government that almost all refugee claimants are bogus and in no danger if they are returned. A November 1991 *Globe and Mail*/CBC poll found considerable support for a more hardline approach to refugee determination and little recognition of the fact the government's approach itself could be construed as unfair and inequitable.

Perhaps more revealing of the government's real agenda is the fact that the same ministerial announcement in November 1991 froze Canada's quota of immigrants for the following year, despite the fact an overwhelming majority of Canadians in the same poll expressed the view that immigration was good for the country and that overall numbers should be increased. At the same time, the family-class definition was to be further restricted, thereby excluding many previously acceptable categories of relatives.

The Mulroney government's lack of sympathy on immigration matters has been echoed in the attitude of several of its ministers of Indian Affairs. With the exception of David Crombie, they have tended to ignore representations of native peoples, reduce government funding and programs, and reject aboriginal claims out of hand. The government's steadfast refusal to live up to the financial terms of the Cree-Naskapi James Bay agreement led that desperate group of citizens to seek redress at the United Nations.

In spite of Conservative rhetoric to the contrary, native people heard the message loudly and clearly that they were a very low priority of the government. After a series of undistinguished ministers served in the revolving door of Indian Affairs, the demise of the Meech Lake Accord and the subsequent eruption of the Oka crisis can hardly be termed surprising. Moreover, public opinion on this issue was unequivocal; Canadians' criticism of their federal government's handling of this matter, and their high level of support for measures related to native self-government in the current constitutional proposals, speak eloquently to their sense of fairness and responsibility, a sense which does not seem to be shared by the Mulroney Conservatives.

In much the same vein, the government has displayed a philosophical and economic aversion to such measures as affirmative-action programs. Like aboriginal peoples, women's groups were the victims of painful and regressive policy decisions such as the funding of REAL Women through the budget of the affirmative-action Women's Program of the Secretary of State's department, severe budgetary cuts to many of their sustaining grants, and the refusal of successive ministers to attend the traditional meeting with national women's representatives at their annual conference.

Perhaps the most unsettling element was the suspicion that these actions were politically motivated, since women, like native Canadians, had been vocal in their criticism of the government's actions. And, of course, neither group was a likely source of support.

In short, in their negative attitudes towards human rights and their unequal treatment of immigrants, refugees, women, and native peoples, the Mulroney government demonstrated a profound lack of commitment to fundamental Canadian values and the formal programs designed to support and nurture those values. Their inability to articulate an alternative national vision provoked public confusion, mass frustration, and widespread rage.

The most damaging result, however, was that many Canadians began eventually to question their own commitment to the political consensus that had been so carefully and painstakingly forged over the previous two decades. Having bought into the "Just Society" and the pan-Canadian vision, they were now being told, in hundreds of subtle and direct ways, that it was both wrong-headed and too expensive. Feeling economically vulnerable themselves after enduring massive tax increases and decreased levels of government services, they began to wonder if they had not been mistaken in their beliefs. Thus, while unifying policies such as bilingualism and multiculturalism received high levels of support in opinion polls throughout the previous ten years, the seven years of Conservative government saw a steady decline in those levels of support, and a parallel decline in the sense of national identity.

This process of decline, it could be argued, was already well under way when the ultimate débâcle of Meech Lake began to unfold.

In undertaking to acquire Quebec's signature on the 1982 constitutional amendment, Brian Mulroney believed he would be making history. He also apparently believed it would enable him to best his arch-nemesis, Pierre Trudeau, along the way. Instead, Mulroney's efforts to achieve this objective became his Waterloo.

Once more his coalition strategy came back to haunt him. Having been elected largely on the basis of his Quebec support, which was nationalist to the core, and having appointed several former supporters of the "Yes" side in the 1980 referendum to his cabinet, Brian Mulroney was unable to articulate a strong federalist vision, even if he had been so inclined. Instead, the premiers of Ontario and Manitoba were forced to speak on behalf of national interests while the prime minister gave away the store.

At the same time, Mulroney's dependence on his western support, particularly of the far right, meant that, when Meech began to unravel, many of his caucus members were especially susceptible to the arguments used by critics about "special powers" and "the distinct society."

But Mulroney had other difficulties on the accord: his government's incompetence and willingness to rewrite the rules of the game were the primary cause of the failure of this major initiative. The way in which Mulroney achieved the failure of the Meech Lake Accord is a monument to his government's record-breaking abuse of parliamentary democracy, ignorance of the Canadian political culture, and disdain for groups of citizens who are neither rich nor powerful.

How this ultimate failure was accomplished in spite of the original and unprecedented approval given by both federal opposition parties and all ten premiers is a remarkable tale, in which Mulroney's political instincts overpowered nation-building considerations.

The accord, while rejected almost immediately by some experts on the basis of content, was not widely opposed by most Canadians at first. Their later opposition was on the basis of process as much as content. In short, while the accord was flawed in content, it was doomed because of Mulroney and his government's strategy to ensure its passage.

It was in the process by which agreement was originally achieved that the seeds of the accord's eventual destruction were sown. This process was typical of Mulroney's approach to governing. Negotiating the amendment of the constitution of a country was, for him, the same as a business negotiation. It involved deal-making and manipulation, and a pressure-cooker environment in which both of these things could be most easily forced.

Determined to go down in history as the man who did what Pierre Trudeau could not by bringing Quebec on side, Mulroney made winning an overriding concern at Meech Lake on April 30, 1987.

This meeting, in turn, had been forced upon the government. Although bringing Quebec to adhere to the 1982 amendment had been outlined in the Throne Speech of 1984, virtually nothing had been done since by the government to achieve this objective.

Eventually the Quebec government of Robert Bourassa, which had been elected in 1985 and had publicly listed a set of five conditions in March 1986, became impatient and began using the forum of provincial premiers' gatherings to press its case. Mulroney responded by sending his federal-provincial relations minister, Lowell Murray, to discuss the matter with the various premiers, taking along a draft proposal from Ottawa responding to the five conditions.

On the basis of a reasonably positive response, Mulroney invited the premiers to a "working dinner" at his residence at Meech Lake to begin to examine the matter in more detail. And so, much like the Free Trade Agreement, which he drifted into almost by accident after his Shamrock Summit with Reagan, Mulroney had once again stumbled upon what would become a cornerstone of his tragic legacy.

It is not difficult to imagine the premiers' astonishment when Mulroney proposed they hammer out an actual agreement at this meeting. When he and the premiers finally did emerge with an "agreement in principle," Mulroney was ecstatic, although this "agreement" bore little resemblance to the original federal position. Any deal would do.

As days passed, however, it became apparent that none of the premiers was really sure what they had agreed to, and their bureaucrats were having great difficulty putting the agreement into appropriate constitutional language. Questions were also being raised by a number of politicians and academics concerned that the deal was flawed and would need to be carefully examined and amended before implementation.

Undeterred, Mulroney proceeded with a second meeting of the premiers in Ottawa at the historic Langevin Building on June 2, a meeting that had originally been scheduled as a mere formality to approve the final text in private before a public signing ceremony later in the day.

Instead, the meeting dragged on for nineteen hours, until the early morning of June 3. Several premiers and their bureaucrats raised serious concerns about the possible implications of the accord. Some threatened to leave, but were cajoled into staying by Mulroney in his role as the master manipulator.[4]

In the end, he wore them down, the deal was signed, and the deed was done. In his eyes, it had taken barely a month to accomplish something more significant than the agreement that had taken Pierre Trudeau nearly two years.

Unfortunately, in his haste, the quality of the "deal" was sacrificed. The increasing dissent of academics, intellectuals, and politicians should also have told him something, but, like the premiers, he dismissed these critics as insignificant, with one exception.

Joe Ghiz and John Buchanan, among others, have recounted how Mulroney spent considerable time at the beginning of the Langevin meeting reading quotations from Pierre Trudeau's broadside against the accord, which had appeared in newspapers across the country the previous week. He then rebutted each criticism in great detail, apparently reading from prepared notes.

As Michel Gratton revealed in his exposé of the early Mulroney years, the prime minister's obsession with Trudeau was long-standing and all-pervasive. Just days before their massive 1984 sweep, Gratton recounted, Mulroney was bitterly unhappy because the media were not accurately reporting the size of the crowds he was attracting. "During this period in mid-August," Gratton writes, "I began to worry the boss was starting to believe his own myth. He'd always been obsessed by the Trudeau legend and . . . thought him overrated. I found it unsettling that, in the midst of a staggering electoral victory, he was fretting because the papers weren't talking about Mulromania."[5]

His diatribe that day in 1987 against Trudeau, whom he accused at one point of "thinking he is still running the country," was so intense and prolonged that several premiers felt obliged to intervene and assure Mulroney they had not been influenced by the former prime minister's arguments. Finally, Richard Hatfield interrupted Mulroney by saying, "Look, will you forget about him!" And for a while they did.

At this point, the first part of the process was complete. A major constitutional amendment had been drafted and agreed to by the prime minister and ten premiers, behind closed doors, in less than two months.

Compared to the previous initiative of Pierre Trudeau, when negotiations had gone on for months and had ended in failure, leading the prime minister to decide to move unilaterally by October 1980, this process was not only far swifter but clearly a "success."

On the other hand, the contents of the proposed federal drafts and counteroffers of the provinces had all been made public in the 1980–82 round. Most of the first ministers' meeting in September

1980 had been televised. As a result, the Meech process was perceived to be far more secretive and elitist. Moreover, since the agreement had been concluded in large measure without or in spite of expert advice, it was a poorly crafted document. Both of these aspects of the initial process — its secrecy and its emphasis on eleven men to the exclusion even of expert advisers — would continue to plague the accord throughout its troubled life, and in the end would contribute heavily to its downfall.

The second phase of the process lasted two and a half years, from May 1987 until early 1990. It could probably best be described as a period of passive indifference bordering on arrogance. Certainly, it was marked by the stubborn intransigence of Brian Mulroney in the face of growing opposition and a changing cast of players.

At the federal level, the Liberal and New Democratic parties, while officially supportive of the deal, had called repeatedly for a parliamentary-committee process similar to the one used in 1980-81 to review, amend, and improve it. Both had introduced considerable numbers of amendments, all of which were defeated by the government after little debate.

When a special parliamentary committee was finally established by the government, with great reluctance, it was on the understanding that no changes of any kind would be accepted. This ludicrous position only served to heighten the degree of antipathy felt by critics of the deal, and the committee's report was viewed as a blatant and hypocritical sham.

Once again the legitimacy of Parliament was being called into question. Compared to the 1980–81 committee process, the Mulroney approach appeared even more unacceptable. In that earlier case, the committee not only heard far more witnesses, representing a greater range of Canadians, but adopted many of their recommendations. The 1981 committee's report proposed several amendments, almost all of which were accepted by the minister responsible, Jean Chrétien, who had played a key role in building consensus during this process, and by the government as a whole.

As a result, in 1981, interest groups representing women, the ethnocultural community, official-language minorities, the handicapped, human rights, and aboriginal issues — all of whom had expressed initial concerns — were overwhelmingly in favour of the final legislation and said so publicly. Despite certain ongoing concerns on the part of some elements of the native community, who at first had agreed as well and then subsequently split on the issue, the level of consensus among key groups in society on the final content was very high indeed, and ordinary Canadians knew it.

Of course, such was not the case in 1987. When the parliamentary committee reported in September, it recommended no changes at all, despite a preponderance of testimony from similar groups calling for major changes to the legislation. Mulroney and his advisers continued to refer to the accord as a "seamless web" in which not one word could be altered without dire consequences. Indeed, his defence of the accord at this point was highly reminiscent of his approach to the Free Trade Agreement. In the face of criticism, he dug in his heels and became irrevocably committed.

Knowing that his overwhelming majority in the House assured him of the accord's passage, Mulroney was apparently unconcerned by the increasing criticism. And the accord did eventually pass in the House of Commons. When it was debated by the Liberal-dominated Senate and then returned to the House with the same amendments the Liberals had introduced earlier, it was passed unamended a second time on June 22, 1988, thereby completing its adoption by the federal Parliament.

However, as Mulroney well knew, it was also necessary for the accord to be introduced into and approved by the legislature of each province. Meanwhile, the government of Manitoba had come very close to being defeated in an election in March 1988. The new leader of the opposition, Liberal Sharon Carstairs, was a well-known opponent of the deal who had declared, upon learning she held the balance of power, that "Meech Lake is dead."

An election in New Brunswick in November 1987 had already cast considerable doubt on the accord's fate. First, New Brunswick, and then Newfoundland, in April 1989, elected premiers who not only had not signed the accord but had stated publicly they were opposed to it. This opposition was critical since the deal still had to be ratified by all ten provinces within a three-year period from the date when the first province did so — in this case, Quebec on June 23, 1987. By late 1989, two provinces — New Brunswick and Manitoba — still had not done so, and Newfoundland's new premier was stating publicly that he would rescind his province's approval if his concerns were not treated seriously. He then revealed that his calls to the prime minister had gone unreturned and that the federal minister responsible, Senator Lowell Murray, had never tried to speak or meet with him.

Not only had other prominent politicians joined Trudeau in his crusade against the accord, but representatives of a number of special-interest groups — official-language minorities, multicultural groups, aboriginal peoples, and women's groups — continued to complain that they had been totally excluded from the process and were threatened by the contents of the deal. In spite of all this, Mulroney and his government did nothing, apparently continuing to believe that their opposition was unimportant.

In November 1989, at the annual first ministers' meeting on the economy — a process begun by Mulroney himself in Regina in 1985 — Meech Lake forced itself onto the agenda, in spite of the efforts of the federal government to avoid it. It was put there by Clyde Wells, who had declared just before leaving Newfoundland for the meeting in Ottawa that either his concerns about Meech would be dealt with at this meeting or he would immediately rescind Newfoundland's approval of the accord.

It soon became apparent that a concerted strategy on the part of Mulroney and the seven supportive premiers was developing. Their plan was to isolate Wells, literally and figuratively. They would ignore Gary Filmon of Manitoba, whose opposition was not serious but merely tactical because of his minority situation, and they would ignore Frank McKenna of New Brunswick, who was viewed as far more conciliatory. They would train all of their guns on Wells, who was expected to crumple under the pressure. This strategy did not sit well with most Canadians. By the time the constitutional issue arose, the public was already psychologically inclined to favour Wells as the underdog. As a lawyer who had served on the Canadian Bar Association's constitutional committee and represented the federal government in the Newfoundland court reference in 1981, Wells was nevertheless more of an expert than Mulroney.

This fact was evident to everyone watching the meeting on television that day, when Mulroney and Wells got into an unscripted shouting match reminiscent of the famous Trudeau–Johnson exchange in 1968. It climaxed when Mulroney, carried away once again by his own rhetoric, attempted to chastise Wells for his position that no one province should be able to hold up progress. To the astonishment of the experts in the room, Mulroney made a reference to the entry of Newfoundland into Confederation, that demonstrated not only an ignorance of history but an apparent ignorance of the logic behind the amending formula contained in Meech Lake itself. An incredulous and furious Wells retorted, "I cannot allow the suggestion to remain on the table that my attitude is somehow that I do not want Quebec to be part of the country, or that I am not being generous in making sure that Quebec is a full constitutional participant, and frankly, Prime Minister, you should check the historical facts before you use the example to which you have just referred. It happens to have nothing to do, no relevance to the constitutional issues that are involved in the Meech Lake Accord."

Mulroney, stung by the telling criticism, quickly changed the subject. The meeting ended inconclusively, with Mulroney promising to send Lowell Murray on a second tour of provincial capitals to see if compromise positions could be worked out. Wells went home to make good on his threat to rescind approval. Reporters went back to their desks to prepare statements that Pierre Trudeau had been reincarnated as a provincial premier.

To the amazement of even the accord's most aggressive supporters, Mulroney's next attempt consisted of setting up yet another parliamentary committee — the Charest Committee — with a mandate to seek a means out of the impasse while always keeping in mind that the accord was a seamless web that could not be altered.

To many, this consistently unbending approach was indicative either of an Alice-in-Wonderland mentality or of desperation. The latter, of course, was caused by Mulroney's overwhelming dependence on his Quebec support base, still nationalistic to the core, and the increasing unrest of his Quebec caucus led by none other than Lucien Bouchard.

Meanwhile, in another move reminiscent of the FTA debate, Mulroney had been raising the stakes on Meech for months. As the going got tougher, he became more adamant. Not only could the accord not be changed, but its acceptance was now described as essential for the survival of the country. What had started as an exercise by the political elite to gain Quebec's signature on an existing amendment had, over time, become a last-ditch attempt to placate a Quebec that otherwise would feel totally rejected and leave Confederation.

While this was all news to the average Quebecker at the start of the process, the incessant repetition of this doomsday scenario began to have an effect. By early 1990, nationalist sentiment in Quebec was on the upswing, and individuals who had little or no idea of the content of the Meech Lake Accord were expressing the belief that its passage was essential for their cultural survival.

At the same time, it was becoming increasingly clear that Mulroney's failure to define the parameters of the debate at the outset, by abandoning the federal draft and acceding to many provincial demands unrelated to Quebec's five concerns, had succeeded in achieving short-term agreement at the expense of long-term discontent. In short, Mulroney had created a crisis where one never needed to exist. Not only did most Quebeckers now believe the rejection of the accord would mean a rejection of their role in the federation, but every special-interest group and other province now believed they had a right to be not only consulted on their concerns but also accommodated. The "Quebec round" had turned into a free-for-all.

When the Charest report's recommendations emerged in May, containing several suggestions for amendments to the accord in a "companion" document, as well as outlining a process for a second round of negotiations on such matters as Senate reform, the crisis escalated exponentially. Bouchard, outraged by the "betrayal" of Quebec by Mulroney and the rest of the Conservatives, resigned from the cabinet and the caucus to sit as an independent.

The issues by now were totally obscured by the "survival of Canada" debate — taking place on an emotional level and exacerbated by Mulroney's hyperbole and doomsday scenarios. The proponents were reduced to the argument that, regardless of the merits of the accord, it must be passed unchanged because the alternative was Quebec's separation. It was in this supercharged atmosphere, brought about by nearly three years of intransigence and apathy, that the third and final phase of the Meech Lake Accord's demise unfolded in Ottawa in June, only three weeks before its deadline for ratification.

Though the mistakes made by Mulroney and Murray in the first two stages of the process were many, they quickly fade into insignificance when compared to the blunders and the cavalier approach taken in this final round of negotiations.

Having been publicly humiliated by Wells in the November 1989 meeting, Mulroney decided to keep the proceedings behind closed doors at all costs. No doubt, he also hoped that doing so would enable him to repeat his success of the initial agreement by sheer will-power and manipulation. As former Manitoba attorney general Roland Penner later described the initial meeting in 1987: "Mulroney just wrote us and said 'Come down to Meech Lake for a little chat,' said the spider to the fly." This time the fly was to be Wells, and the little chat was to be over dinner in a museum restaurant in Hull, overlooking the Parliament Buildings.

Unfortunately for Mulroney, not even the marathon seven days of closed-door meetings that ensued could succeed in changing Wells's mind, although he came very close. As Canadians sat riveted to their television sets for nearly a week, exhausted premiers came and went from the Conference Centre in downtown Ottawa, each giving a different version of events. Federal "officials" also ventured into the fray and further muddied the waters. The event became a media feeding frenzy in which accusations of bad faith, eavesdropping, and deliberate deception were bandied about by both "sides."

In the end, a "deal" was announced on June 9, at the first public event of the entire process. Although Mulroney and the other premiers attempted to put the best light possible on this agreement, it was obvious to the general public that Wells had agreed to nothing except to take the "deal" back to his province for approval or rejection. It was also obvious to Canadians that neither Wells nor the Manitoba delegation, which included Carstairs and the NDP leader, Gary Doer, and which was committed by provincial legislation to examine the deal before ratification, were remotely happy. Nor were aboriginal peoples, who had failed to have their issues placed conclusively on the agenda.

A variety of other special-interest groups feared their Charter rights might still be infringed by the accord, and questioned the validity of the "companion" document. When a number of prestigious legal experts wrote an open letter to the prime minister also questioning the constitutional legitimacy of the add-on proposal, their fears appeared to be confirmed.

Even more significant, however, was the widespread public dissatisfaction with the secrecy of the process, the exclusion of many relevant players, and the uneven treatment of provinces and special interests. In the next few weeks, several blatant attempts by the federal government to blackmail the recalcitrants — notably by Lowell Murray, who at one point suggested Manitoba should ratify the deal and then study its contents, and by John Crosbie, who suggested Newfoundland's failure to ratify could have severe economic consequences for that province in terms of federal transfer payments — further destroyed public acceptance of the deal.

The final death blow ironically was dealt by Mulroney himself. Unable to contain himself once again in an interview with the media, he responded to questions about why he had waited so long to convene the meeting of first ministers with a statement he most likely will regret for the rest of his life. He boasted that the delay had all been part of his plan, which he had confided only to his three closest advisers. "I told them when it would be," he recounted. "I told them a month ago when we were going to start meeting. It's like an election campaign. You've got to count backwards. You've got to pick your date and work backwards from it. And I told them 'That's the day I'm going to roll all the dice.'"

When the accord eventually died on June 23 at the hands of a Manitoba aboriginal MNA, Elijah Harper, who used procedural tactics to delay until it was too late, and a furious Clyde Wells refused to bring the motion to a vote because of last-minute bullying tactics by Murray, the majority of Canadians approved.

In light of these developments, a strong case can be made that the deal, which initially had considerable public support, came to be overwhelmingly rejected by the general public, in large measure because of the way in which it was handled by Mulroney and his government. And this was the case even before the disastrous week-long meetings in Ottawa, which only served to reinforce that sentiment. As a watershed Gallup poll on the issue clearly demonstrated, by May 1990 only one in four Canadians believed the accord "would be a good thing" for Canada. Even in Quebec, where its failure was said by Mulroney to be critical, less than half of the population (41 percent) agreed that it would be good for the country.

The contrast with the 1980–82 process is striking. Two months after the proclamation of the Constitution Act, 1982, in April of that year, Gallup reported: "in a ratio of four to one Canadians feel that, in the long run, our Constitution will be a good thing for Canada." Even more remarkable, especially in light of Mulroney's later attempts to rewrite history and paint a picture of widespread unhappiness and discontent in that province, only 16 percent of Quebeckers believed the 1982 deal would "not be a good thing" for the country, while 49 percent positively supported it.

Clearly the demise of the constitutional-reform package left the country in a state of confusion. Quebec nationalists marched in Montreal the following day, St. Jean Baptiste Day; western nationalists renewed their demands for Senate reform. Mulroney, amazed that the accord had died, gave a subdued speech on national television in which he called for calm. It would undoubtedly have been more effective had it not followed his repeated statements that the failure of Meech would mean economic chaos and the beginning of the end for Canada.

Despite the fact that he was the instigator of and principal player in the Meech drama, Brian Mulroney has consistently refused to accept any of the blame for the current disunity. He attributes the accord's failure to other participants such as Harper and Wells, and even to Jean Chrétien, who had opposed the deal but attempted to broker a solution based on the Charest report in the final days.

Mulroney has also attempted to blame the accord's failure on the amending formula contained in the 1982 agreement, a formula insisted upon by the provincial premiers over the objections of the Trudeau government. Although nothing in that formula forced anyone to wait three years, as he often implied, Mulroney frequently laid the blame for the accord's failure at Pierre Trudeau's doorstep.

He then attempted to spread the guilt around through personal attacks on Chrétien, Trudeau, and "all those who lulled Quebeckers in 1980 by promising them a renewed federalism, only to exclude them from the constitution." In addition to accusing them openly of deliberate bad faith, his unstated premise was that the Constitution Act, 1982, was not the fulfilment of renewed federalism because Quebec did not sign.

As columnist Christopher Young wrote in the *Ottawa Citizen* in December 1990, "This is the separatist myth promulgated by Parti Québécois leader Jacques Parizeau and Bloc Québécois leader Lucien Bouchard. It's become something worse than a myth — a Big Lie, intended by constant repetition to be accepted as the truth." Needless to say, Mulroney's negative tone did nothing to improve national unity and may well have served to make matters worse by playing into the separatists' hands.

It soon became obvious that Mulroney also intended native peoples to pay a price for their part in the accord's defeat. A proposal for a royal commission on aboriginal issues, which the prime minister had "coincidentally" offered in writing five days before the accord was due to expire, was abruptly withdrawn shortly thereafter. As well, both Mulroney and Indian Affairs minister Tom Siddon then boycotted a historic national summit of Indian chiefs.

Meanwhile, in the rest of the country, having attempted to convince Canadians that the failure of Meech would be disastrous, Mulroney failed to articulate an alternative. As a result, Canadians became convinced that no one "was speaking for Canada." They also believed that no one was articulating the vision of Canada that reflected a commitment to a pluralistic, bilingual society in which equality of opportunity and equitable treatment of regions are paramount concerns. They had just rejected a deal they concluded would exclude various groups, call into question rights guaranteed in the Charter, and weaken the ability of the federal government to assure national social programs with minimum standards. They perceived a leadership vacuum at the federal level that neither a parliamentary committee on the amending formula or the Citizens' Forum could fill.

Consequently, Mulroney's constitutional initiative, far from achieving national reconciliation, resulted in an even greater level of hostility and distrust. The centrifugal forces unleashed by this process are undiminished nearly two years later.

And yet many would argue that it did not have to be so. If Mulroney had bargained in good faith, and demonstrated a commitment to the underlying principles of Canadian political culture, the results might have been very different. Certainly, the five conditions set by Quebec could have been resolved in other ways, while the add-on demands of the other provinces could and should have been rejected as inappropriate.

The summer of 1990, following the demise of the accord, was truly remarkable. The consequences of the near total abdication of responsibility on the part of the Mulroney government will no doubt be the subject of lengthy debate among political scientists for years to come. Mulroney's disappearance to Harrington Lake for most of the summer, widely remarked upon at the time, has become even more contentious in retrospect.

Proponents of the accord predictably claimed that the increase in nationalist support in Quebec and in English-speaking Canada after the collapse of the accord were inevitable. In their view, the national-unity crisis that ensued justified their arguments that Meech should have been passed in order to avoid far greater demands for decentralization.

Those who opposed the accord rejected this argument categorically. They pointed to the behaviour of the prime minister and his cabinet in the aftermath of Meech as the real catalyst for the increased dissent and tension. It was not the failure of the accord, they argued, but the failure of the Mulroney government to respond appropriately that produced the current constitutional crisis.

There was greater agreement on the subject of the Oka crisis, which began on July 11 and continued throughout the summer. Virtually all observers agreed that the federal government's actions before and during the Meech crisis led to a heightened state of frustration on the part of native peoples; the federal government's failure to intervene promptly in the Oka crisis was a primary reason for its lengthy duration.

The only contentious point is the degree to which this lack of leadership resulted from incompetence or deliberate abdication of responsibility. Tom Siddon, the weakest minister in that portfolio in decades, remained in British Columbia for the first phase of the crisis. He took several days to issue a statement, and then stressed that the matter fell under municipal and provincial jurisdiction. The federal Department of Indian Affairs, it appeared, had no responsibility in the matter.

The prime minister, forced to address the issue from his retreat at Harrington Lake, simply indicated that he believed the matter was under control. "I'm convinced everything will be settled quickly," he said.

After a week of escalating tensions the government still had no intention of recalling Parliament, appointing a federal mediator, or entering into direct discussions. The leaders of national aboriginal associations, such as the Assembly of First Nations, organized demonstrations on Parliament Hill and actually launched a court challenge in order to "attempt to force Ottawa to assume its legal and constitutional responsibilities."

They were joined in their criticism of the government by organizations such as the Canadian Human Rights Commission and the Canadian Council of Churches, which issued a scathing rebuke of the government's inaction and called for the immediate appointment of a federal mediator.

The government finally did respond, by sending in the army. Canadians were mortified and then outraged to find themselves the subject of criticism by Amnesty International, the United Nations, and the European Community's Human Rights Commission. Although ambivalent about the use of force and the specific actions of certain Mohawk groups involved, Canadians were overwhelmingly supportive of native peoples and critical of the government's handling of this and related native issues. By fall 1990, 85 percent of Canadians were still supportive of Elijah Harper's decision to kill the Meech Lake Accord; over 50 percent identified aboriginal concerns as the most important constitutional issue for their political leaders to address. Over 70 percent believed the Mulroney government had mishandled the Oka issue from beginning to end. Few could understand how a dispute over a golf course could have been allowed to escalate as it did.

Most Canadians also believed Parliament should have been recalled. However, the crisis was evidently less threatening to the government than twenty Tamils in a leaky raft. Parliament, now totally marginalized in the political process, was not reconvened until late September, after the issue had been resolved.

Fall 1990 also saw the creation of the Citizens' Forum, whose purpose was to consult with Canadians, and a joint parliamentary committee on the amending formula, apparently designed to support Brian Mulroney's continued but erroneous claim that the amending formula had been partly responsible for the accord package not being accepted.

Nevertheless, the overwhelming preponderance of expert testimony at the hearings of this committee stressed that the formula had in no way been responsible for the failure of the accord. Most witnesses also stated that, while improvements could be made, the mechanisms in place since 1982 were essentially sound. Noted constitutional expert Stephen Scott put the matter in perspective during his testimony before the committee when he declared: "The failure of the 1987 Constitutional Accord is, in my view, not the failure of Canadian federalism in general; not the failure of the constitutional amendment process; and not the failure of Canadian federalism in the sense of an inability to address Quebec's five stated concerns."

Scott then identified what he believed to be the three primary reasons for the accord's collapse: "perceived substantive defects . . ., the methods by which the [package] was devised . . ., and third, and most important, the extreme methods employed in the attempt to secure its passage."[6]

Undeterred, the prime minister continued to publicly criticize the amending formula and praise the "vital" work of the committee in preparing for some unspecified future negotiations. Given the growing nationalist sentiment in Quebec and the political difficulties of his old ally, Robert Bourassa, Mulroney was evidently realizing that he would not be able to avoid the issue forever.

By November 1990, support for separation had risen to record levels in Quebec. In the rest of the country, the feeling that "Quebec asked for too much" was shared by 67 percent of the population.

In early January 1991, Mulroney was on the rebound. He and his cabinet began to refer to the new agenda that they planned to introduce, first through a budget in late February, and then shortly thereafter in a Throne Speech after prorogation.

To the astonishment of many, both Mulroney and a number of his "unofficial" spokespersons began to suggest that he was the only federal leader able to reconcile Quebec and reunite the country. If necessary, he would fight the next election campaign on the national-unity issue. Coming from the man most Canadians held responsible for the national-unity crisis, these were brave words indeed.

The subsequent reports of the Campeau-Bélanger Commission and Allaire Committee of the Quebec Liberal Party, released in early 1991, forced Bourassa's hand. Mulroney then announced that his cabinet would form a "Unity Committee" under the leadership of the new minister of Intergovernmental Affairs, Joe Clark. Once a package of proposals had been agreed upon by the cabinet, he declared, a new parliamentary committee would be established to consult Canadians on the package.

During summer-long deliberations of the Unity Cabinet, it became apparent that there were serious divisions between Mulroney's Quebec and western ministers. Eventually, however, a set of proposals for constitutional reform was finally hammered out and triumphantly released in fall 1991. But the Canadian public was no longer interested in the national-unity issue, evidently suffering from a type of constitutional fatigue. As countless opinion polls had demonstrated throughout fall 1991, Canadians' positions had hardened along linguistic and regional lines since the failure of Meech Lake. There was less rather than more willingness to compromise in order to achieve a deal. This situation was compounded by the public's now well-entrenched belief that the system had become unworkable. Western premiers were demanding that issues such as Senate reform be addressed in the same round as Quebec's concerns, aboriginal groups were insisting that their issues be placed on the agenda now rather than later, and new issues such as a Social Charter were being added to the list with each passing day.

These developments are especially distressing when compared with November 1982, shortly after the signing of the Trudeau constitutional package, when Gallup reported that Canadians' confidence in the future of Confederation was actually on the upswing. Of those interviewed, some 67 percent expressed the view that Canada was in no danger of breaking up. In Quebec, 58 percent agreed with that statement; only 23 percent feared separation was inevitable.

Now it may be too late to undo the damage. Public-opinion polls consistently reflect fierce public resistance on both sides of the issues. The current set of federal proposals, rejected in November 1991 by a majority of Canadians in Quebec and the rest of the country, were designed to provide something for everyone: Senate reform for western Canada; two references rather than one to the distinctive nature of Quebec.

Yet, despite the public's overwhelming support for strong central government, a man who believes in the "community of communities" approach has been put in charge of the government's plan. The federal package contains proposals for eliminating the federal declaratory and disallowance powers; transferring powers to the provinces; and creating a Council of the Federation, which would have a further constraining effect on federal decision making. The package is not only unpopular, however, but irrelevant to most Canadians, who, even in Quebec, continue to list economic issues as a far greater source of concern.

Meanwhile, the parliamentary committee assigned to consult with Canadians on these proposals has been a fiasco — a model of incompetence, disorganization, and deliberate attempts to exclude "unfriendly" expert witnesses, to say nothing of patronage contract appointments and partisan bickering. Exasperated, both opposition parties threatened to withdraw their participation unless major changes were made. Their threats, in turn, became the subject of media coverage, leading several observers, and, above all, the Mulroney Tories, to accuse them of playing partisan politics with the future of the country. The fact remains that, in almost all of the Dobbie-Castonguay Committee's public hearings, those few

Canadians who were allowed to participate spent most of their time denouncing the government and its leadership.

The vitriolic mood that continues to permeate the country's psyche does not appear to augur well for the type of consensus-building Brian Mulroney and his team belatedly have come to recognize as essential for such an exercise. Despite recent attempts to compare himself with his illustrious predecessor, Canadians know Mulroney is no John A. Macdonald. Nor is he a nation-builder. Having rolled the dice once too often, the prime minister and his government appear to have little credibility left, and no mandate to lead this initiative. The gravity of their situation is all too clear, but the way out remains a mystery. Perhaps the greatest tragedy of this situation is the fact that Canadians, who had developed a genius for consensus and tolerance, have been driven to intransigence by a leader who simply does not belong and who has managed, in seven years, to destroy our faith in ourselves and our country.

NOTES

1. Jackson et al., *Politics in Canada*, pp. 110–2.
2. D. Stasiulis, "The Symbolic Mosaic Reaffirmed: Multiculturalism Policy," in K. Graham, ed., *How Ottawa Spends, 1988–89* (Ottawa: Carleton School of Public Administration, 1989), p. 103.
3. D. Stasiulis, "The Symbolic Mosaic Reaffirmed," p. 102.
4. A. Cohen, *A Deal Undone* (Vancouver/Toronto: Douglas and McIntyre, 1990), pp. 105–17.
5. M. Gratton, *So, What Are the Boys Saying?*, p. 54.
6. S. Scott, Presentation to the Special Joint Committee on the Constitution, August 1990.

5. Winning at All Costs
How the Mulroney Conservatives Destroyed Our Faith in the Electoral Process

> We are at a point where the differences in our political parties require the judgement and decision of Canadians. The differences are clear and substantial; the decision Canadians face on November 21 will make a difference. . . . We intend to run on our record of the past and our plan for the future.
>
> — Brian Mulroney, October 1, 1988

Brian Mulroney may never have spoken truer words than the ones he used to launch the 1988 election campaign. There was, indeed, a substantial difference between the positions of the Conservative and opposition parties, and the Conservatives did, in fact, believe they could run on their record and win.

Given the nature of that record after the government's first term in office, Canadians might well have been forgiven for questioning their confidence. With the Mulroney Conservatives at third place in the polls for most of the two years prior to the election call, while the Liberal Party stood around 40 percent, an even more significant question is how they were able to convince Canadians to give them a second mandate and another majority government.

The explanation for these election results appears to be complex and unusual: political scientists, media strategists, and pollsters are still debating the relative importance and potential long-term implications of a number of factors.

Many would argue that the 1988 election was a unique event in recent Canadian history. Certainly, it was essentially a single-issue campaign, a phenomenon rarely seen in Canadian politics.

It was unusual as well in that, for the first time in its history, one of the two major parties was unable to finance a full-scale campaign. Another peculiarity was the significant financial resources expended on advertising by special interests, which had the effect of benefiting a political party, something the Elections Act had intended to avoid. The regulations of the act limit the total amount of spending any party can undertake in order to ensure a level playing field for all the contestants. In this election, however, the tilt was considerable.

Unprecedented as well was the importation by the Conservatives of American-style negative and personalized communications strategies.

Yet, the campaign began simply enough, with the prime minister announcing the dissolution of Parliament on October 1. The announcement was not unexpected. This time the Conservatives held all the cards, including incumbency, and they had chosen the date with care. The decision on when to call the election, and how to run it, was the culmination of several months — indeed a solid year — of behind-the-scenes planning by Conservative party strategists and advisers appointed by Mulroney and operating under the direction of the campaign co-chairs, Senators Norm Atkins and Michel Cogger.

A secret campaign strategy group had been meeting since early December 1987 to devise an election plan. By January 30, 1988, the group was presented with a position paper that addressed a number of areas in which the government would have to remedy its perceived poor performance. The free-trade initiative was not one of them. On the contrary, the paper argued that the free-trade deal was a problem for the Liberals: "The negative appeal against free trade, and in particular that our cultural identity and other distinctive features of Canadian life are endangered, has failed. . . . Unequivocal opposition to free trade is John Turner's big gamble, and it appears to have failed." How wrong this prediction was amazed and consternated the campaign team.

The position paper did correctly predict the Liberals would not be able to remain in first place in the polls throughout the year (long before the disastrous failed coup attempt on Turner's leadership in April ensured that result). It also concluded that the Conservatives would be best served by a strategy based on polling results showing a high level of anxiety among Canadians concerning changes in the economy and the world. The paper argued that the Tory campaign should therefore emphasize not only their solid record, but their ability to "manage change." Few Canadians remember that "managing change" was to be the major theme of the Conservative campaign, for, although the Tories started out with clear intentions to focus on their record, things did not go as planned for very long.

On October 1, the Mulroney team believed they were in very good shape to fight an election campaign. Certainly, they had more money than they were allowed to spend, and an organization superior even to the one they had had in place during the 1984 campaign.

Although their standing in the polls remained a source of concern, it had recently improved noticeably, as their pollster Allan Gregg had predicted. Just days before the announcement of the election, on September 26, an Angus Reid poll actually put the Conservatives in first place, at 40 percent, with the NDP in second position, at 31 percent, and the Liberals trailing at 26 percent.

Many accounts of the 1988 election describe two separate campaigns within it. Before the leaders' debate the Tories, as Graham Fraser wrote in *Playing for Keeps*, attempted to cruise to victory. The second strategy, devised in the last half of the campaign to avoid snatching defeat from the jaws of victory, saw the Tories use every available tool at their disposal, and invent several new ones. However, no account has analysed the Conservatives' behaviour from the twin perspectives of their increasing aptitude for bending or breaking the rules, and their longstanding ability to conceal their neoconservative agenda behind liberal rhetoric.

Yet, it is only when seen from this viewpoint that the 1988 election can be understood in terms of its subsequent impact on Canadians and the country. Simply put, the 1988 election was a repeat performance of everything the Mulroney Conservatives had already demonstrated in office — deception, deliberate misrepresentation, and disregard for convention. As a result, their victory, while impressive in terms of the numbers, was a Pyrrhic one, bound to disappoint in record time as the people learned they had been duped again.

The 1988 Conservative election campaign was, if possible, an even greater logistical success than that of 1984. Lacking nothing in the way of financial resources, personnel, or experience, the organizers of Brian Mulroney's second electoral outing set new standards of efficiency and luxury on the campaign trail. Given the beautifully appointed private jet with all the trimmings, it was not surprising that journalists preferred to be assigned to the Conservatives rather than to the poverty-stricken Liberals, leapfrogging across the country in rented planes and on public transit, or to the NDP.

In spite of masterful logistics, however, there were problems almost from the beginning. The seeds of the Conservatives' problems lay in their failure to predict the importance of the trade issue. They had not bothered to develop a substantive game plan to defend the deal; they simply had no intention of discussing it, and apparently believed the opposing parties could not force them to do so.

That they clung to this view, despite the Liberal-dominated Senate's forcing the election on this very issue, is remarkable, to say the least, but they apparently believed the advantages of incumbency would allow them to set the agenda. This fundamental error was matched only by their underestimation of John Turner, particularly in the leaders' debates. After a dismal performance in 1984 and four years to prepare himself, his desire for revenge in a rematch might reasonably have been expected, particularly if the Tories had paid attention to his greatly improved public appearances in the year leading up to the election. But the Conservative strategists ignored Turner, just as they did the trade deal.

A third problem was their unrealistic strategy for managing their own leader. Mulroney, viewed by some Conservative strategists to be a handicap, was to be "cocooned." His every campaign appearance was to be stage-managed, his every performance scripted. The absurdity of the controlled approach was sarcastically exposed by journalist Linda Diebel, among others, in describing the scheduled event in Dundurn, Saskatchewan, in the *Toronto Star*: "With not another farm as far as the eye could see and only a herd of Black Angus cattle on the horizon, the Mulroneys followed a meticulous little route behind ropes, while Conservative farming families watched from a respectful distance."

And strategists couldn't control the early candour of the cabinet and Conservative candidates. Finance Committee chairman Don Blenkarn quite truthfully assured reporters that the proposed goods and services tax (which other Tory hopefuls were studiously ignoring as a campaign plank) would produce considerably more revenue for the government than had been previously indicated. The minister of Housing, John McDermid, told the *Toronto Star* just days after the election call that the homeless would not receive any additional support from the Mulroney government. He then noted that "they can always get off the street and find a warm place to sleep and be taken care of on a temporary basis." Having only recently ascended to the cabinet, McDermid had not yet learned that believing in the neoconservative agenda and articulating it during an election campaign were two very different things.

The prime minister made a few candid remarks himself. Speaking at a luncheon of women's health advocates, he repeated several times: "The best social policy is a job." He then announced that "a buoyant economy is a higher priority for the Conservatives [than childcare]." Later the same day, unrepentant, he told another group that his government would not have introduced a proposal for a national childcare plan (which had died with the election call) if the economic recovery that began once they took over in 1984 had not been so strong.

By the time they reached the leaders' debates, at roughly the midpoint in the campaign, the Conservatives nevertheless believed they had little to worry about, and the polls certainly appeared to support that premise. A mirror image of the 1984 event, the debate again proved to be a turning point in the campaign. But this time the results were reversed. As journalist Peter Maser has written: "In his exchange with Mulroney, Turner did more than just reverse the standing in the polls. He succeeded in transforming a normal election campaign into a referendum in which the dominant issue became free trade. . . . [Turner] had managed to wrest control of the public agenda from the Conservatives and turn it to the one issue on which he was the most credible leader."[1]

Within days of the debate, after discussions with pollster Allan Gregg and a number of communications advisers, the Conservatives swung into action and implemented a totally new strategy. Ruthlessly implemented and devastatingly effective, this second strategy caused many of the ongoing problems of the Conservatives' second mandate, largely because it relied so heavily on winning at all costs. Overconfidence had landed them in this predicament, and underhanded tactics would rescue them.

Allan Gregg later admitted Mulroney's advisers were stunned by Turner's sudden rise in credibility and popularity. They soon became convinced he would have to be destroyed personally in order for them to recover. How they chose to accomplish this objective is highly instructive; their pride in recounting the details of the plan is perhaps equally revealing.

As Gregg recounted, the strategists viewed Turner as a "bridge" between anti–free trade sentiment and support for the Liberal Party. "What we had to do was bomb the bridge," Gregg stated nonchalantly, "and that is precisely what we proceeded to do." Looking south of the border to the vicious American presidential campaign that was unfolding simultaneously, the Conservatives' advertising and media gurus began by devising a similar type of strategy for the remainder of the campaign. A no-holds-barred attack similar to the sleazy campaign of George Bush left many observers seriously concerned for the nature of future elections in Canada.[2]

First, they devised a strategy to challenge Turner's veracity. They developed an ad campaign focused on "The Ten Big [Liberal] Lies" about free trade. Then they sent Brian Mulroney, at heart a self-proclaimed street fighter who "loves a good scrap," into the fray with a "myth a day" plan to discredit Turner and opponents of the deal. Even Michael Wilson accused Turner of "lying" to the Canadian people and of being a "traitor." Mulroney himself referred to Turner as "deceitful" or "dishonest" in virtually every speech he gave after this point in the campaign. Referring to

Turner's claim that jobs would be lost, not gained, if the deal were implemented, a favourite Mulroney line became: "The only job John Turner is interested in protecting is his own." Turner, meanwhile, in a stance typical of his old-school approach to politics, flatly refused to retaliate, despite considerable urging from his handlers.

This unprecedented personal attack on an opponent and the theme of lying and treason were picked up by a group of "experts" orchestrated by the Conservatives. They included Simon Reisman, the negotiator of the government's free-trade deal and still a public servant on the government payroll, and retired justice Emmett Hall, a noted Saskatchewan Conservative who, while an expert on medicare, was hardly a trade specialist.

Not content with this character assassination of the Liberal leader, however, Mulroney targeted various Liberal MPs, asking rhetorically how putting John Nunziata, Sheila Copps, or Brian Tobin in charge of a department would appeal to Canadians. Even more viciously, he took on the NDP's Svend Robinson, a veteran British Columbia MP who had publicly announced his homosexuality shortly before the election was called. Mulroney smirkingly asked the public to picture Robinson as minister of National Defence.

Nor was the prime minister above "shading the truth." During a swing through Quebec, Mulroney stated that electing a Liberal government would "kill the Free Trade Agreement and the Meech Lake Accord." The first part of the statement was not debatable, but Mulroney's audacity in suggesting that Turner, a man whose unswerving commitment to the accord had cost him caucus and party support, was actually *opposed* to Meech Lake was quite remarkable. Equally remarkable was that this claim, like many of his misleading statements, went largely unchallenged.

All this, of course, leads logically to the question of how it was possible for the Conservatives — after years of the neocon-servative agenda, high-level corruption, deceit, and the antics of Mulroney himself — to successfully employ this smear campaign. It also raises the issue of how they were able to reconvince the public that their team was honourable and competent, that they were not planning an all-out attack on social programs, and that the trade deal would result in prosperity, not McJobs, for Canadians.

There are four underlying reasons for the success of the second Conservative strategy, and all of them are related to their ability to take advantage of the weaknesses of the electoral process in Canada.

The first of these reasons was money. The Conservatives had more than they could legally spend. The Liberals hadn't enough to run a national campaign, and the NDP barely enough. It is difficult to overestimate the importance of this factor, given the high cost of television advertising and the degree of technological sophistication possible if a party has the money and the time to organize.

Under the Elections Act, parties are currently limited to an expenditure of $8 million for an election campaign, assuming that they field candidates in every riding. There is no limit on how much may be spent in advance of the writ being dropped, and certain expenses are exempted, even during the campaign. After an election, each party must submit a detailed accounting of its expenditures.

Needless to say, the Mulroney Conservatives reported that they spent the total amount allowed under the act. What they were not obliged to report were huge expenditures in advance of the campaign call, something made possible by their wealth of funds and by the fact that they alone knew when the writ would be dropped.

The federal Liberals, meanwhile, spent considerably less (at $6.8 million) than the allowable amount, and less than the NDP (at $7.1 million) for the first time in their history. The lack of money undoubtedly affected the Liberals the most. With limited resources, they were unable, for example, to finance a second set of advertisements to respond to the new Tory strategy and package of ads that emerged after the leaders' debates, even though there was clear evidence that such ads could have been invaluable in stemming the flow of votes from the Liberals to the Tories.

However, the Liberals' inability to finance a full campaign was not the only financial first of the 1988 election. There was also the unprecedented involvement of special-interest groups financing ads related to the free-trade deal. What was most significant about their involvement was the large sums of money they were able to expend on this "third party" advertising, through a loophole in the Elections Act.

Indeed, the wording of the act had specifically been framed to exclude outside financial assistance for any political party during an election campaign, since there would be no point in assigning limits for party expenditures if interest groups could step in to assist parties indirectly. Although an earlier court ruling had thrown the entire question of campaign advertising by third parties into question, no one had anticipated a situation in which ads in favour of an *issue* — in this case, the Free Trade Agreement — would have the effect of supporting one party. The degree to which these expenditures aroused public anger in the 1988 campaign can be clearly seen from the way in which the issue of third-party advertising subsequently came to dominate presentations to the Lortie Commission on Electoral Reform. Many intervenors argued strenuously that such activities should be banned or severely limited in future elections. In a study prepared by the commission's research director, Jane Hiebert, the importance of these expenditures to the eventual outcome of the election is graphically demonstrated. Hiebert concludes: "the last week of [pro–FTA] advertisements resulted in a net 5.5 point change in voters' intentions." She further states that "independent expenditures in the 1988 election undermined the principles of fairness and equity."[3]

While third-party involvement would likely be undesirable under any circumstances, during the 1988 campaign the gravity of the problem was attributable to the fact almost all of the money was on one side of the issue. The pro–free trade forces spent nearly as much as the Conservative party, at least $3.6 million on ads supporting the deal, thereby virtually doubling the Tories' advertising budget without affecting their total limit under the Elections Act.

These pro-trade special-interest groups were funded, in turn, by big business. Together, the recently created Alliance for Trade and Job Opportunities ($2.3 million), the National Citizens' Coalition, and the Alberta government spent seventy-seven cents for every dollar spent on advertising by the Conservatives. The only real organized opposition to the deal, the volunteer-run Pro Canada Network, spent only eleven cents for every dollar of national advertising by the Liberals and NDP.

Hiebert also notes that "65 percent of the [pro–FTA] funds were spent in the final week of the campaign, mainly in newspaper advertisements." She goes on to conclude: "The principal effect of the advertisements was to mobilize those FTA supporters intending to vote for the Liberal Party to change their minds and support the Conservative Party."[4]

But money was not the only factor working to the Conservatives' advantage in the 1988 election. Given the degree of their incompetence during the first half of the campaign, money alone may not have saved them. A second factor was the role of the media.

Clearly, the calibre of reporting in general left much to be desired. Most major newspapers and networks decided to send relatively inexperienced personnel on the three leaders' tours. The CBC felt obliged to examine its own reporting practices after the election in light of several unfortunate events that cast considerable doubt on its evenhandedness. The most significant media "event" of the election was undoubtedly its "exposé" on an alleged mid-campaign attempt to replace John Turner as leader of the Liberals. Although vehemently denied by all of the senior Liberals "implicated" by the CBC report, the incident was a profoundly damaging one from which the party never recovered. It was also one the Mulroney advertising team relied on for additional ammunition during the latter part of the campaign.

More significant, however, was the media's apparent determination after the leaders' debates to report their comments on the trade agreement to the exclusion of all other issues. Ironically, this one-track reporting could be argued to have penalized the Liberals and the NDP more than it did the Conservatives. For, once trade was established as an issue and the respective positions of all parties were known, the public wanted to evaluate the positive agendas of their alternative choices. Yet, despite repeated attempts by both the Liberals and the NDP to open up other "fronts" in the campaign, notably to discuss the Tories' proposed second phase of tax reform, the GST, and their own plans for social-policy initiatives, the media, for the most part, were unwilling to focus on other issues. The public was therefore in the dark about Liberal and NDP proposals. As many frustrated strategists in both Liberal and NDP camps observed, in the age of mass-media elections, an event or a statement that is not reported did not happen. As Conservative strategist Hugh Segal noted, the consequence of this single-issue campaign was that, "when the concerted [Conservative/third-party] barrage flattened Turner's credibility on free trade, it wiped out his chances of winning the election."

Given the widespread concern a year later over the media's perceived biased reporting of the Meech Lake débâcle, and the refusal of several networks to provide interviews for the authors of best-selling works critical of the prime minister and Quebec premier Robert Bourassa, the extent of the Mulroney government's ability to influence the media during the 1988 election is a subject that may well warrant further investigation.

Meanwhile, Mulroney's alliance with Robert Bourassa and the Quebec Liberal party proved an invaluable third source of support. Although they came to the Conservatives' aid early in the campaign, Bourassa and his organization redoubled their efforts once things began to deteriorate after the debates. Mulroney's support for the Meech Lake Accord, as well as the Quebec business community's support for the Free Trade Agreement, motivated Bourassa to effectively sabotage the Liberal campaign, allowing his troops to work for the Conservatives while publicly declaring he would remain "neutral." Given the federal Liberals' traditional reliance on their provincial counterparts for organizational support, this desertion proved a fatal blow to their chances in Quebec.

Last, but not least, the opposition parties themselves inadvertently aided the Conservative cause. By failing to put their own houses in order and to provide what the public perceived as an effective alternative, they literally ceded victory to the Conservatives by default.

The Liberals were most culpable in this regard, since it was the cumulative effect of many unfortunate events and decisions, rather than one momentous incident, that gave the Conservatives enough ammunition to ensure their downfall. Indeed, many of their image problems, of which the Conservative "communications experts" took such effective advantage in their advertisements after the debates, began long before the campaign started: the numerous attempted but unsuccessful leadership coups destroyed the image of Liberals as competent managers and loyal team players; the widely publicized antics of the so-called Rat Pack, originally thought by some caucus members to be a valuable tool for attacking the government, also contributed to this negative image; the many ghastly nomination battles involving instant members and rival ethnic groups were rightly viewed by most Canadians as inappropriate, undemocratic, and unseemly displays of partisan politics at its worst; the inability of the party to attract impressive candidates, and its failure to ensure the nomination and/or election of the few significant new stars it had recruited — Patrick Johnston of the National Anti-Poverty Organization, Maude Barlow of the Pro Canada Network, and Bill Graham of the University of Toronto — hurt its image as the "natural governing party" even further.

Then there was the problem of Quebec. With the dismissal of their most competent and experienced organizer, Senator Pietro Rizzuto, in early 1988, a number of organizational and fundraising attempts over the year leading up to the election culminated in disaster. These failed attempts, primarily under the direction of Turner's likeable but hopelessly inept Quebec lieutenant, Raymond Garneau, left the party in a shambles and several warring factions fighting over non-existent spoils.

During the campaign itself, Liberal fortunes in Quebec plummeted. The national campaign co-chair, André Ouellet, was in such serious difficulty in his own riding that he was increasingly unable to devote much time to the supervision of the campaign. This left his co-chair, the popular Senator Al Graham, whose role had always been seen as cheerleader rather than organizer, and the novice campaign director, John Webster, to soldier on with their limited resources and staff.

Despite these constraints, an impressive amount of excellent material had been prepared by the time the writ was dropped. A national platform and a comprehensive package of documents for individual candidates, far exceeding that which had been available in previous elections, was provided by the Liberals' Research Bureau. The Liberal ad campaign, under the direction of David Morton, was described by independent observers as superb. Webster and his team at the party's national headquarters had orchestrated an extensive and, given the lack of funds, technologically acceptable communications network. Like the Conservatives, the Liberals had been gearing up, primarily under the auspices of the Liberal Strategy Committee, chaired by Senator Michael Kirby, for at least a year.

In short, the fatal flaws of the Liberal campaign were not the result of poor advance planning, but of a number of bad decisions taken during the campaign itself, decisions that, in retrospect, proved to be their downfall. These included the initial decision of the campaign committee to exclude a policy expert from the leaders' tour (resulting in the childcare fiasco, where everyone from Turner's principal secretary to a press assistant attempted to explain a document they had not written or understood), and the committee's decision to avoid releasing the details on the costing of the Liberal platform, despite the fact that a full accounting had been prepared in advance of the campaign and was available for their use at any time. As Strategy Chair Senator Michael Kirby later recounted, "the big mistake . . . was not catching the extent of public unease about the costing issue soon enough." Kirby admitted that the failure to release costing details in a timely fashion increased the leader's vulnerability to Tory charges of incompetence, and added to the Liberals' problems in successfully opening up a second front on the Tory tax-reform issue, as they had planned.

Meanwhile, the NDP was faring no better. In fact, its situation was actually worse than that of the hapless Liberal Party. Having had early expectations of assuming the mantle of official opposition (quickly scuttled by their leader's pompous comments to that effect), after a bland, almost innocuous start the NDP proceeded to fade even farther from the picture with the poor performance of Ed Broadbent during the leaders' debates.

Coupled with the inexplicable failure of the NDP strategists to devise an approach that would capture the anti–free trade sentiment for them — an issue widely viewed as the one that would appeal most naturally to their constituency and beyond — the NDP campaign basically went nowhere.

Hampered further by problems in Quebec, where their slim hopes of taking any seats faded with internal squabbling among executive members and surprising indecision on the part of the leader regarding the Constitution's notwithstanding clause, they were obliged in the final days of the campaign to focus heavily on Ontario if they were to see any significant increase in their standings in Parliament.

This focus led to the ill-fated Main Street/Bay Street theme of the final few weeks, an overly orchestrated and futile attempt to shed the moderate "mainstream" image the party had been attempting to cultivate for more than a year, in the hopes of attracting significant middle-class support away from the Liberals. Instead, they found themselves desperately attempting to regain lost ground with their more traditional working-class constituency in order to stave off total disaster.

As long-time NDP strategist Gerry Caplan noted in *Election*, an exposé he coauthored with Liberal Senator Michael Kirby and Tory adviser Hugh Segal, the NDP was the biggest loser in the 1988 campaign. Although they had won more seats than ever before, the party and the caucus were dismayed by the results because of their initial high expectations. Caplan concluded, "The Liberals had fought the good fight and lost. But as Ed Broadbent was pushed to the shadows of irrelevancy by the fireworks surrounding the free trade issue, the New Democrats seemed to have lost a clear sense of exactly what they were fighting for."

And so it was that the Mulroney Conservatives, having almost lost the election through overconfidence, survived to fight another day. With the help of overfull coffers and third-party advertising, the media, their alliance with the Quebec Liberal Party, and the opposition parties themselves, they roared to the finish line well ahead of their closest rival.

Not only did elements of the electoral process work to the advantage of the Mulroney Conservatives in the 1988 campaign, but, as the election results clearly reveal, the electoral *system* itself was extremely helpful to them.

With 169 seats to the Liberals' 83 and the NDP's 43, the Mulroney Conservatives were returned on November 21, 1988, with a second successive majority. But this was not the massive *popular* victory it might appear. An examination of some of the most significant election numbers suggests the Conservatives were more lucky than they thought to find themselves, once again, in charge of running the country.

A majority of voters did not cast their ballots for Brian Mulroney and his team, or for the Free Trade Agreement. However, in our "first past the post" electoral system, the winner, regardless of the margin of victory, takes everything. Also, in our multi-party system, a single issue, however dominant it may have been during the campaign, cannot be clearly translated into support for a particular party.

The results of the 1988 National Election Survey demonstrate that, while the Free Trade Agreement motivated some voters to support the Conservative party despite their unhappiness with the Mulroney government, there is conclusive evidence that more Canadians rejected than supported the deal. The issue itself was mentioned as the "most important election issue" by 82 percent of the electorate, while most of the remainder chose it as the second-most important issue. Of those for whom the issue was also the determining factor in their final choice (some 50 percent of voters), those opposed to the deal outnumbered those in favour by a significant margin — 29 percent compared to 21 percent.

In addition, the trade issue produced a much higher level of "strategic" voting in this election than is normal. In other words, voters attempted to compensate for the electoral system as best they could. Thus, the NDP suffered a substantial loss of voters to the Liberals in the final weeks of the campaign, as those most violently opposed to the trade deal attempted to avoid the "split vote" scenario so common in our three-party, winner-take-all electoral system and ensure their vote counted as much as possible to prevent a Conservative victory.

In comparison with the 1984 survey, the 1988 results also found that voters based their decision in 1988 on the factors of "party" and "stand on the issues" to a far greater extent, while "leaders" and "local candidates" were far less important considerations in this campaign. Again, the reasons are very revealing. The leadership factor, which had been so important in the 1984 campaign, was largely ignored by voters in 1988, primarily because of the perceived lack of *any* acceptable candidate. Jon Pammett of Carleton University has noted that "the depth of public displeasure with the leaders in 1988 was extraordinary. Since measurement with the thermometer technique began [in 1968] we have never before experienced a federal election in which *no* leader scored above the neutral mark." While incumbent prime ministers always do badly on these tests and the last incumbent prime minister to receive a higher-than-neutral rating was Pierre Trudeau in 1980, Pammett found that "Brian Mulroney's nosedive in public appeal is unprecedented; he fell fully 13 points in four years, eclipsing any previously registered declines, including Robert Stanfield's 10-point drop between 1968 and 1974."[5]

The regional breakdown of the actual election results is also significant. The Conservatives paid the price for their mistreatment of Atlantic Canada and Manitoba, while reaping the rewards of Robert Bourassa's assistance in Quebec. As a result, their overall support was much less nationally representative than in 1984. Their seats in Atlantic Canada fell from 25 in 1984 to 12 in 1988, in the West from 58 to 48, and in Ontario from 67 to 46. By contrast, they actually *increased* their representation in Quebec, from 58 to 63, reducing the Liberals to 12.

The discrepancy between the percentage of the popular vote and the number of seats a party receives has been a subject of contention in Canada for some time. In 1988, the Conservatives received 43 percent of the vote, compared to 52 percent for opposition parties combined — the Liberals receiving 32 percent and the NDP 20 percent. Nevertheless, the Tories received 57 percent of the seats, for a margin of 14. This failure to more closely reflect the distribution of the popular vote produced calls for changes to the electoral system, most notably the introduction of some type of system of proportional representation. Ironically, the skewing of seats in 1988 was actually less severe than in 1984, when 50 percent of the popular vote for the Conservatives translated into 74 percent of the seats, a margin of 24.

Within the Tory vote, a significant gender gap and income-distribution gap (61 percent of their support came from those with incomes over $50,000, as compared to 21 percent of the Liberal support and 15 percent of the NDP support) also emerged from a survey of the results. Put another way, upper-income Canadian males formed the backbone of the Conservatives' support in the 1988 election.

The most significant conclusion, however, can be drawn from combining voters' reasons for supporting a particular party, namely, that Canadians reluctantly accepted that the Mulroney team was less objectionable than the alternatives.

As Pammett has concluded, the 1988 election "was decided by the ultimate judgement that the potential alternative governments offered by the opposition parties were not credible. . . . The public devoutly wished for an alternative [, but,] faced with a series of unattractive choices, Canadians gritted their teeth and made the best of it."[6]

Given these results, Canadians might have expected Mulroney and his team to see their return to power for what it was — a close call, in which they had been given a second chance by default.

An election in which more votes left the Tories than went to them, and in which they were successful primarily because of the split majority vote, should never have led Mulroney and his team to gloat. For Brian Mulroney, a man still intent on building a dynasty, the last-minute reprieve should not have been interpreted as a ringing endorsement of their first-term performance, but as a second chance in which they had the opportunity to rectify past mistakes.

Yet, as he told his caucus innumerable times over the next few years when their popularity sank to new lows, he alone had pulled the fat out of the fire during the campaign and, no matter what the polls might say, he could do it again.

This redoubled arrogance was directly responsible for Mulroney's intransigence on the Meech Lake Accord and his willingness to back Wilson on the GST, despite public opposition. It was also responsible for the black mood that quickly descended over the country, as Canadians perceived that, the electoral system having failed to translate their frustrations and discontent with the choices offered, they would be subjected to another four years of his government. (This mood, of course, deepened to something near despair when Mulroney, who had publicly declared in 1983 that a government was morally bound to call an election every four years, repeated several times in the summer of 1991 that the next federal election would not be until 1993, or the fifth year of his second mandate.)

Having dispensed with the formal adoption of the Free Trade Agreement in a brief session in December 1988 shortly after the election, the newly returned government adjourned Parliament until April. That a government would choose to delay the introduction of its new agenda for nearly four months did not bode well. Coupled with its failure to convene Parliament and meet the opposition, it showed once again its contempt for the parliamentary system. The omens were not positive for a new and improved Mulroney government.

Indeed, far from turning over a new leaf, the government seemed determined to provide Canadians with more of the same — more deception and dishonesty, more broken promises, and even greater lack of respect for parliamentary democracy.

But the damage the Mulroney government has inflicted in the past seven years through its abuse of the instruments and processes of government is only half of the story of its unpopularity and the country's profound discontent. Its neoconservative agenda, and the initiatives that have flowed from it, have further outraged and embittered ordinary Canadians, and it is to this agenda that we now turn.

NOTES

1. P. Maser, "On the Hustings," in A. Frizzell, J. Pammett, and A. Westell, eds., *The Canadian General Election of 1988* (Ottawa: Carleton University Press, 1989), p. 67.
2. G. Caplan, M. Kirby, and H. Segal, *Election* (Scarborough, ON: Prentice-Hall, 1989).
3. *Ottawa Citizen*, April 19, 1991, p. A12.
4. Ibid.
5. Frizzell et al. *The Canadian General Election*, p. 121
6. Ibid., p. 115.

Part II

BREAKING PROMISES

How the Neoconservative Agenda Destroyed Our
Faith in Canada

6. Withdrawing from the Marketplace
How the Neoconservatives Dismantled the Economic Infrastructure of Government

Free trade affects Canadian sovereignty and we will have none of it, not during leadership campaigns or any other time.
— Brian Mulroney, June 1983

We would not raise taxes. Tax levels are already too high.
— Michael Wilson, House of Commons, March 6, 1984

By late fall 1990, even Finance minister Michael Wilson admitted the Canadian economy was in a recession. Prior to that, he and Brian Mulroney were telling anyone who would still listen that there was merely an "economic slowdown" that they, in fact, had "induced." In a television interview on October 14, 1990, Wilson stated, "We had serious inflationary pressures that we had to control." He then misquoted his own budget forecast of April 1990, in which he had predicted a six-month slowdown followed by a rebound in fall 1990. "I said recovery would start in the beginning of 1991. In fact we now expect it will be halfway through 1991." Implying that everything was still under control, he concluded, "If we had ignored the inflationary problem it would have gotten out of hand and that would have led us directly to what we had in 1981–82."

Unfortunately for Wilson and Mulroney, it was soon apparent that the country was already in the throes of a recession that, in several respects, eventually equalled or exceeded that of 1981–82. The unemployment figures for December 1990 — the ninth month of the recession — were higher in terms of both percentage

(9.3 percent compared to 9 percent in the equivalent month of March 1982) and total numbers (1,281,000 people compared to 1,100,000).

Bankruptcies by January 1991 stood at record levels, up 69 percent over the previous year. Housing starts and car sales plummeted 12 percent and 19 percent, respectively, from August to September 1990, declines that outstripped those of 1981 by considerable margins. Plant closures, layoffs, and overall levels of job losses (some 237,000 jobs lost in the manufacturing sector alone during 1990) were far ahead of the levels for the same period during the previous recession.

At the same time, the Canadian dollar remained strong, and interest rates, which had fallen rapidly during the last recession, declined much more slowly and less significantly. The Mulroney government's introduction of the GST in January 1991 then added to inflationary pressure.

Worse than the actual numbers at a given time, however, were the trend lines. The deficit, which Wilson had focused on reducing with single-minded determination for nearly six years, was increasing. Canada's balance-of-trade surplus was decreasing, as was our competitiveness relative to other OECD nations. In September 1991, the economy registered its first trade deficit since the 1960s, the result of increased imports and greatly decreased exports.

In short, the Canadian economy was in serious difficulty long before the recession began. Moreover, the majority of economists and analysts believe the recession was caused primarily by the domestic policies of the government, rather than by external global forces, as had been the case in 1981–82. Put another way, this was a "made in Canada" recession, the first of its kind.

Despite the initial strong support of the business community for the Mulroney government and their direct intervention in the free-trade debate in the 1988 election, almost all the heavyweights in the financial community agreed with this assessment. Criticism of the government's monetary and fiscal policies by the business elite exploded in 1990, much to Michael Wilson's chagrin.

Virtually every major representative of the business community, from the Chamber of Commerce to the Canadian Federation of Independent Business, criticized specific measures in the government's GST and the way in which it was implemented. Concerned as well about continued high interest rates, the business community was expressing its lowest level of confidence in the economy since 1982.

On the issues of the deficit and fiscal policy, the business community's outlook was equally bleak. Former staunch ally Tom d'Aquino of the Business Council on National Issues, a pro-free trade lobbyist, declared in October 1990 that the federal government had "lost control of spending." A report released in February 1991 by the right-wing C.D. Howe Institute criticized the federal government's "irresponsible" policies and pointed out that "the level of debt to GDP . . . was just shy of 55% at the beginning of the current fiscal year — almost double its level at the beginning of the previous recession."

The international community did not fail to observe these developments either. The European monthly gospel sheet *Euromoney* rated Wilson among the three worst Finance ministers in the world in their 1990 year-end review.

Canadians, of course, were only too well aware of the practical implications of these statistics. Lost jobs or concern about job security, less disposable income, high credit-card interest rates, and increased uncertainty about their future were the stock in trade in Canadians' replies to pollsters about the state of the economy. Consumer confidence in 1990 was at an all-time low, and remained so throughout 1991. A *Globe and Mail*/CBC poll in November 1991 saw Canadians rank the economy as the most serious problem facing the country, far outstripping all other concerns, including the constitutional crisis.

This level of concern should hardly have come as a surprise to the government, since the official "end" of the recession declared by the new Finance minister, Don Mazankowski, in early September 1991 was followed by news of further increases in the unemployment rate and consumer bankruptcies, continuing declines in the job-prospect index, and low consumer confidence. The jobless rate hit 10.6 percent in August and remained virtually unchanged throughout the fall of 1991; the October help-wanted index of Statistics Canada fell for the second straight month, to a seven-year low of 70 (on a scale of 100 set for 1981). Another Stats Can survey released the same month reported bankruptcies were running 50 percent ahead of 1990, which itself had been a record year for consumer failures.

What surprised many Canadians was the government's apparent lack of interest in these statistics. Don Mazankowski seemed determined to follow Michael Wilson's lead, pursuing the monetarist priority of inflation-fighting at all costs. While Statistics Canada was warning that a decline in interest rates reflected an extremely weak economy, in which "the recovery could be the slowest escape from recession in Canadian history,"[1] Mazankowski was happily declaring that "as long as we continue to dampen the fires of inflation we have the potential of seeing further reductions in interest rates." In a lengthy speech to Japanese investors in Tokyo earlier in the month, the new Finance minister had covered virtually every economic issue except unemployment, yet when he returned to Canada he conceded that levels could well remain at or above 10 percent until 1993, an "unfortunate" but apparently necessary outcome of the monetarists' crusade against inflation.[2]

Despite such statements, it is only very recently that the cumulative effect of seven years of Conservative economic policies is being recognized as the primary source of our troubles. Yet, not only has the Mulroney government's approach to the economy plunged the country into a severe recession and hampered its recovery, but its neoconservative agenda has produced three profound and unintended consequences — the demise of the manufacturing sector, the demise of the middle class, and the demise of the regions.

The effects on the manufacturing sector are, of course, most visible in the Canadian industrial heartland of Ontario and Quebec. Analysts disagree about the extent to which particular government policies — the Free Trade Agreement; high interest rates; tax increases; and the lack of financial incentives for research and development, and technology transfer — are the primary culprits, but no one disagrees with the figures that paint a depressing tale of plant closures, layoffs, bankruptcies, and manufacturing-job losses. A March 1991 analysis by the Centre for Policy Alternatives estimated that some 435,000 jobs had been lost in twenty months. A more conservative estimate by the Canadian Manufacturers' Association placed the figure closer to 300,000. Virtually all analysts agreed that many of these jobs would never return.

The demise of the middle class is becoming increasingly visible as well. Personal bankruptcies, up 37 percent in 1990 and 50 percent higher again in 1991, were increasingly affecting people in higher-income brackets. The Metro Toronto childcare system, dependent on a mix of subsidized and paying customers, was on the brink of collapse by January 1991. Almost all non-subsidized children had been removed by parents unable to continue paying fees. Restaurants, car dealers, and retail-clothing outlets and manufacturers suffered substantial drops in business throughout 1990–91 as the disposable income of the middle class shrank yet again.

A comprehensive report released by Statistics Canada in February 1991 demonstrated that the rich became richer during the 1980s. These wealthy high-income earners, those with incomes in the top 20 percent, increased their share of total income exclusively at the expense of the middle class.

As the *Ottawa Citizen* reported, one of the agency's analysts, Michael Wolfson, expressed considerable surprise at the findings: "This seems to be contrary to the conventional wisdom up until now that Canada has been immune, from the mid-60's to the mid-80's, to changes in inequality, unlike the U.S. where inequality increased." The implications of these comments are painfully evident. Inequality has increased in Canada since the mid-1980s and the arrival of the Mulroney Conservatives.

There is little or no dispute among experts as to the root cause. Thirty-two tax increases, the introduction of "temporary" surtax measures, the clawback of family benefits, and the imposition of the GST, all contributed to the substantial drop in the disposable income and the standard of living of the middle class.

The demise of the regions of this country has also been evident. Unemployment levels never returned to those of pre-1981 recession days in many areas despite six years of alleged economic growth under the Mulroney government. For economic growth occurred unevenly, creating a boom period in the central core of the country and leaving the regions to fend for themselves. With the advent of the recession in 1990, the unemployment figures once again took off.

This increased disparity among the regions was exacerbated by deliberate Conservative policies in the area of fisheries, forestry, and transportation. Atlantic Canada, for example, was, first, deprived of the transportation infrastructure on which it relied to maintain economic links with the rest of the country, and, then, forced to absorb a series of chaotic and uncoordinated changes in fisheries and forestry-management policy as well as the adverse effects of the defensive American trade posture and the Free Trade Agreement.

These unintended consequences, however, are only part of the overall picture of Conservative economic mismanagement. The Mulroney government's steadfast refusal to deal with the structural weaknesses in the Canadian economy and our rapidly declining competitiveness have been directly responsible for the severity and length of the recession, and the devastating impact of the trade deal on Canadian workers and the manufacturing sector. Having failed to prepare Canadians for the new realities of globalization and international competitiveness, the government has attempted to blame the results of their inaction on factors beyond their control. Yet, it is precisely their failure to respond to these new economic realities that is the real culprit. Rather than adopting proactive solutions — increased training and adjustment assistance to improve the calibre of the work force, or more incentives to industry to adapt to new technology and specialize in value-added products — they have focused their efforts on an intensive propaganda campaign to convince Canadians that the neoconservative option is the only option. Not surprisingly, the neoconservative vocabulary of competitiveness is a negative "lean, mean" approach that blames workers for declining productivity and calls for lower wages, fewer benefits, and a declining standard of living for everyone but the corporate elite.

And so, just when the increasing globalization of markets and emphasis on knowledge-based, technologically advanced economies call for a decisive restructuring and modernization of the Canadian economy, Canada finds itself unable to compete and struggling

painfully and slowly to recover from a massive recession for which
the government was largely responsible and appears to have no
remedies.

In short, the past seven years of Conservative government have
proven conclusively that a reliance on "market forces" does not
work. Here, as in Britain and the United States, it is becoming
apparent that neoconservative economic policies not only foster
inequity, but are ineffective, even by their own standards.

In the 1984 election campaign, Brian Mulroney and his Conservative
party were the beneficiaries of massive public discontent with the
governing Liberals, but even Mulroney knew that Canadians did
not want drastic changes in policy direction. Rather, what was
needed was a new crew to steer the ship of state.

To this end, detailed Conservative policy pronouncements during
the campaign were kept to an absolute minimum. When forced
to address an issue, they kept it vague enough that almost any
interpretation would be possible at a later date. General but liberal-
sounding rhetoric was aimed at soothing a somewhat sceptical
electorate.

In essence, the Conservative platform on economic policy had
three main elements: a commitment to (1) deficit reduction, (2)
economic growth, and (3) less government intervention in the
marketplace.

The first two objectives were considered desirable by most
Canadians and, indeed, by the other two political parties. The third,
while more contentious, might have been acceptable, depending
upon how it was interpreted. Clearly, the difficulty with any of
these objectives would come with the way in which it was to be
achieved.

Since the 1940s, Canadians had seen governments of all political
stripes implement economic policies based on the liberal economic
theories of Keynes and Galbraith, which essentially stressed the
need to pursue growth through full-employment strategies. More
recently, right-wing economists have argued for an emphasis on
controlling inflation — primarily through monetary policy tools
such as interest rates — as a better way to encourage economic
growth. It is this monetarist approach that has been advocated

by Michael Wilson and his supporters, marking the first time a federal government has not supported a full-employment strategy since the Great Depression. The implications of this new approach have been significant and far-reaching.

However, in 1984, recognizing the reluctance of Canadians to embrace "drastic" solutions, the Conservatives made no mention of monetarism or the "supply side" economics championed by Republicans under Reagan and Bush. They kept their campaign material bland and upbeat. For example, the *PC Pocket Handbook* stated: "A PC government would embark on a program of responsible deficit reduction through such means as improved public sector productivity and reform of crown corporations. We can reduce the deficit without increasing taxes or reducing the level of social services."

On economic growth, Mulroney himself used all the appropriate "liberal" or Keynesian vocabulary, stressing such areas as training, education, and, most importantly, research and development. In a rare burst of specificity he would later regret, he even declared to his riding association in Central Nova that "another cornerstone must be a firm undertaking to double our commitment to research and development."

Once in power, the Conservatives addressed the three objectives of their economic policy under the rubric of "Economic Renewal," the first of the four pillars in their overall strategy outlined in the November 5, 1984, Throne Speech. The first two objectives were presented essentially as they were during the campaign, but subtle differences began to appear in their vocabulary.

On deficit reduction, for example, the speech proposed "a plan designed to reduce the deficit in an orderly, balanced and fair manner, and to control the growing burden of the public debt." However, it also noted that "the need to deal urgently" with the deficit was "beyond dispute."

Similarly, measures to achieve economic growth included a mention of research and development, but the new and overwhelming emphasis here was on the private sector as the "engine" of such growth. As a result, there were also references to a number of specific policies that had rarely, if ever, been raised during the campaign. The Mulroney approach to economic growth, according to the Throne Speech, would focus on ways "to improve the flexibility and efficiency of our capital markets; market-oriented training programs," and proposals to "improve the market environment by changes in competition laws and the regulatory framework of the financial services industry." There would also be initiatives to "stimulate both domestic and foreign investment" so that Canada would be seen as a "profitable place to do business."

The third objective, removal of direct government intervention in the marketplace through privatization and deregulation, was not mentioned at all.

The opposition parties were hard-pressed to find fault with much of the Throne Speech, as it was sufficiently vague to allow for many different interpretations. But the actions that followed these reassuring words produced a considerable degree of public resistance and anger. The obvious question is: Why? Prominent experts on the process of government have observed that there is a two-way relationship between politics and policy. That the philosophy of the party in power influences its policies is not surprising. That the policies of the government have an influence on the political environment, or *realpolitik*, is less often recognized and less well understood. American political scientist Theodore Lowi has explored this phenomenon in terms of economic policies. Noting that there are three basic types of policies — distributive, redistributive, and regulatory — he has argued that the type of policies pursued by a government will make a difference in terms of its influence on the political environment. Specifically, redistributive and regulatory policies are more likely to result in conflict and confrontation, particularly if policies that are significantly different from previous ones are being implemented.[3]

For the past seven years, the Conservatives clearly have pursued economic policies that fall primarily into the last two categories. Their attempts to remove government from the marketplace have required a number of redistributive and deregulatory initiatives, all of which are a contradiction of previous government-policy directions.

In the 1988–89 annual assessment of federal economic policies published by the Carleton School of Public Administration — *How Ottawa Spends* — editor Katherine Graham specifically notes that the Mulroney government's redistributive policies, such as tax reform, have met with considerable resistance and a mounting degree of scepticism.[4] This latter reaction appears to be based on the fact that Canadians do not believe the rationale for these initiatives, namely, that they will be progressive.

Graham goes on to note that the government's deregulatory interventions, whether in transportation, fisheries and forestry, or cultural industries, have been met with "particular frenzy." Graham's colleague Seymour Wilson points out that Michael Wilson's attempts to portray his approach to deficit reduction as "fiscally responsible" and "cutback management" fly in the face of "all public opinion survey data [, which] indicate the public is not prepared to make deep cuts or cancel government social programs."[5] Graham herself concludes "the government still seems to be unaware of one of the central truths of the Canadian political environment."

Although Graham's conclusion undoubtedly applies to much of their first term in office, the Mulroney Conservatives did, in fact, learn something of these fundamental truths. Yet, the *realpolitik* they encountered did not change the objectives of the committed neoconservatives in Mulroney's cabinet. Only their tactics changed.

Shortly after the Speech from the Throne, the Conservatives had unveiled a flurry of initiatives designed to accomplish their three economic objectives. Almost immediately, they were met with considerable resistance, not only from the opposition parties and special-interest groups, but from the Canadian public in general. The problem once again, as with their commitments on patronage, was the gap between their rhetoric and their actions. Their campaign promises had attempted to be all things to all people. But, after the election, apparently believing their overwhelming electoral majority gave them a mandate to implement their hidden neo-conservative agenda, they aggressively introduced significant redis-tributive and regulatory changes.

Only when it became painfully obvious to the prime minister that public resistance was unacceptably high from a political perspective (moving him to contradict his own ministers and reverse cabinet decisions) did the neoconservative element begin to devise a less-direct approach to accomplish their objectives. An important feature of this second approach was to continue to use liberal rhetoric, even when their objectives were clearly illiberal.

After this second strategy was adopted, they began to make considerable progress in implementing their policies. In fact, they achieved by the "back door" method much of what they had failed to do directly. While introducing numerous incremental changes that had the effect of eliminating universality, for example, the Mulroney government continued to sing its praises and insist it was unaffected by their policies. Part of the delay in recognizing the effect of their policies, therefore, can be explained by the fact that much of what they have done has been either deliberately misrepresented or misunderstood at the time each individual policy was introduced.

Nevertheless, the cumulative effect of neoconservative economic policies has been disastrous for the Canadian economy. Moreover, their implementation has not achieved the Conservatives' original objectives. As an examination of the record in each of their three target areas demonstrates only too well, their policies have been both inequitable and inefficient, a failing compounded by incompetence, lack of coordination, and, more than once, the introduction of policies with competing objectives.

As even Michael Wilson would have been forced to admit, on leaving the Finance portfolio, he had virtually no success with deficit reduction; economic growth had remained at a standstill after a lengthy recession; and the removal of government from the marketplace, while reasonably successful, had produced unfortunate and unanticipated consequences.

The failure of the Mulroney government's economic policies can most easily be seen in the area of deficit reduction. Every budget since 1984 declared deficit reduction to be a priority. Yet, in 1990–91, at $380 billion, the public debt was more than double that ($170 billion) inherited from the Liberals in 1984. The economic legacy of the Mulroney government includes half of the total debt accumulated since Confederation.

In its pre-budget submission to the Finance department in 1990, the Chamber of Commerce scathingly declared, "The staggering federal debt proves that the government, despite its protestations to the contrary, has failed miserably to address the problem. Virtually every measure it considered unacceptable in 1984 has been surpassed."

Unfortunately, Wilson's commitment to deficit reduction was accompanied by specific goals and timetables, both as an opposition critic and later as Finance minister. In his first Budget Speech, on May 23, 1985, he stated categorically, "Our actions will directly reduce the annual deficit at the end of the decade by more than $20 billion [to $18 billion]."

Yet, the deficit for 1991–92 was expected to be well over $30 billion. This figure was forecast despite attempts by Wilson in November 1990 and again in his February 1991 budget to make "adjustments" to take into account the decreased revenues and higher costs brought about by higher-than-predicted interest rates, a continuing strong dollar, and the recession itself.

Both Mulroney and Wilson still attempt to lay the blame for their fiscal woes on the doorstep of the Liberal governments of the early 1980s, but this argument has worn thin with the general public, even though they cannot dispute the specifics of this rewriting of history. If Mulroney wanted to assist his critics in this regard, he would no doubt remind them, for example, of his speech to the Chamber of Commerce in Montreal, in March 1984, while still Leader of the Opposition, when he declared, "By next April the debt will have reached $180 billion. Despite a decade of rhetoric, this government now borrows over $20 billion a year just to meet its interest payments."

By contrast, Michael Wilson, in his February 20, 1990, budget, planned to spend $41.2 billion to pay the interest on the national debt. In his November "corrections," he predicted it would actually be $43.7 billion. By then, the cost of the interest on the debt was not only the largest item in the federal spending plan, but the fastest growing. In 1990–91, with federal spending overall predicted to rise by 7 percent, the cost of servicing the debt was rising by 11 percent.

All of this was the more distressing, as the Tories had received far more revenue than the Liberals would have, as a result of Wilson's many changes in the tax structure. Indeed, federal tax revenues had increased by $50 billion since the Mulroney government came to power. Given Wilson's campaign promises, this increased revenue has caused the Tories considerable difficulty. Having emphasized their determination to reduce or eliminate the deficit through expenditure cuts, not increased taxes, they promptly ignored this promise once in office. Indeed, in the past seven years, they have introduced the most massive tax increases in Canadian history.

Canadians know at a visceral level they are making less money or barely treading water, compared to ten years ago. This is not surprising, given the many small but insidious changes to the tax system that Wilson introduced in the first few years, long before the GST. The Michael Wilson who, as opposition Finance critic in 1984, declared that taxes were already too high became Michael Wilson the Finance minister, who introduced thirty-two separate measures to increase taxes during his seven-year tenure.

Wilson introduced many changes in personal income tax in early 1985-86, including the de-indexing of family allowances and personal tax credits, the elimination of the federal tax reduction for low-income earners, the elimination of the RHOSP deduction, and "temporary" surtaxes, which have now become permanent.

Phase I of the Tory tax-reform plan was allegedly designed to make the system fairer. The effect has been to make the income-tax system less progressive, notably by collapsing the five categories of income into three. By 1989, the wealthiest Canadians, with incomes over $100,000, were paying less income tax than in 1984, while every Canadian family with an income over $10,000 was paying more, according to a study prepared for the Institute for Research on Public Policy by Alan Maslove.

Indirect taxes, such as the excise tax on gasoline, alcohol, and tobacco, as well as increased air transport taxes also contributed substantially to the increase in federal coffers. But the most significant change in indirect taxation was undoubtedly the increases introduced by Wilson to the manufacturers' sales tax (MST) each year from 1984 to 1986. The MST rose from 9 percent under the Liberals to 12 percent by April 1986. When he began to speak of replacing this tax with a more broadly based GST in 1987, Wilson could therefore claim that the 9 percent rate he was proposing was a 3 percent *decrease* from the existing level of MST.

The one component of the economy not paying substantially more in taxes to the federal government was the corporate sector. Between 1984-85 and 1988-89, federal revenue from corporate tax increased by roughly 28 percent, while revenue from individuals through income tax and sales and excise taxes increased by 62 percent.

The inequity in Tory tax policy and, indeed, in their deficit-reduction strategy generally was becoming evident. Both opposition parties as well as countless special-interest groups representing low-income and disadvantaged Canadians accused the Mulroney government of attempting to reduce the deficit on the backs of the middle class and the poor. The February 1991 Stats Can report proved the Tories were indeed reducing the standard of living for all but the wealthiest and the poorest of the poor.

Phase II of the Tory tax-reform plan, the GST, only heightened this perception of inequity and unfairness: consumption taxes are by definition regressive and most damaging to low-income earners. Wilson's half-hearted attempt to deflect this criticism by offering a GST tax credit to the lowest-income earners convinced no one, particularly as the level at which the credit ceased to apply was ludicrously low and would be phased out over time.

At least no one could deny that Michael Wilson, in his arch neoconservatism, was consistent and persistent. It was Brian Mulroney, with his lack of any philosophy other than winning, who threw more than one spanner into Wilson's works, adding incompetence to the government's image of unfairness and helping to obscure the right-wing agenda. In 1985, when Wilson openly attempted to de-index seniors' pensions, he was staunchly defended by the prime minister until a diminutive pensioner from Quebec accosted him in front of the national media on Parliament Hill. Mme Solange Denis's now-famous "You lied to us. You got us to vote for you and then it's Goodbye, Charlie Brown" was too much for Mulroney. Humiliated, Wilson was forced to back down.

Brian Mulroney hung Wilson out to dry again on an open-line show and in a meeting with university students in Vancouver. Until then, Mulroney had staunchly defended Wilson's GST proposal, including the Finance minister's firm position that no exemptions could be allowed. Yet he responded to severe criticism of this position by the B.C. students by saying that he personally agreed it was unfair to tax books, and hoped it would be possible to correct this error in the near future.

Despite the introduction of the GST, which produced far more revenue for the government than had been predicted, the federal deficit for 1991 was still pegged to be $30.5 billion and the public debt a staggering $419 billion, more than $220 billion more than when the Conservatives took office in 1984.

On September 16, 1991, the *Financial Post* painted a stark picture of the extent of the Conservatives' failure to deal with the deficit. Referring to the "crippling" burden that "overwhelms most other fiscal policies," the article described the "fiscal crisis" that now threatened the economy and the "slow strangulation" to follow as worldwide pressures for increased competitiveness were forced to go unheeded.

The second objective of the Mulroney Conservatives, economic growth, has fared no better than their top priority of deficit reduction. There was a period of real growth in the first years of their mandate, for which they eagerly took credit, but most analysts believe it would have taken place regardless of government policies because Canada and the world were coming out of a recession. Then the economy stalled. By April 1990, it was in freefall, with little prospect of an early recovery.

But even before the recession began, the Canadian economy was in serious difficulty. We were losing our competitive edge. Deficit financing was caused, in part, by maintaining our standard of living artificially, as a country's standard of living automatically declines with its ability to compete in the global economy.

By 1990, Canada's real wages were stagnant, with the average weekly earnings of industrial workers at 1975 levels. We had fallen from second to fifth place among G-7 countries in productivity, and our balance-of-trade surplus was declining rapidly. Despite deficit financing, our standard of living had fallen from second to eighth place among industrialized countries.

Was this inevitable, or could this decline have been avoided?

The majority of analysts believe that the 1990–91 recession was brought about largely by the high-taxation, high-interest-rate, and high-dollar policies of the government. Many also feel that the overall decline in economic growth and competitiveness was exacerbated by the Mulroney government's failure to respond appropriately to changing economic realities and its refusal to deal directly with structural problems in the Canadian economy.

Some critics argue that the laissez-faire neoconservative approach, which depends on market forces to correct problems, is incompatible with current realities, such as the globalization of markets and increased corporate concentration. In Canada, with its sparse population, huge distances, and lack of investment capital, the marketplace has never been able to function well without a level of government intervention to correct imbalances and fill the gaps. These critics of the laissez-faire approach argue the new economic trends have only served to highlight these problems and require increased government intervention — perhaps in new and innovative ways — in order for the economy to adapt successfully.

Others maintain that neoconservatives recognize the need for some remedial measures in times of significant economic change; the mechanisms they use differ from those of liberal Keynesian or socialist economics. Instead of regulation or direct intervention in the marketplace, for example, the neoconservative approach would be to provide assistance and incentives to the private sector. The problem with the Mulroney government, these critics maintain, is that, in lieu of incentives or assistance, it provided rhetoric.

The government's monetarist approach to declining competitiveness has also produced a new economic vocabulary in Canada. When the Mulroney Conservatives speak of the need to increase productivity, they invariably refer to the "exorbitantly high" wages and generous benefits Canadian workers receive, implying that these will have to be reduced before the economy can prosper. Wilson and Mulroney rarely refer to the other elements of the productivity equation — a skilled work force and high-value-added products — both of which would require intervention of some kind in terms of training and research and development.

Yet, competitiveness, the key to economic growth and prosperity, depends primarily on a country's ability to create, innovate, and adapt technology, not the resource base on which Canada has always been dependent. The competitive standing of nations is therefore dependent on the training and skills of their work force and the amount of research and development being undertaken, as well as the ability of the industrial and manufacturing sectors to adapt new technology.

This is not news to many Canadians. It was not news to Jean de Grandpré and Pierre Lortie, handpicked by Mulroney and put in charge of special commissions mandated to report on these issues in light of the FTA and election promises on R&D.

It was not news even to Brian Mulroney, who spent considerable time in *Where I Stand* describing the need for more research and development. On December 9, a few months after being elected leader, he gave a speech in the House of Commons in which he outlined his understanding of this issue once again. "There are profound structural deficiencies in this economy," he stated. "One is productivity. One is research and development. . . . One is the lack of recognition of the entrepreneurial spirit which governs small businesses, farmers and fishermen. . . . They have to be rewarded, not penalized."

Once in power, Mulroney appeared to lose sight of these issues as the "market forces" theology of his cabinet took hold. Despite his campaign commitment to double Canada's R&D expenditures, total R&D spending *declined* under Mulroney. As of 1990, it had fallen to 1.32 percent (proportion of GRD to GDP); other industrialized countries invest well over 2 percent and are moving towards increased investment.

The decline in R&D expenditures was almost exclusively attributable to public-sector cutbacks, not decreased investment by the private sector. Massive cuts or outright elimination of government in-house research facilities — the National Research Council and research programs in the federal departments of Agriculture; Environment; Communications; and Energy, Mines and Resources — were followed by systematic reductions in funding to the scientific granting councils. Next came reductions in the transfer payments to the provinces for education and training.

These decisions were taken by the Mulroney government at the very time when the Economic Council of Canada was releasing reports calling for more public-policy involvement in these areas. The council's analysis of the employment prospects for the rapidly growing service sector, for example, highlighted the need for "effective training and labour adjustment programs and for other programs that influence the economic security of workers." This was followed in its 1990 annual report, *Transitions for the 90's*, by a plea for full-employment policies rather than a single-minded emphasis on deficit reduction and inflation control.

But the government did not heed this advice from its leading economic adviser; nor did it consider the recommendations contained in the comprehensive (and critical) reports by de Grandpré and Lortie, calling for increased government spending or incentives in R&D, and training and technology-transfer assistance. And it completely ignored the report of a special conference held in Saskatoon on the future of post-secondary education.

In short, while continuing to mouth liberal rhetoric about government involvement to encourage competitiveness and research and development, the Mulroney government was abandoning the field. It expected the private sector to train workers and invest in research and technology, yet few incentives were provided for them to do so. The Canada Jobs Strategy, for example, placed the emphasis on short-term employer requirements to the exclusion of almost everything else, including job training. Biology students spent their summers working at McDonald's, and engineering students were lucky to find work at their local gas stations.

The economy and Canadian workers paid the price. The 1990 Competitiveness Report of the World Economic Forum ranked Canada sixteenth of the twenty-three OECD countries on "future prospects," down from ninth place in 1986. The report specifically noted that Canada's R&D effort had dropped from tenth place in 1984 to seventeenth in 1990.

By May 1991, even Michael Wilson had admitted the recession was longer and deeper than he had expected. So the Mulroney government dusted off its liberal rhetoric on competitiveness and presented it as a new element of neoconservatism in its Throne Speech. Focusing exclusively on national unity and prosperity, the speech echoed countless earlier promises by Mulroney and Wilson for a renewed emphasis on education, training, and research and development. Neither the opposition nor the scientific and educational communities believed a word. This may have had something to do with the cabinet shuffle that immediately preceded the Throne Speech. Putting Michael Wilson in charge of the new "superministry" of Industry, Science and Technology was, as Jean Chrétien aptly countered, "putting the fox in charge of the chickens."

The Mulroney government's laissez-faire approach to economic growth has not been any more successful than its approach to deficit reduction. The neoconservative emphasis on market forces creating economic growth has not only failed to help achieve that objective, but has resulted in unintended and undesirable consequences. Simply put, their dogmatic reliance on the marketplace meant the Mulroney government developed no industrial strategy. Instead, their approach to economic growth was based on negative measures — the elimination of restrictions on foreign investment, the elimination of "irritants" to big business, and the removal of tariff barriers, all of which fit the neoconservative objective of less government intervention.

The government's encouragement of foreign investment, at first glance wildly successful, has not produced significant benefits and may have a number of decidedly negative implications for our future as a technologically advanced nation.

After its election in September 1984, the Mulroney government moved swiftly to introduce legislation to abolish the Foreign Investment Review Agency (FIRA), a creation of the Trudeau Liberals that the Conservatives viewed as anti-business and anti-American. It was replaced, in spring 1985, by a new body, Investment Canada. The stated objective of this organization was to simplify and streamline foreign business applications while maintaining some degree of control over vital Canadian interests.

In its first six years of operation, Investment Canada approved some 5,400 foreign-investment proposals. It did not reject a single application, although some applications underwent a review process in which "undertakings" or guarantees were required, usually concerning the maintenance of local employment levels or R&D facilities. However, these undertakings could not easily be enforced, especially if the company was resold. The Boeing deal for de Havilland, for example, which the government proudly announced in 1986, resulted in lost jobs and a net cost to the government because of subsidies paid to Boeing on purchase. Five years later, Boeing was attempting to unload de Havilland on a European consortium that was demanding more federal money as an incentive.

Not surprisingly, foreign investors were quick to respond to the government's "open door" policy. Direct investment doubled from

$4.5 billion annually in the early 1980s to a record $12 billion under the Mulroney Conservatives. Acquisitions of Canadian assets, as opposed to new investment and business expansions, traditionally accounted for roughly 10 percent of this direct foreign investment. In 1990, acquisitions accounted for over 55 percent of the total.

Although this shift to acquisition might not in itself be cause for considerable alarm, the nature of the assets being purchased is. Among the better-known of these foreign takeovers are several Canadian high-technology firms, including Mitel, Lumonics, and Connaught BioSciences. Others include firms in the energy and utility fields, notably Consumers Gas in Ontario, and domestic publishing companies.

There has also been a dramatic increase in foreign-held debt, primarily through the purchase of bonds. Over 38 percent of marketable Government of Canada bonds were held by foreign investors in 1991, up from 15 percent in 1978. As economic analysts have anxiously observed, the Mulroney years have seen the emergence of substantial "twin" deficits — budgetary and current account — as the federal government increasingly finances its debt by borrowing abroad.

At the same time that its own financial situation was deteriorating, the Mulroney government was eliminating "irritants" and providing direct assistance to multinational corporations and financial institutions. Beginning with the replacement of the pharmaceutical legislation implemented by the Trudeau Liberals — legislation that lowered consumer costs by balancing patent claims with the benefits of generic products — the Conservative government showed itself more than ready to accommodate big business.

The lifetime $500,000 capital-gains exemption introduced in 1985 was originally designed to benefit even those who invested outside Canada; although subsequently modified after public outcry, it remained a boon to the rich. Similarly, the corporate tax burden, as noted earlier, remained low, while revenues from personal income tax and consumption tax soared.

One of the government's most prominent gestures was the issuing of a banking licence to American Express in April 1990, despite repeated assurances by the minister that no such approval would be granted before the long-awaited reform of financial institutions was accomplished. Moreover, the Amex organization did not meet five of the nine requirements for licensing under the existing Bank Act. This about-face has led many critics to suggest that the licence may have been part of the price the Mulroney government paid in order to secure the Free Trade Agreement.

The FTA was the ultimate weapon in the neoconservative arsenal to achieve economic growth. Of course, this aspect of the Mulroney government's economic policy is a complete contradiction of earlier Conservative party positions, including that of Brian Mulroney during the 1983 leadership race and afterwards.

Having closed down Schefferville as president of Iron Ore, Mulroney seemed sincere when he referred in 1983 to the dangers of free trade. It was, he said, like sleeping with an elephant — "If it ever rolls over, you're a dead man. And I'll tell you when he's going to roll over; in times of economic depression, they're going to crank up those plants in Georgia and North Carolina and Ohio, and they're going to be shutting them down up here." As late as 1985 he was still stating categorically that "there is no question of us seeking an agreement with the United States in the domain of free trade."

The trade agreement is one of only two major initiatives undertaken by Mulroney personally. It is also the perfect example of the internal tensions between neoconservative and pragmatic forces in the cabinet, and of the general incompetence of the government. Much has been written on the origins and process of the free-trade negotiations, which many believe were entered into almost by accident. Concerned about increasing protectionism in the U.S. Congress and the rising number of trade disputes, Mulroney apparently raised these issues with Ronald Reagan during the famous "Shamrock Summit" in March 1985, an event that Mulroney's own organizers believed was to be essentially a public-relations exercise from which no specific results would emerge. Always the temporizer, however, although agreeing in principle to closer economic ties, Mulroney continued to refer to "fair trade, not free trade."

In May 1985, a foreign policy Green Paper called for enhanced trading access to American markets; on September 5, the long-awaited, Liberal-appointed Macdonald Commission report on the

Canadian economy called for, among other things, a full-fledged trade agreement. Mulroney decided to act. Announcing his decision to open negotiations on September 26, he stated that "both sides understand there are no preconditions and that nothing is taken off the table."

In effect, as York University political scientist David Leyton-Brown concludes, "Mulroney gambled the future of his government, and indeed of the country, on the conviction that a closer economic relationship with the United States would yield economic benefits without threat to Canada's independence or interests."[6] Mulroney would, of course, gamble with the country's future again in his second initiative, on constitutional reform.

The next two years saw the Mulroney government's position on free trade evolve dramatically, and not in a linear fashion. Despite the dedication of considerable resources and manpower, including the assignment of public-service mandarin Simon Reisman to head the Canadian delegation, the two years following this decision were marked by confusion, repudiations, and outright contradictions expressed by Mulroney, several ministers, Reisman, and his American counterparts, Clayton Yeutter and Peter Murphy. As the Americans imposed countervails (notably on softwood lumber) to raise the stakes in the negotiations, the two opposition parties hammered away publicly at the government's apparent incompetence, inconsistencies, and lack of comprehensive strategy.

For example, the Macdonald Commission had called for a free-trade agreement only as part of the implementation of recommendations related to competitiveness and the restructuring of the economy generally. In particular, the report and several supporting studies specifically called for a massive program of training and retraining to reshape the work force in advance of such a move. Typically, the Mulroney government ignored this crucial component of the report.

On October 6, 1987, when challenged on this point in the House of Commons, Michael Wilson repeated his stock answer: "We do not expect there will be a need for any significant programs of adjustment. We have a number of programs in place right now." Yet, the next day, Mulroney told the *Toronto Sun*: "That's why this government . . . has undertaken with the provinces to ensure a massive program to assist those workers affected by dislocation and adjustment."

Issues such as the use of subsidies for regional-development purposes, the sale of Canadian water, and the fate of national energy initiatives were all brought into question, and each received different responses from different players. Shortly before being appointed chief trade negotiator, Simon Reisman was quoted in the *Ottawa Citizen* as favouring the export of Canadian water. Trade minister John Crosbie stated in the House on July 11, 1988, that "water itself as a natural resource is not dealt with in the agreement." He also declared no amendments could be made to the legislation implementing the deal, or it would mean the end of the agreement. Two days later his colleague Flora MacDonald stated that "we have introduced a water policy with regard to diversion . . . prohibiting it . . . so the next step will, of course, be legislation."

While Brian Mulroney was praising the Auto Pact, stating: "If it ain't broke, don't fix it," Peter Murphy was declaring: "This is one of the very serious issues we have to look into."

Small wonder the public was confused and apprehensive. Earlier, when Simon Reisman had stormed out of Washington in a huff, only months before the negotiating deadline expired, it appeared the deal was off. Reisman was furious because the Americans continued to put new items, such as regional-development programs, on the bargaining table.

Both Mulroney and Wilson had repeatedly stated, in response to opposition pressures, that social programs and regional development were not "on the table," although initially Mulroney had said, it will be remembered, that everything was, in fact, up for negotiation. Reisman eventually returned to Washington after consultations with Mulroney, and a deal was concluded.

Although the opposition parties continued to express concerns, and a formal opposition movement emerged at the grass-roots level, the government felt things were under control. It was not until the launching of the election in October that the roof fell in. The election, which Mulroney expected to fight on his record, quickly became a single-issue campaign that galvanized public support around the pro– and anti–free trade forces. John Crosbie set the tone when he admitted on June 29: "I haven't read every page of the free trade agreement because it's totally unnecessary. It's too long. Some sections are far too complicated." Such comment heightened the public's distrust of the Mulroney government, already renowned for incompetence and deception. Concern among the general public was so high that an unknown retired judge from Alberta, Marjorie Bowker, became a household name with the publication of her easy-to-read analysis of the deal and its implications.

Essentially the deal contained three components: a dispute-settlement mechanism, which, of course, had been a primary concern of the Canadian team; an agreement to reduce and eventually eliminate tariff barriers in a number of substantive areas; and a framework agreement establishing the process by which future substantive areas could be negotiated. The government argued originally that the dispute-settlement mechanism was the most important element of the deal in the face of American countervail and duties. It also argued that the agreement would provide additional jobs for Canadians and improve economic growth because of the removal of such tariffs. As the debate progressed and Mulroney began to feel threatened, he upped the ante and began to paint the agreement as essential for Canada's economic salvation. Without it, he now argued, jobs would be *lost* and the economy would go into decline in the face of global competition.

These arguments, of course, were being made in the face of statements by economists and think tanks that the deal, while possibly desirable, was not the miracle cure for the Canadian economy. The Economic Council of Canada stated categorically in its 1987 annual report that "the failure to reach a Canada–U.S. free trade accord would be unfortunate but . . . not catastrophic." Moreover, like the opposition parties, the council was promoting a multilateral approach to trade remedies.

In addition, arguments were being advanced by numerous trade experts that the dispute-settlement mechanism that had been agreed to might be worse than useless because existing American laws would continue to apply. Trade minister John Crosbie helped the cause of these critics with his June 28, 1988, statement that the trade deal was "risk-free," but, nevertheless, "it would have been better for us if we had been able to agree with the Americans on a common definition of what a subsidy is or on what proper and reasonable countervail measures would be."

Of particular concern to opponents of the deal was the lack of a specific guarantee of exclusion of social programs, energy, and cultural policies. In the absence of such written guarantees, they concluded that these areas were not protected, either from interpretation under current arrangements or from succeeding rounds of negotiation. It was this argument, notably with respect to social policy, that fuelled the debate during the election. Time and again, Brian Mulroney was forced to declare that social programs were not on the table, that there were no secret deals, and that no "harmonization" of social policies would take place in the future.

In the end, despite John Turner's "fight of his life" speech during the debates, which seriously derailed the Conservative game plan for a brief time, the combined strength of the Liberals and NDP was not enough. Although they received 52 percent of the popular vote to the Tories' 43 percent, the split of the anti-trade vote between the two opposition parties allowed the Mulroney government to return to power.

Numerous studies have analysed the consequences of the deal. The Canadian Labour Congress has published lists of job losses and plant closures that they attribute to the deal. Perhaps because they could see jobs would soon evaporate, the government quickly introduced legislation to "privatize" the unemployment-insurance program, reduce regional assistance, compromise the universality of several social programs, and "harmonize" safety and bilingual labelling standards with American standards. Critics of the deal saw these actions as proof their criticisms and fears were well founded.

Meanwhile, the 500,000 jobs that Brian Mulroney promised would flow from the deal have not materialized. Instead, unemployment rose to over 10 percent and remains there, and the number of jobs listed with federal employment centres steadily declines. The government has blamed the recession, fuelled by high interest rates and the value of the dollar, for the inability of the economy to benefit from the trade deal. Critics suggest the high interest rates and dollar value not only are the responsibility of the federal government, but may also be the direct result of unspecified agreements between the government and the Americans in order to close the deal in the first place. These critics point in particular to the sudden return of Reisman to Washington and the equally sudden American agreement to put regional subsidies aside for a future round of negotiations. In her analysis of events during and after the signing of the deal, Maude Barlow of the Council of Canadians also suggests that the worst is yet to come, as not all tariff reductions have yet been phased in.

Others have noted that the trade dispute mechanism has not prevented a continuing string of American countervail measures (most visibly on steel, sugar, lobsters, and pork), while recent rulings against Canada on fish processing and lobsters by the new panel have put in jeopardy our ability to manage our renewable resources. During 1989, the first year of operation of the FTA, 179 Canadian corporations were taken over, a record current-account deficit of $20 billion was rung up, and 100,000 fewer jobs were created than in 1988.

In short, although it may still be too soon to state conclusively that the FTA has had a net negative effect on the economy, it is certainly possible to conclude that its vaunted merits have not materialized. By November 1991, Canadians' opposition to the trade deal, at 54 percent, had reached the highest level ever recorded by Gallup since it began polling on the issue in 1988. A majority of Canadians in each region of the country believed the deal had been detrimental to the economy.

Equally troubling is the FTA's effective limitation of the federal government's ability to intervene in the economy. As former Trade minister Pat Carney was fond of telling western audiences, the FTA ensured that no federal government would ever again be able to enact a National Energy Program.

But, caught in a recession of its own making, with an escalating public debt and little room to manoeuvre, the Mulroney government now appears not only unwilling, but unable to institute proactive measures to assure the recovery. Instead, it seems to have concluded that the failure of the Free Trade Agreement to produce economic growth should not preclude further negotiations. As a result, John Crosbie announced in early 1991 that Canada would participate in ongoing American negotiations with Mexico on a North American

Trade Agreement, ignoring ample evidence that such a move alone, regardless of its merits, will do nothing to increase competitiveness or prevent further decline.

Neither deficit reduction nor economic growth, the first two economic objectives of the Mulroney government's Economic Recovery plan, has been accomplished. We can also see that the failure to accomplish the second objective has been in large measure the direct result of the neoconservative preference for non-intervention. Last, but not least, the government's hands-off approach to economic growth has resulted in several unintended consequences, including a massive increase in foreign ownership and foreign-held debt, and the demise of the manufacturing sector.

However, the Mulroney government's third economic objective, the removal of government from the marketplace, has largely been achieved. Indeed, through the Conservatives' policies of privatization and deregulation, Canadians have witnessed a literal dismantling of the government's economic infrastructure. The question here, of course, is whether this has been a desirable accomplishment. In neoconservative theology, the privatization of Crown corporations and other government bodies is innately good. Thus, while Liberal and even NDP governments had said for some time that Crown corporations ought to be re-examined in light of changed circum-stances, but that each case should be treated separately on its merits, the neoconservatives expressed the dogmatic conviction that all Crown corporations, at all times, should be dismantled.

In making this case, its proponents have cited four essential reasons, namely: the greater efficiency of the private sector, the potential for more direct ownership by individual Canadians, the reduction of the federal deficit through the profits of sale, and the reduction in the size of government.

Unfortunately, few of these desired effects have materialized. Ownership of privatized companies has passed in considerable numbers to foreign interests; the sale of many assets has produced little or no profit to the government at considerable cost to taxpayers, and with no effect on the size of the deficit; and the overall size of government has been reduced marginally, if at all, since use of contract personnel increased to replace lost permanent positions.

Such evidence has not stopped the relentless drive by true believers in the cabinet. By fall 1990, the Mulroney government had completely or partially divested itself of eighteen corporations, and was in the process of selling off five more, including Petro-Canada and Telesat. Most of these corporations were in the transportation, energy, and communications sectors. This should come as no surprise, especially to students of Canadian history, precisely because the original rationale for creating these corporations was to assure a national infrastructure that would preserve the country from the natural north-south pull.

All Liberal and Conservative governments in the past believed that Canadians needed to be able to travel throughout their country and to communicate with one another if they were to develop a national identity and survive next door to the United States.

Yet, as noted earlier, many of the Mulroney Conservatives do not share this view. As we have seen, Sinclair Stevens and others were considering the privatization of most Crown corporations in the deliberations of their transition team, even before the Tories came to power. Brian Mulroney, in contrast, is on record on many occasions defending some of these key instruments of the national infrastructure. Ever mindful of appearances and popular opinion, he has vacillated in the face of possible political costs. More than once in the past seven years, he thwarted or put on hold the plans of his ministers, after agreeing originally with them in cabinet; more than one minister came to fear Mulroney's impromptu declarations such as "Air Canada is not for sale."

As a result, major sell-offs, most notably of Petro-Canada and Air Canada, were delayed until the end of the first mandate or the start of the next, although they were high on many Tories' hit lists. Similarly, the CBC, roundly detested by cabinet ministers and Conservative backbenchers alike, was eventually emasculated through numerous financial cuts, but not eliminated entirely. Via Rail and Canada Post have been so severely restricted that they, like the CBC, may soon be unable to function. Canada Post, ordered to balance its books, has closed or privatized all 5,221 rural post offices and implemented a two-tier class of citizen with the elimination of door-to-door delivery and the introduction of community mail boxes in new suburban areas.

In the transportation industry, deregulation and privatization have produced unmitigated disasters. Via Rail has eliminated 51 percent of its network, depriving countless rural communities in Atlantic and central Canada of their principal means of access. Furious environmentalists point to increased use of passenger rail service in Europe and the United States as the way of the future in terms of energy conservation and pollution reduction.

Meanwhile, the airline industry, which was supposed to benefit from deregulation through increased competition, has been brought to its knees. A series of mergers and takeovers resulted, so that there are now only two major airlines controlling the market; Air Canada and Canadian International increased their combined market share from 65 percent in 1984 to almost 98 percent by 1990. By 1991, many transportation experts were declaring that only a merger of the remaining two airlines could ensure the existence of a domestically owned carrier for Canada. Others are more pessimistic; they believe that a merger with a U.S. airline will be inevitable to guarantee the survival of either player.

Contrary to neoconservative theology, reductions in air fares and improved service have not followed deregulation. Instead, the Canadian pattern has mirrored the American experience. Consumer costs for air travel are actually on the rise, while service, and possibly overall safety standards, have declined.

The trucking industry, already hit with deregulation and higher energy costs, was dealt a death blow by the GST. By spring 1991, the few remaining independent Canadian truckers were staging massive anti-government rallies to focus attention on their plight. One major trucking firm, GTL, quietly closed its doors and declared bankruptcy. Others moved to the United States, leaving the vacuum to be filled by huge U.S.-based trucking conglomerates.

Similarly, the government's prompt dismantling of the National Energy Program, an admittedly unpopular if largely misunderstood Liberal initiative to ensure a measure of price stability and secure source, left a vacuum in which "market forces" did not perform well. The Conservative commitment to non-intervention in the oil and gas sectors of the energy industry succeeded in decreasing Canadian ownership from 50 to 43 percent by 1990, *before* the proposed sale of Petro-Canada was factored in, while Canadian *control* declined to just 39 percent. Thus, when global prices plummeted, and later when the Gulf War increased market uncertainty and prices fluctuated wildly, the federal government had no leverage to moderate effects, and both producers and consumers suffered.

Apart from the economic consequences of these actions, however, the dismantling of much of the national infrastructure has had other, more profound effects on the country and its citizens. The outpouring of frustration over the ruthless emasculation of Via Rail, the CBC, and Canada Post has been accompanied by less-publicized protests by those affected in the artistic, cultural, and scientific communities. The Canada Council, the National Research Council, and other vital elements of these policy areas have been subjected to brutal and repeated cutbacks. The 1991 five-year plan of the National Research Council paints a clear picture of the effects of neoconservative policy: its budget, including approved increases during that period, will still be nearly $100 million less than it was in 1985, and that figure does not take inflation into account.

Clearly the Mulroney government's approach to all three elements of economic policy has not worked. They have failed to achieve either deficit reduction or economic growth. There is also persuasive evidence that reduced government involvement in the marketplace through privatization and deregulation has been not only a financial disaster, but also a significant drain on national morale.

Seen in this light, the February 1991 budget and May 1991 Throne Speech continuing these efforts can only be viewed as a recipe for disaster. In a time of rising inflation and a deepening recession, Michael Wilson continued his dogmatic pursuit of deficit reduction through more spending cuts, increased taxes, and privatization. He did so despite his own admission that these measures would lead to higher unemployment and greater hardship for many Canadians. Indeed, less than a week after his budget was introduced, the unemployment rate had risen from 9.7 to 10.2 percent. (It stubbornly remained above 10 percent for the remainder of 1991, leading his successor, Don Mazankowski, to speculate that it would be 1993 before rates began to significantly decline.)

Even more astonishing was Wilson's refusal to introduce positive initiatives for recovery and economic growth. There were to be no new programs or monies for training, education, or research and development. Indeed, there would be cuts. Yet, liberal rhetoric about the importance of these types of measures for improved competitiveness was repeated at great length, both in the Budget Papers and in the Throne Speech.

On February 26, 1991, Michael Wilson brought down his last budget. As the first budget he would table during a recession, it was expected to be a grim, belt-tightening exercise attempting one last time to wrestle inflation and the deficit to the ground before a cabinet shuffle and Throne Speech would mark the start of the Tories' "New Agenda."

The budget was indeed bad news for most Canadians. Taxes were increased by $3.4 billion to pay for the Gulf War effort and the revenue shortfall brought about by the recession. In the midst of the recession, it offered virtually no relief to the 1.3 million unemployed and more than 0.5 million Canadians utilizing food banks. Unemployment, which the budget documents accurately forecast would rise above 10 percent, would now be paid for through increased employer and employee contributions to UI. The Canadian Jobs Strategy, meanwhile, was to be cut by $100 million.

The budget also continued the federal strategy of shifting the deficit to the provinces: $411 million was slashed from federal housing assistance; the 5 percent cap on the Canada Assistance Plan for certain provinces was extended for a further three years. By freezing Established Programs Financing (EPF) transfers to the provinces, a further $2.3 billion was cut from health care and education.

The Budget Speech acknowledged that education and scientific research are keys to competitiveness, and then introduced an additional 3 percent cap on all science and technology programs and granting councils as of 1992. Following, as it did, on the heels of the 1990 budget's 5 percent cap on all science programs except the granting councils, this new funding restriction put Canadian research and development on the endangered species list.

In another symbolic attack on the federal public service, salaries were capped at 3 percent and 2 percent over a three-year period, with the threat of a legislated return to work if labour unrest developed as a result of these measures — which, of course, it eventually did. The bitter public-service strike in early fall 1991 left government-employee relations and public-service morale at an all-time low.

Yet, despite the increased revenues and expenditure reductions, federal spending was predicted to rise by 6.9 percent, and the deficit was allowed to remain at $30.5 billion. The government's friends, the business community, were dismayed and infuriated. The Canadian Manufacturers' Association, the Canadian Chamber of Commerce, and the Canadian Federation of Independent Business roundly criticized many budget measures, most notably the 24 percent increase in employers' UI premiums, as well as the government's persistent failure to make any headway on the debt.

Nor was criticism of the budget limited to its economic impact. As premier of one of the most severely affected provinces in terms of federal transfer reductions, Ontario's Bob Rae was quick to make a connection with the national unity issue. He struck a responsive chord in many Canadians when he said, "Mr. Mulroney can't talk national unity one day and then cut back on national programs the next. That's a contradiction that strikes at the very heart of the social contract that is Canada. If we can't look to our national government for leadership . . . I think people's faith in the country will be affected. You can't dismember social programs and then turn around and say 'Let's work to keep Canada together.'"

Claude Lajeunesse, president of the Association of Universities and Colleges, pointed out that failure to invest in human resources through education and training would mean more than decreased competitiveness for the Canadian economy. "If Canada does not have its human resources in line," he warned, "there will be no [new wealth] generated to support social programs in Canada within the next generation."

Other consequences of expenditure reductions were also becoming more and more evident. CBC management announced that they would be forced to close a number of regional and local stations, in order to meet the budget shortfall caused by greatly reduced federal funding over the past several years. The government was unmoved, and the stations shut down.

The Canadian people were outraged. Editorials across the country spoke of the government's insensitivity in effectively shelving one of the few remaining vehicles for national unity, just when the effects of the FTA and the failure of Meech Lake were causing an unprecedented identity crisis. Mayors from affected municipalities joined forces and took their case to Ottawa, local groups offered to buy stations, and hundreds protested in regionally organized demonstrations, but to no avail.

The government and Michael Wilson persevered, believing short-term criticism would be worth the benefits that would eventually accrue from the increased revenue at their disposal — revenue acquired from the restraint in expenditures and the GST cash cow. These benefits, they calculated, would coincide with an economic recovery just in time for the next election.

The burden of the recession budget quite clearly fell on workers, and Canadians evidently knew it. Unimpressed by the clarion call to tighten their belts and diminish their expectations to pay for the Gulf expedition, they continued to reject the government's approach. By late March 1991, several polls had shown that the government's credibility was seriously eroded: over 75 percent of Canadians rejected the GST, which they saw as unfair and inequitable; nor did they believe the increased revenues it would produce would go towards deficit reduction. Over 80 percent of Canadians indicated they believed the government's economic policies had actually made matters worse and would continue to do so. After seven years of Wilson's "medicine," they were unprepared to swallow any more.

Still the government appeared unconcerned, its attention focused on the upcoming Throne Speech in May that would reveal the "New Agenda." But, when it was unveiled, this new agenda proved to be merely a repetition of past promises, almost all of which had been broken. Columnist Jeffrey Simpson charitably described the Throne Speech as a "remarkably stand-pat speech for a government stuck in the mud," and rightly concluded the government's new course was "straight ahead. At the half-way mark in the full five-year period in office, the Mulroneyites intend to slog ahead, emphasizing the same themes that brought them to power in 1984 . . . for a government in the dumps, quite a gamble."

It was more than a gamble. It was a tragic abdication of responsibility by the national government for the economic future of the country and ordinary Canadians. As Michael Wilson's fellow neoconservative Ronald Reagan used to say in his early years, the way for citizens to evaluate the success of a government's economic policies was to ask themselves whether they were better or worse off than three, four, or five years ago.

The answer, for virtually all Canadians except the very rich, and large corporations, is a resounding "worse." Subjected to massive tax increases and made increasingly vulnerable by high interest rates and decreased job security, they sense that their future prospects are declining rapidly. The answer, for Canadian workers and for the Canadian economy, is also "worse." Canada is more rather than less dependent on the U.S. economy, more vulnerable to the forces of globalization, and less prepared. Uncontrolled foreign investment and foreign-held debt are reducing the scope of policy making, and the declining support for R&D will limit our future options even more. With the transportation and manufacturing infrastructures weakened and no new programs in place to improve the educational and training skills of our work force, the country is less well equipped now than it was seven years ago to meet the challenges of the future.

As the next chapter demonstrates, there have also been social consequences of this economic decline, consequences that have been greatly exacerbated by deliberate neoconservative policies designed to reduce government involvement in that area as well.

NOTES

1. *Financial Post*, September 14–16, 1991, p. 1.

2. Ibid., p. 4.

3. T. Lowi, "American Business, Public Policy, Case Studies and Political Theory," in *World Politics* 16/4: 677–715.

4. K. Graham, "Heading into the Stretch: A Pathology of Government," in *How Ottawa Spends, 1988–89*, pp. 1–22.

5. S. Wilson, "What Legacy? The Nielsen Task Force Program Review," in *How Ottawa Spends, 1988–89*, p. 24.

6. D. Leyton-Brown, "The Canada–U.S. Free Trade Agreement," in Gollner and Salee, eds., *Canada Under Mulroney*, pp. 106–7.

7. Repudiating Sacred Trusts
How the Neoconservatives Abandoned Our Commitment to Social Justice

Universal social programs are a sacred trust, not to be tampered with.

— Brian Mulroney, August 18, 1984

Canadians who lived through the Great Depression can still picture the bread lines and the transients riding the rails. Most thought they would never see such sights again in their lifetime; yet, by the late 1980s, food and shelter once again became unattainable luxuries for a growing number of their fellow citizens.

More than half a million Canadians, 40 percent of them children, depended on food banks in 1990 to survive each month. Across the country, some 1,200 community food programs — soup kitchens, food banks, and school lunch programs — were established. Originally believed to be a temporary measure to weather the worldwide recession of 1981–82, they became a permanent fixture of Canadian society.

By 1989, after five years of sustained economic recovery, estimates placed the number of homeless Canadians between 100,000 and 250,000. Large urban centres such as Vancouver, Montreal, and Toronto were unable to cope with the influx of those needing shelter, despite a proliferation of emergency-housing centres and hostels. In Toronto, the numbers on the waiting list for public housing had reached 10,000 and showed no signs of abating.

Moreover, the nature of the homeless — once elderly men and those with alcohol- or drug-related addiction problems — had changed dramatically in less than a decade. One study found that slightly more than half (51.5 percent) of those seeking temporary shelter in 1989 were recipients of social assistance, unable to find affordable housing. Youth, single-parent families headed by women, and single elderly females comprised a growing percentage of the homeless. Even more striking was the growing number of the "working poor" obliged to seek temporary-shelter assistance. Another report concluded that between 30 and 40 percent of the homeless had psychiatric problems, insufficient funds having led to the de-institutionalization of patients. Slightly fewer than 30 percent were suffering from drug or alcohol addiction.

With the advent of another recession, one that in many ways proved to be more severe and lengthy than that of 1981–82, these statistics become the good news. With the loss of benefits after prolonged unemployment and the decreasing buying power of welfare payments, the number of homeless and the number of Canadians receiving assistance from food banks over the course of 1991–92 continues to mount.

The common denominator in all of these statistics, of course, is poverty. Canada's efforts to deal with poverty began in earnest with the Great Depression. The federal government, acceding to provincial requests for assistance, stepped in to coordinate nation-wide recovery and social-assistance efforts. Given the provinces' inability to finance these efforts and the perceived advantages of minimum national standards for such programs, particularly for disadvantaged regions, this federal coordinating role, once assumed, became firmly entrenched.

The first elements of the Canadian social-security system as it existed in 1984 were introduced by Prime Minister Mackenzie King in a program that implemented sweeping economic and social reforms designed to protect Canadians from the worst effects of future economic downturns. Successive Liberal and Conservative governments built upon King's foundation to create an impressive array of programs. Unemployment insurance, old age security, the guaranteed income supplement, the Canada Pension Plan, the

Canada Assistance Plan, family allowance, and medicare were implemented to lessen the effects of poverty.

There is irrefutable evidence that these programs were effective. From 1969 to 1981, the number of poor Canadians fell from 4.8 million to 3.5 million, an overall decrease from 23.1 to 14.7 percent of the total population.

Among the most important factors contributing to this decline were the improvement in social-assistance benefits and the introduction of pension measures for senior citizens. The latter alone produced a dramatic decrease in the number of elderly Canadians living below the poverty line, a group that had traditionally represented the largest segment of poor Canadians.

These programs, while successful in moderating the effects of poverty, did not significantly narrow the gap between rich and poor or achieve their ultimate objective of eradicating poverty. Nevertheless, the social safety net prevented any *increase* in poverty levels, in addition to alleviating the conditions of those falling below the poverty line.

It should also be noted that the overall objective of these programs had broadened from the original concern with avoiding the worst consequences of another depression. Over time, the concept of the social safety net evolved into one that aimed to alleviate the effects of poverty, however caused, by assuring a minimum standard of living for all Canadians as a right of citizenship. This principle, in turn, resulted from the growing importance of the twin principles of social justice and equality of opportunity in liberal thinking, objectives that earlier had been seen as secondary to individual liberty. As Anatole France reportedly remarked, the importance of individual liberties fades rapidly where rich and poor are equally free to sleep under bridges.

In incorporating this expanded approach within its philosophy, Canadian liberalism successfully evolved in a unique direction. The measure of its success can be found in the degree to which Canadians became profoundly committed to the concept of the social contract.

As the free-trade debate so conclusively demonstrated, Canadians support an interventionist role for the federal government in social as well as economic areas, not only as a means of ensuring equality of opportunity and a better standard of living for all citizens, but also as a unifying and distinguishing element of the political culture. The social safety net, Decima polls confirmed, was seen as one more way in which Canadians were different from and superior to Americans.

Of course, social programs alone were never expected to eliminate poverty. Indeed, it was clearly recognized that economic factors, and in particular unemployment levels, determined poverty levels. As a result, federal governments in Canada traditionally pursued full-employment strategies as a high priority, again with considerable success. The decrease in unemployment between 1969 and 1981, for example, contributed significantly to the decline in the number of Canadians living below the poverty line during the same period.

It is not surprising, then, that the advent of the 1981–82 recession, with its sharp increase in unemployment, reversed the trend of the previous twenty years and brought about a substantial increase in the number of Canadians living in poverty.

While the recession was devastating, it is undeniable its effects would have been much worse had it not been for the existence of the social safety net, which automatically kicked in to prevent a recurrence of the Great Depression. With the recovery in late 1983–84 and the subsequent decrease in unemployment, poverty levels fell. By early 1985, 3.9 million Canadians, or 16 percent of the population, lived in poverty, down from a recession high of 4.2 million. But this initial decline soon slowed and then levelled off. It is this unexpected flattening of the trend line that makes the numbers cited at the beginning of this chapter so significant.

According to conventional wisdom, economic recovery should have brought about another period of significant decline in the poverty rate. Although the total number of those living below the poverty line did decrease from the 1980–81 recession highs, by 1989 poor Canadians comprised some 12.2 percent of the population; one of every six children in Canada was living in poverty. In other words, despite five years of sustained economic growth, the number of Canadians living in poverty did not decrease at the rate that might have been expected based on earlier experiences. Instead, the decline was gradual and modest, barely returning after several years of recovery to pre-recession levels.

Moreover, the conditions of many of those living in poverty actually deteriorated. The number of homeless and those dependent on food banks increased. At the same time low-income Canadians' access to services and facilities that traditionally moderated the effects of poverty decreased. In 1989, for example, when over 14 percent of the population was living below the poverty line, only 12.2 percent of the population was housed in low-income family units, down from 13 percent in 1988 and 14 percent in 1987. This downward trend began in 1984–85.

Meanwhile, unemployment had risen steadily in the late 1980s. Before the 1990–91 recession, it stood at 7.3 percent, the level at the start of the 1981–82 recession. Regional unemployment levels, as the preceding chapter noted, never declined to pre-1981 levels.

In short, the "recovery" of the Mulroney era was extremely uneven. Regionally and individually, it did little to benefit those most in need. As the above statistics demonstrate, many low-income Canadians were worse off before the 1990–91 recession than at the end of the previous one. Given the extensive social safety net that existed when the Mulroney Conservatives took office, why did the condition of those living below the poverty line deteriorate? Given five years of economic recovery in which overall employment figures improved, why did poverty levels not decline more significantly? Put another way, what was different about the economic recovery of the Mulroney years?

The simple answer is that government policy was different. For the first time since the Depression, a federal government was not committed to the two fundamental objectives of its predecessors with respect to social policy. As we have seen, the Mulroney government effectively abandoned the goal of full employment in favour of economic policies driven by the objectives of inflation control and deficit reduction. It also abandoned the traditional goal of national social programs — that of ensuring a minimum standard of living for all Canadians — in favour of efficiency, rationalization, affordability, and deficit reduction. It even abandoned the federal coordination role in national social programs, transferring financial and administrative responsibility to the provinces.

The end result was a job market favouring employers rather than workers, with a steady increase in poorly paid temporary and part-time jobs at the expense of permanent full-time employment, and the dismantling of the social safety net, largely without the knowledge or informed consent of Canadians. What was different about the Mulroney "recovery" was that the reduction in overall unemployment masked a dramatic change in the nature of the jobs being created, leading to increasing numbers of working poor. The government's concerted attacks on the social safety net then ensured those caught in the poverty trap would see their standard of living and opportunities for improvement decrease dramatically.

The legacy of the Mulroney government in the area of social policy is therefore a litany of broken promises and deliberate misrepresentation that began with the 1984 election and continues to this day. The convoluted process by which the neoconservative element of the cabinet accomplished these ends, and the consequences of their decisions for Canadians generally and the poor in particular, are chronicled below.

If there was one area in which Brian Mulroney knew he had to be careful during the 1984 election campaign, it was social policy. He knew Canadians tended to distrust Conservatives on these issues, and he knew that his right-wing supporters within the party did not help his image on that score. As the campaign unfolded, it became clear this would be the area in which John Turner and Ed Broadbent would focus much of their attack, playing on the inherent doubts Canadians still harboured about his intentions. In typical Mulroney fashion, long on rhetoric and hyperbole but short on substance, the future prime minister addressed Canadians' concerns frequently over the course of the campaign, attempting to reassure voters of the sincerity of his commitment to the social safety net.

Worried about the seniors' vote, Mulroney assured voters in Sherbrooke his party would "reinstate complete indexing of Old Age Pensions to the actual cost of living." To control the damage caused by his widely publicized statement the previous March that "I have no hesitation in reviewing the concept of universality," he declared in Winnipeg in August that universal social programs were a "sacred trust, not to be tampered with." His statement was so categorical it appeared the matter had been laid to rest.

This was not the first time he had used the now-infamous expression, nor would it be the last. In a 1983 year-end interview with the CBC, he had already referred to medicare as a "sacred trust." He further volunteered that "I have never been in favour of user fees . . . the problem is one of underfunding and so . . . there has to be new money of course go into medicare." By November 1984, even his minister of Health and Welfare, Jake Epp, had adopted the expression, however awkwardly. "Medicare is not only a sacred trust," Epp ventured, "but one that we will maintain."

Canadians could surely be forgiven, then, for failing to recognize the real Tory agenda on social policy when they elected the Mulroney Conservatives in 1984. It had been a very long time since they had been exposed to a politician who was prepared to mislead voters so deliberately and cavalierly. Understanding the Tory agenda was made even more difficult because it had two aspects — one proactive and one passive — and Canadians were not prepared for either. The first agenda was promoted by the extreme right wing of the party, to whom Mulroney owed the leadership. This wing consisted of a sizable proportion of his back bench, primarily from western Canada and rural Ontario. This group had an agenda born of years languishing in opposition and watching "liberal" innovations "destroy" some "fundamental" societal values. Not surprisingly this group, which came to be known in Ottawa as "the dinosaurs," wanted to proceed full steam ahead, changing the laws on such matters as capital punishment, pornography, prostitution, abortion, and young offenders, all of which, in their view, had been handled by the previous government with a distressing degree of laxity and merited a more punitive approach.

The problem these supporters presented for Mulroney cannot be underestimated. On the one hand, they represented half of his winning Quebec–West coalition and a substantial part of his personal power base; as such they needed to be accommodated. On the other hand, neither he nor most of his cabinet, or the more sophisticated caucus members from Ontario and Quebec, shared these views. For, in spite of their abysmal ignorance of the underlying values of the political culture, Mulroney and several senior cabinet colleagues were closer to the mainstream on societal values. As a result they were acutely aware of the fact most Canadians did not share the dinosaurs' views.

Indeed, most Canadians did not think these were issues that needed to be addressed. There was no burning cry in the land to reopen the capital-punishment debate, which had been resolved more than a decade earlier. Nor was there any overwhelming concern on the part of the majority of Canadians that prostitution and pornography threatened the very fabric of the nation. Certainly there was no desire on the part of the moderate majority to revisit the painful question of abortion. In short, most Canadians were content with the status quo and astonished when the government vigorously pursued these issues instead of attending to more pressing matters.

The first years of the Mulroney era therefore saw the emergence of a new social-policy agenda that made many Canadians uncomfortable. Sensing this, but obliged to accommodate his supporters, Mulroney attempted a delicate balancing act between the two social-policy agendas. The right wing was selectively placated or rewarded with legislation on a number of "their" issues in exchange for internal caucus harmony and their support on other issues.

On the whole, the balancing act was successful in maintaining caucus unity, but it produced several public-relations setbacks. The government feared lengthy examination of these issues would distract it from its second agenda; in many cases, it therefore introduced legislation as inoffensive as possible, only to have its own members publicly condemn its failure to go far enough. On other issues, the initial legislation, designed to reflect accurately the position of the caucus, was too Draconian for the public, leading to embarrassing "redneck" image problems Mulroney was trying so hard to avoid.

Among the first of these legislative initiatives was that related to prostitution. Ironically, although the issue had developed some visibility in certain cities, notably Vancouver, it was Conservative backbenchers from largely rural areas and fundamentalist backgrounds who were determined to pursue the matter quickly, fomenting discontent at their breakfast "prayer meetings" and caucus events. As a result, the Mulroney government somewhat hastily introduced far-reaching and harsh new legislation in 1985 that banned "any communication for the purpose of prostitution in public places" and provided for the prosecution of both prostitute and customer.

Unfortunately, the legislation disregarded a long-standing Supreme Court ruling (1978) declaring that solicitation could be considered a criminal offence only if individuals were "persistent and pressing" in their advances. It also ignored the findings in 1985 of the Special Parliamentary Committee on Prostitution (the Fraser Committee), which recommended that the government focus on eliminating the social and economic causes of prostitution rather than on introducing punitive measures, and strongly urged that solicitation be removed from the Criminal Code entirely.

Shortly after it was enacted, the new legislation was challenged as unconstitutional and struck down by a number of courts. Several studies since then have also demonstrated a dramatic increase in the number of "escort" services, suggesting that the primary effect of the legislation was simply to drive prostitutes underground.

However, the public's adverse reaction to the prostitution legislation paled in comparison to their response to the government's next attempt to legislate morality. In the pornography issue, the Mulroney government came in for considerable criticism and public ridicule.

Bill C-114, tabled in June 1986 by Justice minister John Crosbie, was allegedly aimed at violent and degrading pornography and child pornography, but failed miserably to confine itself to those issues. Instead, the legislation included a lengthy shopping list of every conceivable type of sexual conduct and concluded, apparently to ensure comprehensiveness, with the words "or any other sexual activity." Bill and minister swiftly became the object of public derision and scorn; the former died on the order paper and the latter moved on to another portfolio.

Not content, the moral minority in Mulroney's caucus insisted on another effort. Bill C-54, introduced by Crosbie's successor, Ray Hnatyshyn, in May 1987, received no more support than had C-114. It was rejected outright by more than two-thirds of Canadians, according to an Angus Reid poll, largely because of the puritanical attempt to include "depictions of sexual intercourse between consenting adults" among the list of proscribed activities. However, it was incompetent drafting that led the artistic community and librarians across the country to rise up in arms at the apparent attempt to emulate developments in the United States and impose new community standards, first, by placing the onus on the accused individual or organization to defend a work's "educational, artistic or scientific merit," and, second, by allowing local enforcement officials to determine who should be charged.

Over the years, the radical right also attempted to reinstate capital punishment, overhaul the Young Offenders Act, create a George Bush–style "war on drugs," and water down Justice minister Kim Campbell's gun-control legislation.

The general public, while largely indifferent or opposed to most of these efforts, was nevertheless quite supportive of two initiatives of this agenda, namely, legislation to ensure greater provision for the victims of crime and to confiscate the proceeds of illegal activities.

Indeed, the most noteworthy long-term effect of this agenda may have been to heighten public concern about criminal activity and the justice system. Unfortunately, this perception, stimulated by sensationalized media coverage and the widely publicized campaigns of several Tory backbenchers, is largely inaccurate.

Canada compares favourably with most other Western industrialized nations in terms of our low levels of violent crime, yet recent polls have demonstrated that growing numbers of Canadians believe their personal safety is at risk. Similarly, despite a criminal-justice system that is far more punitive than those of almost any other Western nation, more and more Canadians are coming to believe our legal system is "too lenient."

This discrepancy between fact and opinion has grown dramatically in the past few years. A Decima poll in 1989 asked respondents in major urban centres to identify aspects of their quality of life that had been "getting worse" in the past two or three years. Fully 89 percent of respondents in Montreal and 72 percent in Toronto listed "illegal drug use and related crimes," while 58 percent and 71 percent, respectively, also chose "violent crime."

In reality, the overall level of drug-related crime was lower in 1987 than in 1980. Drug-related criminal offences *including simple drug offences such as possession,* constituted only 2 percent of all recorded crime. Violent crimes of all kinds constituted only 8 percent of all criminal offences; the vast majority of these were for simple assault, where no weapons had been used.[1]

Although the percentage of violent crimes rose marginally during this period, the rate of commission of the most serious offences — including homicide and armed robbery — actually declined. More important than data from a particular year, however, are the longer-term trends: over the decade of the 1980s homicide levels varied from year to year, but the fluctuations were not statistically significant. A study released by the Canadian Centre for Justice Statistics in August 1991 noted a similarly modest increase in levels of violent crime over the longer period from 1975 to 1989, and again noted no appreciable increase in homicides.[2]

According to Paul Sonnischen, a criminologist with the Canadian Federation of Municipalities, "Canada enjoys relative peace and comfort in terms of safety in the streets." Mr. Sonnischen's statement received support from an unusual quarter in the comments of Gary Rosenfeldt of Victims of Violence, who believes "many people have an exaggerated fear of violence because sensational crimes are given so much attention."[3]

Nevertheless, the issues of crime and drug use continue to receive high priority from voters in large Canadian municipalities; in Toronto, the November 1991 mayoralty race was dominated by such "law and order" issues. The federal government, quick to respond to this outpouring of public concern, immediately devoted a week of the parliamentary agenda to such issues, proclaiming the week of November 4 "Public Safety Week."

In a typical move to curry favour rather than lead public opinion or educate, the government failed to address the underlying issues: youth unemployment, family violence, and drug abuse. Nor did they restore funding for a number of programs they had previously reduced or eliminated in those areas. Instead, they planned to introduce legislation to amend the Young Offenders Act, rework Criminal Code provisions on the criminally insane that had been struck down by the courts, and introduce a Psychoactive Substance Control Act, whose purpose was merely to simplify and consolidate existing legislation.

The unfortunate effect of this negative focus on law enforcement and the judicial system by the Tory dinosaurs may well have been an unwarranted lack of public confidence in that very system. Certainly, the emotions generated by these issues diverted the public's attention from the second, more important social policy agenda of the Mulroney government.

The second social-policy agenda is the classic neoconservative one in which less government intervention and decreased spending are the primary goals. Like Brian Mulroney's approach to economic policy, characterized by his declaring that Canada was "open for business," the goal of the neoconservative approach to social policy is to focus on the financial bottom line.

This objective could be achieved largely through cuts to federal programs and withdrawal of services; thus, it could be implemented quickly in many program areas. For the most part, it could also be handled through the regular budgetary process and the main estimates for federal expenditures, where it could be buried among countless other measures. With some notable exceptions, this second Tory agenda was therefore less visible than the first, and Canadians were unable to discern its implications for some time.

The first program areas affected highlighted the Mulroney Conservatives' attitude towards affirmative action, equality of opportunity, and the plight of disadvantaged groups. Basically, Canadians were on their own. It was up to individuals to assume more responsibility for their well-being, and for voluntary charitable organizations to assume responsibility for activities that had been mistakenly funded by government.

Thus we were treated to the spectacle of a minister of Health and Welfare who failed to understand that his primary responsibility was to protect Canadians, not the mussel industry; a minister responsible for the Status of Women who declared that "we are all mistresses of our own destiny" and refused to meet with the annual National Action Committee (NAC) lobby of her client group; and Tory members of a parliamentary committee on childcare who expressed the view that women should stay at home and look after their own children.

We also witnessed a chairman of the Finance Committee who suggested that unemployment insurance and the Canada Pension Plan should be abolished, and status Indians should pay income tax and move off reserves to urban centres; a minister of Housing who declared that the homeless had plenty of emergency shelters; and a prime minister's wife who attended ribbon-cutting ceremonies at food banks.

Beginning with expenditure cuts in November 1984, and proceeding through seven budgets and two economic "corrections," the Mulroney Conservatives reduced or eliminated support for specific groups of citizens. The Women's Program in the Department of the Secretary of State, for example, saw successive reductions in its funding for sustaining grants to voluntary organizations. Moreover, some of the precious remaining funding was to go to a favourite right-wing Conservative lobby, REAL Women, an organization diametrically opposed to the affirmative-action mandate of the program.

Similar cuts were made to programs supporting native peoples, including Friendship Centres, sustaining grants for national native organizations, and funds for newsletters and other communications projects. Funding for native housing and post-secondary education were frozen. The implementation of Bill C-31, which restored status for certain native women, was a disaster because the government refused to allocate funds for the extra accommodation and other expenses needed by bands receiving these women.

In the case of most of the affected social programs, including the women's and native peoples' programs, these debilitating cuts were incremental, and therefore failed to attract much attention. One expenditure cut that did attract public attention and disapproval was the outright elimination of the Katimavik youth program. The furore over that decision, and the hunger strike of Katimavik's founder, Senator Jacques Hébert, convinced the Conservatives that gradual erosion was the safer strategy for future program reductions.

The other side of the funding coin was the government's failure to live up to campaign promises by implementing new programs, particularly in childcare and public housing. It originally masked its lack of commitment to these policies by establishing committees and task forces, and, in the case of childcare, actually tabled legislation. However, the Mulroney government carefully ensured that its version of these programs would be cost-effective and involve minimal state intervention.

The Tory proposal for a "national" childcare plan was a classic example of this approach. A far cry from what proponents had been demanding, it was hardly a national plan as it did not provide for minimum national standards. It was also an unusual "government" plan in that it relied heavily on the private sector. Worse still, it attempted to placate the right wing of caucus by providing special compensation through the taxation system for women who remain in the home to look after their children, completely ignoring the fact that homemakers are already compensated through the spousal deduction, and hence would be doubly advantaged by this provision. By providing funding directly to individuals, rather than focusing on the lack of infrastructure, the government also ignored the critical problem — that not enough childcare spaces are available, at any cost.

To reduce the costs of their "comprehensive" childcare proposal even further, the Tories linked their plan to existing Canada Assistance Plan (CAP) arrangements with the provinces. In so doing, the government effectively limited the plan to a small group of low-income earners, excluding the middle class from it entirely. The effects of their approach not only would be inequitable and inadequate, but, within a few years of implementation, would cost the federal treasury far less than the existing system of subsidies.

Such deliberate obfuscation, praising the concept but delivering nothing of substance, became a trademark of the Mulroney government's approach to social policy. It contributed greatly to the public's confusion, as government statements were telling Canadians these were major initiatives for which they should be grateful.

The childcare plan was a perfect example of this subterfuge. Despite widespread criticism by women's groups and childcare activists, the Conservatives convinced the public during the 1988 campaign that the activists were nitpicking on details. They also claimed that their plan had not received final approval only because the Liberals in the Senate had blocked it, when in reality the government could, of course, have obtained passage had it wished, but did not bother to do so. The Conservatives also promised to reintroduce and implement the plan immediately upon their return to office. Instead, Michael Wilson announced in his first budget after the election that the plan had been postponed indefinitely because of a lack of resources, making it a casualty of the renewed thrust on deficit reduction.

An equally shameless lie was directed to the government's own employees. By fall 1991, most Canadians were aware the federal public service was on strike over the government's refusal to bargain on wage increases, but few realized other issues were at stake. Among the most important was the government's four years of stalling and delaying tactics to avoid meeting its legal obligations to implement equal pay for work of equal value.

The federal government has long been seen as a role model for the private sector. The concept of good-faith bargaining between the government as employer and its employees had historically been supported and enhanced through the acceptance of unionization and collective bargaining. Both these principles were violated by the government in its handling of the equal-pay issue, long before the strike began. In the 1988 leaders' debates, Brian Mulroney told NDP leader Ed Broadbent that equal pay was an important issue for the government. Money was being budgeted to cover the expected costs, which would be identified by the joint equal-pay study the government had commissioned. "The commitment is there, the money is there," Mulroney replied in response to Broadbent's probing.

Yet, less than a year later, the government rejected the results of the four-year study it had commissioned and called for a new study. It then claimed there was no money to implement any plan. Instead, it offered small interim "adjustments" to some, but not all, of the female-dominated groups identified by the report as seriously underpaid. The unions responded by filing a complaint with the Human Rights Commission, and placed equal pay on the bargaining table in the next round of negotiations. The Mulroney government refused to discuss equal pay in bargaining; that, they said, was an issue for the Human Rights Tribunal. Federal representatives then argued before the tribunal that it did not have jurisdiction and attempted to have the federal court prevent the tribunal from hearing the case.

In an open letter to the prime minister during the strike of September 1991, the president of the striking union, Daryl Bean, concluded: "It is not just a question of fairness. It is the law." A week later the striking employees were legislated back to work, the question of equal pay unresolved.

But reductions in program expenditures and non-action on others were a minor part of the second Tory agenda. The strategy was useful for curbing activities of which it did not approve, but produced little additional revenue for deficit reduction. The real target of the neoconservative agenda was the money expended by the federal government on social benefits, both directly to individuals and indirectly in the form of transfer payments to the provinces for post-secondary education and health care. It was here that the greatest potential for significant savings existed and here that they were most often exposed, caught in the blatant contradictions between the prime minister's rhetoric and election promises and Michael Wilson's determination to cut social spending.

In retrospect, there can be little doubt that Wilson's game plan was in place from the beginning. It was only the implementation that caused him difficulty, as the comical miscues of Wilson and Mulroney on the universality issue in fall 1984 and early winter of the following year demonstrated so well. No sooner had Wilson convinced Mulroney of the need to be firm on the elimination of universality than a negative article or aggressive question would send Mulroney into flights of pseudo-liberal rhetoric, confusing the public and setting the neoconservative cause back several months.

On November 9, 1984, Mulroney first repeated his campaign pledge on sacred trusts: "My Party and I view with favour the principle of universality." Later in the same press conference, he caused more than a few journalists to wonder if he understood the meaning of universality when he declared, "We want to get more money into the hands of those who need it most. . . . We want to make the best possible use of taxpayers' money. A legitimate question arises: Are we making the best use of that money by giving a bank president, say, at $500,000 or $600,000 a year, a baby bonus?"

With Wilson's apparent prodding, he persevered with this line throughout much of the next month, although he was clearly ill at ease with the increasing criticism of it. By December 13, he was still pursuing the mythical bank president in the House of Commons, where he reiterated that "the poor and the dispossessed in our society need more benefits than the bank president at $500,000 a year."

Michael Wilson was only too glad to assist Mulroney the following day: "What we're saying is that there are people who don't need it. Upper- and middle-income social programs cannot be afforded today." On December 18, Health minister Jake Epp entered the debate, suggesting that curtailing benefits for those with incomes over $26,000 "might have appeal for the future."

The uproar that followed these comments caused Mulroney to retreat in disarray. By December 20, he completely reversed himself and assured the House of Commons that "we are going to protect the integrity of universality in this country. I will guarantee it." By January 2, he was flogging the bank president again, apparently believing that Canadians could not distinguish between universality and charity: "We are in favour of a formula that allows us to withdraw entirely or give less money to a bank president who makes $500,000 a year and to give that money to the less well-off members of society."

By now the media and opposition parties were as confused as the general public. Where did the Conservatives stand on the issue? It appeared the only thing to do was to wait for the first Wilson budget. This would surely clarify the contradictory statements about universality, user fees in medicare, and whether savings from any changes to social programs would be used to increase benefits for the poorest Canadians or put towards deficit reduction.

The budget removed any uncertainties. On May 23, Michael Wilson introduced extensive measures to partially de-index a wide range of pension and family benefits, and broke several campaign promises at once. The outcry from senior citizens was particularly virulent since the prime minister's campaign pledge to reintroduce full indexing of pensions had been reiterated by Health minister

Jake Epp as late as December 1984, when he announced in the House of Commons: "I can confirm the regular indexing of Old Age Security, Guaranteed Income Supplement and Family Allowance benefits will be increased as of January 1, 1985."

Mme Solange Denis's famous encounter with Brian Mulroney during a demonstration by senior citizens on Parliament Hill was too much for the man who liked, above all, to be liked. Mulroney ordered Wilson to back down on the pensions portion of his package.

In this case, the Conservatives fled the field because senior citizens are a cohesive and sympathetic group, vocal and easily organized. The same could not be said for the millions of disparate Canadians affected in one way or another by the de-indexing of various family benefits. In addition, the Tory rhetoric successfully masked the reality. The government repeatedly referred to the package of measures as progressive and claimed that they would provide significant assistance to all poor Canadians.

As a result, the rest of Wilson's plan went ahead, despite widespread criticism from experts and social agencies who clearly understood the implications. For the reality was very different from the government's claims. Although it was true that they had introduced certain measures, such as the child tax credit, that would benefit the very poorest of poor Canadians, the vast majority of those on low incomes would be worse off.

Even the *Globe and Mail*, editorially very supportive of Wilson's emphasis on deficit reduction, was moved to publish a lengthy article denouncing the benefits package as regressive and the government's description of it as deliberately misleading. Referring to extensive calculations on the impact of the budget that had been revealed by Canadian Press a few days earlier, the *Globe*'s article on June 13 concluded that this evidence called into question "the validity of Conservative promises to help those most in need, and sheds a different light on figures the government chose to make public on Budget Night."

Noting that Wilson's figures showed family benefits rising through to 1989 for a family of four earning $27,500 annually, the article countered that "what Wilson neglected to mention was that the increase would have been even larger for many of those families if the government had left the current system alone." The article continued: "Far more families will be losers than winners under the proposed new system, and the line that separates the winners from the losers is actually just under $20,000, not $27,500."

Terrance Hunsley of the Canadian Council on Social Development agreed, noting that the hardest hit by these measures would be families earning $30,000 annually. They would lose $1,089 in disposable income by 1990, while wealthy Canadians would *increase* their disposable income by $4,500 during the same period. Ken Battle of the National Council of Welfare, accusing the government of making "social policy by stealth," also noted that the child tax credit that the government was touting would be available only to families with incomes below $23,500; the provision it was replacing had applied to families up to $26,330.

Perhaps the best indication of the real Tory agenda could be found in the government's unpublished budget papers, which indicated the total effect of the family-benefits measures would be to save the government more than $550 million annually by 1990–91. The rest is history. For the next seven years, successive budgets insidiously eroded the universality and progressivity of family-benefits provisions.

These efforts increased after the 1988 election, partly in response to the "deficit crisis" Michael Wilson had discovered, and partly as a result of the Free Trade Agreement. Almost immediately after the election Wilson indicated that ordinary Canadians, indeed all Canadians, would be called upon to make "sacrifices" in order to save the country for "future generations."

The nature of these sacrifices could be gleaned from the section of the 1989 Throne Speech dealing with social justice. Instead of concrete initiatives to implement campaign commitments, it contained, at best, vague statements paying lip-service to those commitments in the abstract — "my government remains committed to a national childcare program" — or, at worst, contemplated changes antithetical to those commitments.

The speech also concealed another planned attack on universality under platitudes: "My government believes fundamentally in those social benefits which support the family and the elderly, while recognizing the need to direct more assistance to those with low incomes." Similarly it gave notice of the government's intention to introduce "amendments to the Unemployment Insurance plan to improve the program's effectiveness and fairness." This would later prove to be the privatization of the unemployment-insurance system.

The budget that followed shortly thereafter confirmed many Canadians' worst fears. It not only pursued deficit reduction through tax increases and program-expenditure cuts, but gave early evidence that the Free Trade Agreement would indeed result in changes to social programs and regional development. As opponents of the deal had feared, the "level playing field" the Mulroney government and the Americans had been seeking was to be accomplished by diminishing Canadian standards rather than raising American ones.

During the campaign, Brian Mulroney had declared in Summerside, P.E.I.: "As long as I am Prime Minister of Canada, social benefits, especially those for the elderly, will be improved not diminished by our government." The 1989 budget reduced old age pensions, family allowances, and health and post-secondary education funding.

On October 13, 1988, campaigning in St. John's, Trade minister John Crosbie stated categorically: "The federal government has no plans to make changes to the unemployment insurance system. You're damn right I asked him [Mulroney] about it and he said no. No one is planning any changes in the unemployment insurance program." On April 11, 1989, Employment minister Barbara McDougall announced massive changes to the UI program, which, in effect, removed federal government participation and privatized it.

In October 1988, Mulroney promised in Winnipeg that "we will be reintroducing childcare legislation and passing it as soon as Parliament comes back after the election. . . . Our program will add at least 200,000 new subsidized spaces to our existing childcare facilities, doubling the present number." The 1989 budget cut $4 billion for childcare spaces and stated that no legislation was contemplated in the foreseeable future.

Referring to the tax burden of the middle class, Michael Wilson promised on the campaign trail, "There will be further income tax reductions for middle-income Canadians. And the income surtaxes will be removed." Asked about this commitment in May

1989, Wilson replied, "At this point, I would not want to hold that one out." Small wonder, as he subsequently increased rather than eliminated the surtax and extended its application to more taxpayers.

On October 3, 1989, Brian Mulroney told the Saint John Board of Trade that "we will not have one Canada that is prospering at the centre while other regions do not receive a fair share of economic opportunity." Both the West and Atlantic Canada then watched in dismay as the April 1989 budget cut the western diversification program by $55 million and the Atlantic Opportunities program by 25 percent, reduced regional development and forestry agreements, closed armed forces bases and ports, reduced Via Rail service, eliminated rural post offices, increased freight rates, and altered UI regulations to the detriment of fishermen and other seasonally employed workers.

By 1989, the government had become so confident that its contradictions and "incremental" approach hadn't been noticed that it dared to tackle the question of pensions again. This time its public-relations exercise was far more successful.

Engaging in a well-crafted game of semantics in which Wilson and Mulroney insisted that universality was not affected as all seniors would continue to receive the benefits, they then destroyed universality through a clawback provision, all the while insisting that they were taxing back the entire benefit only for those "rich" Canadians with incomes above $55,000. They carefully neglected to mention that the level at which taxpayers were defined as "rich" would decrease each year, and might well be reduced to the poverty line, as had a number of previously universal family benefits.

In sum, Wilson and Mulroney eliminated many of the benefits of the social safety net for all but the lowest-income Canadians. In particular, they eliminated these benefits for the vast majority of middle-income Canadians whose tax dollars were paying for them. Last, but not least, the huge amounts of revenue saved by these cutbacks did not return to the social programs as increased benefits for those who needed them most, and in some cases were not even put towards deficit reduction.

Yet, all of these measures were imposed in the name of deficit reduction, a tacit admission by Wilson and the neoconservative elements of the government that, after more than four years of economic growth, they had not achieved their primary objective of "economic recovery." Instead, they had presided over the doubling of the national debt, and now needed further revenues to service that debt.

Not surprisingly, given such demands on the federal treasury, a very similar pattern emerged with respect to such low-priority programs as the indirect federal funding of post-secondary education, medicare, and the Canada Assistance Plan.

Beginning in 1985, Wilson engaged in a smoke-and-mirrors exercise in which he insisted that federal funding for these programs was increasing, when in fact he was decreasing the amounts the provinces ought to have received under a long-standing formula. In short, by unilaterally changing the rules, he decreased the level of their increases, a concept that was difficult for the provinces and the opposition parties to communicate to the general public. But the end result was not difficult to understand. Each year the provinces would receive less and less money to finance their costly health and educational systems. What the Mulroney government was really doing, of course, was transferring responsibility for the federal deficit to the provinces. Provincial premiers were left with two choices — to reduce services or raise their own revenues through increased taxation. Either choice would hurt their chances at election time, but would not rub off on the federal government.

Some provinces criticized this strategy and laid the blame where it belonged, but there was no concerted action by provincial leaders. Many were Conservatives, and all understood the federal government's penchant for retribution in other areas if they were to criticize too openly. Finally, two western provinces and Ontario launched an (unsuccessful) court challenge of one of Wilson's measures, which discriminated against these wealthiest provinces by significantly reducing their entitlement under the CAP program, even though most welfare recipients resided in these provinces.

By 1991, when Michael Wilson's final budget once again reduced transfer payments, describing it as a "freeze on growth payments," provincial leaders led by Clyde Wells of Newfoundland finally began to speak out emphatically and directly about the consequences of seven years of these measures. Unable to absorb such massive cutbacks, province after province announced cutbacks of their own, both to programs and to the size of their public service. Many also indicated they would have to raise taxes substantially. In all cases, they directed their anger at the federal government and the Wilson budget.

Only Ontario's NDP government chose to buck the tide by increasing its deficit rather than raising taxes or cutting back on services. However, Premier Bob Rae made it clear that his government was being forced to take these measures because of the federal budget's "inexcusable" emphasis on deficit reduction rather than full employment, even in a time of recession.

The numbers speak eloquently of the Mulroney government's successful withdrawal from social programs. In 1986, federal transfer payments were $2.3 billion lower than they would have been under the old formula, to which the federal government had previously agreed. In 1987–88, that "savings" had risen to $400 million.

Perhaps the best summary of this situation came from a long-time Conservative MP, David Kilgour, who was so disenchanted with the government that he took the dramatic and difficult step of crossing the floor to sit as a Liberal member in early 1991. Speaking in the House of Commons on Bill C-20, the latest Tory attempt at freezing transfer payments until 1994–95, Kilgour pointed out that the cutbacks meant these payments had barely increased in real terms in almost twenty years.

"It is estimated," he said, "that EPF entitlements in 1991–92 will top $20.4 billion. It seems like a lot. However, if we look at the amount the federal government actually contributed to those programs in 1977–78, in 1991 dollars [that] spending already came to $16.4 billion." Kilgour noted that, with the implementation of Bill C-20, by the year 2000 "the federal government will be denying Canadians $97.6 billion worth of services and resources provided by health care and post-secondary institutions."

Even more disturbing to David Kilgour and all those concerned with maintaining these programs was the fact that the federal government was buying provincial support with tax points. In other words, more direct tax income, rather than federal transfers, would be available to the provinces. As a number of national health and educational organizations had noted, this meant no control over the way in which the money would be spent and less control of, or even the end of, national standards.

The provinces were not slow to understand the implications of this situation either. Quebec decided to implement user fees for visits to hospital emergency clinics. A number of provinces began to speak openly in 1991 of the fact that the withdrawal of federal funding for health care and education would make it unfair and unacceptable for the federal government to impose standards. As one premier allegedly put it in a private meeting with the new federal minister, Don Mazankowski, "He who pays the piper calls the tune."

And the federal government most definitely was not paying the bills. Indeed, it has been estimated that, by the year 2005, with the present plan in place, the federal government will no longer provide any direct funding to these programs; its only contribution will be through tax-point transfers.

Through program cuts, reductions in social benefits, and decreased transfer payments to the provinces, the federal government was able to significantly reduce its expenditures. But this did not produce sufficient revenue for the deficit-reduction exercise Michael Wilson had planned. As the economic policies of the Mulroney government proved disastrous and the debt doubled in seven years, interest payments became a major problem that only greatly increased revenues could alleviate.

The tax reforms Michael Wilson had implemented not only failed to simplify the system or make it fairer, as he had promised, but actually made it *more* regressive. The one thing the reforms did accomplish, however, was to provide a huge increase in federal revenues. The numbers speak for themselves. Between 1984–85 and 1991–92, total budgetary revenues were projected to increase by 8.8 percent per year, a full two percentage points higher than the projected increase in GDP over the same period. Revenue from personal income tax increased by 11.9 percent per year, while that from corporate taxes increased by only 3.9 percent per year. Of the total additional revenue raised since 1984 by federal tax and transfer changes — some $17.2 billion — federal income tax produced $1.6 billion, federal surtaxes another $3.8 billion, and federal commodity taxes, the most regressive type of taxation, $11 of the remaining $11.8 billion.

Tory tax reform consisted of two phases. First, revisions were made to the personal income tax system: the compression from five to three marginal rates reduced taxes for the rich and greatly increased the rate of taxation on middle-income earners. In Phase II, the Goods and Services Tax (GST) accomplished more of the same. Simply put: government revenue increased; simplicity and fairness decreased for individuals, and improved marginally for corporations and the business community.

Among the most comprehensive and authoritative studies is a paper presented to the 1991 annual meeting of the Canadian Economic Association by economist Patrick Grady of Global Economics Ltd. Mr. Grady, a former Finance mandarin, relentlessly compared Michael Wilson's three stated objectives with the reality after seven years of his stewardship of the economy. Grady concludes: "the personal income tax system has deteriorated under the Tories. . . . It is less equitable and more complex. . . . The introduction of the GST will probably shift the tax mix further in favour of regressive commodity taxes and away from income taxes." Grady rejects the government's argument that the poor have been protected from the regressive effects of the GST by the sales tax credit; the credit will be almost entirely consumed by inflation by the end of the decade as a result of the limitations on indexation and on the threshold. He also notes that the government itself has admitted the sales tax is a cash cow rather than the revenue-neutral mechanism originally promised.

The *implications* of Tory tax policy have become abundantly clear. A Statistics Canada report in February 1991 concluded the rich got richer and the poor remained poor, while the middle class became much poorer as a result of the thirty-two separate tax increases introduced by Wilson over the seven-year period under review. Put another way: the top 20 percent of income earners increased their share of the national economic pie by a full six percentage points, from 35.9 to 41.9 percent. This increase came entirely at the expense of the middle class. The lowest 20 percent of income earners maintained their 5.2 percent share. For the first time since the advent of the social safety net and progressive personal-taxation measures, a major *upward* redistribution of wealth occurred in Canada as a result of governmental policies.

This fact did not go unnoticed internationally. The 1991 United Nations Development Program's (UNDP) annual report placed Canada in second place in terms of overall quality of life, slightly behind Japan. Nevertheless, the report pointed to "a number of inequitable and discriminatory aspects" of Canadian society. Speaking to the report, the UNDP's chief information officer, M. Jean Fabre, noted that Canada had one of the widest gaps between the rich and poor. "In that respect," M. Fabre said, "Canada is one of the worst countries. It's not as bad as the United States, but it's still nearly twice as bad as the best countries in the industrialized world."

Slightly more than 12 percent of Canadians were living in poverty before the outset of the 1990–91 made-in-Canada recession. In West Germany and Sweden, the figure was less than half of that.

Given the above situation, one of the most amazing aspects of the Mulroney Conservatives' approach to social policy may well be their apparent sincerity in declaring that Canada "can no longer afford" universal social programs and a national health-care program, and their ability to convince many Canadians that this is so.

Putting aside entirely the question of priorities in the allocation of existing resources (especially since social policy has been such a low priority of this government), an examination of Canadian social-policy expenditures in comparison with those of other Western industrialized nations shows that Canadians are being significantly misled by the statements of Wilson and others that these programs place disproportionate demands on the total federal budget.

An International Monetary Fund (IMF) study published in 1986 put the Canadian situation in context. The Canadian ratio of total social-program expenditures to GDP was 20 percent, the lowest of the seven major industrialized countries. The study analyses figures for 1980, before the Mulroney Conservatives began their systematic reductions.

Recognizing that varying demographics from country to country would have a significant effect on the timing of increased pressures for social expenditures, notably for seniors, the report also analysed each country separately. It concluded that, "in Canada and the U.S. the expenditure ratio will *decrease* until 2010. In both countries the rate would then increase in the following fifteen years, but in Canada the increase would still be very limited." Again this projection did not take into account the later Tory initiatives.

So the argument that Canada's social programs as a whole are unaffordable, and their financial demands out of proportion, is simply not an accurate one, Tory rhetoric to the contrary. This is not to suggest, of course, that there is no need to attempt to stem the growth in health-care costs, or to rationalize a number of income programs and services, in order to make better use of existing resources. On the contrary, social activists agree that a number of long-standing programs may no longer serve their original purpose, and that the complex web of existing programs could be simplified to everyone's advantage.

Indeed, the Ontario Social Assistance Review Committee (SARC) argued in its seminal report that a rationalization of social programs, beginning with increased support for the working poor but eventually moving towards a guaranteed-income system, would not only go a long way towards eradicating poverty but, in the long run, cost less than the current system.

Similarly, most health-care analysts agree that limitations on the increase in health-care costs are desirable and possible. But they do not accept the government's view that reductions in funding or decreases in service are necessary. Rather, the prevailing attitude among experts focuses on the better utilization of existing resources, primarily through the provision of alternative-care facilities, the diffusion of health-care services, and the promotion of preventative medicine.

The problem with the Mulroney Conservatives' approach to social policy, then, has not been that they wanted to introduce reforms, but rather that they did not really support the concept of comprehensive government involvement at all. Therefore, they reduced or eliminated much of it. As in other policy areas, they were not forthright about their agenda and, in many cases, were patently dishonest. Instead of engaging Canadians in a dialogue about how the system could be modified and improved, they denied they were interested in major changes, and then proceeded to dismantle the system.

As Keith Spicer concluded in his foreword to the June 1991 report of the Citizens' Forum he chaired, Canadians "don't like being lied to." Unfortunately, while the public suspected Mulroney and his team were misleading them on various initiatives, fewer Canadians understood the overall effect of these changes or recognized the weaknesses in the government's "affordability" argument.

In *The Resurgent Liberal* American economist Robert Reich describes the successful "conservative parable," in which liberal "permissiveness" and "laxity" are believed to be redressed by economic restraint and social discipline. In Canada, this parable is told in the vocabulary of federal deficit reduction: "restraint," "competitiveness," and "lean, mean" operations in which workers, not employers, must make sacrifices. Columnist Thomas Walkom's March 25, 1991, article in the *Toronto Star* carried this analogy somewhat farther, referring to "restraint" as the "new religion" of Canadian political discourse: "Restraint has become a code word for cutting spending. Not all spending, but certain types. Restraint advocates usually want unemployment and welfare benefits slashed so as to dampen wages. Restraint advocates do not usually want depletion allowances and other obscure but important tax breaks removed, for these breaks are said to encourage global compet-itiveness." In short, Walkom concludes the language of restraint "is biased against wage earners, the poor and the unemployed. It is biased in favour of those who already have."

Clearly the Mulroney government's neoconservative approach to social policy has little in common with its liberal-minded predecessors, who believed that economic growth and wealth creation were not ends in themselves. Rather, they are a means to achieve the ends of social policy — equality of opportunity and quality of life. The determination of Michael Wilson and others in the cabinet to reduce federal responsibility for social justice has had profound consequences, not just for individuals, but for the national identity. The social safety net has always been financed by the middle class, but it has nevertheless enjoyed their strong support, in large measure because they, too, were recipients of universal benefits.

This was no accident. As Michael Ignatieff has indicated, it was part of a deliberate plan on the part of politicians and bureaucrats after the Depression and the Second World War to "provide the essential legitimacy of the civic pact." It was understood that the role of the state was to "foster enhanced civic solidarity as the foundation of national unity." The welfare state could assist in this role by reinforcing legal and constitutional rights of citizenship with "entitlements to economic and social security." Sociologist Andrew Love examined the approach of the Mulroney government from this perspective and argued, "We cannot escape the fact that our national [and provincial] governments have willingly delegated responsibilities to the private sector at the expense of national reconciliation and unity."[4]

Universality became a part of the glue that bound Canadians together as a nation. Its removal has created profound anxiety in the middle class, making them particularly vulnerable to the "affordability" issue, as they are no longer stakeholders. The extent of this damage to the social contract became evident with the widespread positive response to Ontario premier Bob Rae's proposal to entrench a social charter in the constitution. This proposal followed on the heels of a Supreme Court decision denying the three provinces' claim that the federal government had no right to unilaterally restrict the amount of its transfer payments. On the contrary, the Court argued, it is clear that the federal government retains control over such matters.

The anger at the Court over this decision, which seemed to condone further cutbacks on the part of the Mulroney Conservatives, was, of course, misplaced. Once again it was not the political system, or the constitution, that needed to be changed, but rather the players. Federal governments obviously need to retain such control in order to improve plans or introduce new ones, a point made by several social-policy experts who supported the Court's decision.

Nevertheless, the social charter concept appeals to Canadians feeling increasingly at the mercy of the federal government. Once again a provincial premier has been cast in the role of nation-builder by a federal government ignorant and disdainful of the underlying values of the Canadian political culture. As the next chapter demonstrates, this ignorance extends even to the international stage.

NOTES

1. A. Gregg and M. Posner, *The Big Picture* (Toronto: Macfarlane Walter and Ross, 1990), pp. 72–86.

2. *Toronto Star*, August 24, 1991.

3. *Ottawa Citizen*, August 24, 1991.

4. A. Love, "Multiculturalism Can Spur National Unity," in *Policy Options*, January 1991: 23.

8. Following the Leader
How the Mulroney Conservatives Gave Up Our Independent Foreign Policy for a "Special Relationship"

Good relations, superb relations with the United States of America will be the cornerstone of our foreign policy.
— Brian Mulroney, 1983

Foreign policy has rarely, if ever, been the determining factor in Canadian politics. Political parties have consequently spent little time on foreign-policy issues in their election platforms, and Canadian voters have paid even less attention to such matters when casting their ballot. Americans, however, identify their two political parties with very different foreign policies, and these differences have often proved important if not decisive factors in the outcome of federal elections.

The different role that foreign-policy issues play in the domestic politics of the two countries is directly related to the unequal importance of these two countries on the world stage. Unlike the United States, a superpower by any definition since 1945, Canada has been seen by the world and by its own citizens to have a generally positive, but low-key and unassuming role to play.

The Cold War occupied centre stage in the United States during the 1950s, and the Vietnam War and its aftermath played a predominant role in national politics for the next two decades. In Canada, unthreatened and secure, a somewhat insular approach to international relations developed in which there was little perceived need to articulate a "Canadian position" on every foreign-policy issue.

However, Canadians were developing certain expectations of their limited role. Since Canada defined itself, via Lester Pearson, as a "middle power," Canadians expected their leaders to pursue initiatives they felt were in keeping with this title. Indeed, Canada's image as a middle power came to be a positive element of the Canadian identity. Canadians also valued their well-defined international image as peacekeepers. They prided themselves on being seen as generous providers of development aid to the Third World. Finally, Canadians believed that, on foreign-policy matters, their country's positions were taken independent of those expressed by the United States.

As we have seen, this last point is highly significant in terms of political culture and national unity, since much of the Canadian identity is rooted in the idea that Canadians are, first and foremost, "not American."

Political parties and politicians contributed to this perception of our international image. Canadians thought of Lester Pearson not only as the bow-tied Liberal nemesis of John Diefenbaker, but as the prime minister who won a Nobel Peace Prize for his role in Canada's peacekeeping initiatives in the Suez. Similarly, even Canadians who disapproved of several of Prime Minister Pierre Trudeau's domestic initiatives were consistently proud of his prestigious international image, friendships, and status. They overwhelmingly applauded his 1983–84 peace and disarmament initiative, for which he won the Albert Einstein Peace Prize in 1984. Indeed fully 85 percent of Canadians surveyed in a 1983 Decima poll enthusiastically supported Trudeau's peace efforts, despite the fact that only 50 percent believed he might be successful.

This high level of support for the veteran prime minister was clearly related to the growing concern Canadians were expressing about the nuclear-arms race. The same 1983 poll found 58 percent of Canadians feared there would be a nuclear war in their lifetime, while 84 percent believed there could be no such thing as a "limited" war.

An overwhelming majority also agreed with Trudeau's statement that "it is not Communism of which we should be afraid, but rather of the fact that people are starving to death." Slightly more than 40 percent of respondents identified global poverty and hunger as the world's most serious problem; the nuclear-arms race placed a strong second.

It was only on the question of Canada's relations with the United States, which deteriorated dramatically during Trudeau's last term, that Canadians began to question his approach. They had solidly supported his independent path in foreign relations up to that point — whether it was in recognizing China and travelling to Cuba and the USSR, or criticizing various American activities abroad. However, they did not endorse the antagonistic relationship that developed between Trudeau and American presidents in the final years. What Canadians wanted in 1983 was still what Mackenzie King had described as a "businesslike but neighbourly" relationship with the United States that did not stray too far in either direction.

One of the great ironies of the 1984 election was that Canadians unwittingly elected a man and a government who shared none of these concerns. Brian Mulroney and his colleagues had no interest in the issues of global poverty and development aid; indeed, they appeared for most of their first term of office to be caught in a time-warp. Their Cold War rhetoric on the Communist Menace and the need for increased defence spending was not only ludicrously out of touch with events unfolding in Eastern Europe, but completely at odds with the public's concern with peace and disarmament issues.

Worse still, Mulroney personally did not share the public's avowed mistrust of close ties with the United States. Following his natural instincts as an admirer of all things American, Brian Mulroney not only erred on the side of overly friendly relations with the United States but, over the past seven years, has been instrumental in undermining Canada's reputation at home and abroad for independent policy positions.

Attempting to capitalize on concern over the dismal state of Canadian–U.S. relations during the 1984 election campaign, Mulroney characteristically overstated his case. Promising "superb relations" with the United States as a cornerstone of Conservative foreign policy, he completely misread the Canadian psyche. Luckily for him, virtually no one was paying attention to these flights of fancy during an election campaign dominated by patronage scandals and bum-patting incidents.

Once in power, however, he quickly alienated or embarrassed voters by wrongly assuming that his massive electoral victory represented an endorsement of a Canada–United States love-in. From enthusiastic support for the American invasion of Panama to his heavy-handed and single-minded emphasis on trade relations as the crux of Conservative foreign policy, to his continual references to his "personal friendship" with the U.S. president, Brian Mulroney embraced a level of intimacy with the Americans that most Canadians found quite unacceptable.

This alone may serve to explain Mulroney's failure to capitalize on several modest but admitted successes on the international scene over the past seven years. In each case, he failed to achieve public recognition or respect for his accomplishment domestically and, in the most recent example of the Persian Gulf War, he failed to benefit personally, despite widespread public support for the position taken by his government. Unlike George Bush, whose personal approval rating soared to an unheard-of 90 percent-plus rating in the wake of the stunning military victory in the Gulf, Brian Mulroney enjoyed no similar resurgence in personal popularity.

Before the war brought a measure of respectability to foreign-policy matters in the eyes of the Mulroney government, the conflict between the twin neoconservative objectives of enhanced defence policy and deficit reduction had offered nothing but amusing examples of internal conflict and confusion: from the nuclear-submarine fiasco to more recent attempts to cut deeply into the Defence department's budget and eliminate military bases across the country, it became clear to Canadians that the Mulroney government had no coherent agenda.

Only in the area of international human rights, and most notably in the case of South Africa, has the Conservative government demonstrated Canada's traditional leadership role as a middle power over the past seven years. This achievement is largely explained by the willingness of Mulroney and the cabinet to let Joe Clark have free rein, the fact that little if any financial commitment was required and, most importantly, that the issue was of little importance to the United States.

Indeed, Mulroney's personal understanding of international relations other than trade issues has seemed to be one in which the various meetings abroad offered him an opportunity to meet and be seen in the company of the world's important leaders. Mulroney's interest in and grasp of the fundamental global issues of our time appears to have been minimal, while his interest in photo opportunities has never flagged.

Foreign policy did not play a major role in the 1984 election platforms of either the Liberals or the Conservatives. Although the Conservative program did include the reference to "superb relations" with the Americans, it was not something on which the party or its leader dwelled.

The one non-traditional area in which the Conservatives decided to comment during the election campaign was defence policy, but, as usual, their promises were deliberately nebulous. In an obvious attempt to win the votes of towns with military bases or interests, Mulroney and the Conservatives vowed to increase the size of the armed forces and spoke often of their intent to "honour the commitments of the Canadian Armed Forces and our obligations to our defence allies." The clear implication was that the previous Liberal government had not done so. Once in power, of course, the Conservatives were even less prepared to finance military expenditures than the Liberals had been.

With respect to peacekeeping and development aid, the Conservatives formally committed themselves to harmless promises such as "pursuing world peace" and to the traditional aid-funding target of 0.7 percent of GNP. In an unguarded moment, Mulroney himself attached a specific timetable — 1990 — to that goal, something he later regretted.

The Throne Speech that followed their election in November 1984 also contained a brief section on this fourth pillar of their platform, which they referred to as "Constructive Internationalism." Having dismissed peacekeeping, foreign aid, and Canada's role in NATO in the first paragraph, the speech turned to matters of real importance, such as "a spirit of goodwill and true partnership between Canada and the United States" and "exploring with our neighbour new approaches to a better and mutually advantageous trading relationship."

Indeed, much of the foreign-policy theme focused on trade and economic relationships. Even the brief reference to development aid was couched in such a framework. After recognizing that "Canada's record in official development assistance has on the whole been constructive," the speech returned quickly to the trade theme: "It is striking . . . how much economic activity has been held back in developing countries because of world recession, unstable markets and trade barriers. A successful attack on these problems will accelerate economic development and social progress in many of these countries." No mention was made of the fact that Canada could contribute to a resolution of these problems by reducing tied aid, eliminating barriers to the importation of Third World products, and forgiving debt.

The only other point of note in this section of the speech related to defence policy — "Canada will once again play its full part in the defence systems of NATO" — was followed by a passing nod to the desire to "halt the spread of nuclear weapons" and a promise of a comprehensive examination of the role of Canada's defence forces "to clarify the mandate of the military and give them the resources they need to do their job."

Finally, and typical of this government's approach on a range of policy matters in which it lacked both interest and remedies, a special parliamentary committee was established to "conduct a full review of the main components and objectives of our international relations."

Compared to the lengthy sections on economic policy and national unity, the brief time devoted to foreign policy in the Throne Speech was a clear indication of the lack of importance attached to international relations by the government. This attitude partially serves to explain the almost casual way in which the prime minister and his secretary of state for External Affairs, Joe Clark, approached their first real encounter with a foreign-policy issue.

In the summer of 1985, the unauthorized voyage of the American Coast Guard icebreaker the *Polar Sea* through Canadian-claimed waters of the Northwest Passage provoked a level of public concern that clearly caught both men off guard and unprepared. Canadian sovereignty, it seemed, was not something about which they felt considerable urgency, particularly when it involved Canada's "closest friend and ally." Had it been a Russian vessel the government's response would no doubt have been more precipitous. However, it merely became the first of many examples of Canadian acquiesence to American foreign-policy initiatives and objectives. The Mulroney government demonstrated little concern over the incident and, when forced by public concern to act, it made minimal efforts to prevent its recurrence.

Recognizing somewhat belatedly that the opposition parties were scoring political points with their attack on the government's lack of response, Joe Clark eventually developed a four-point plan to deal with the issue of Canadian sovereignty in the disputed waters. He announced that Canada was drawing straight baselines around the Canadian Arctic archipelago, in an attempt to acquire international legal recognition of the waters as Canadian. The government also announced a plan for the construction of the world's largest icebreaker, to be deployed in the Arctic, and a Vancouver shipyard was designated to build the vessel. (A subsequent announcement in June 1986 by Defence minister Perrin Beatty that the government would acquire ten to twelve nuclear submarines was also linked to Arctic surveillance and security.)

Meanwhile Joe Clark had stated there would be no further cooperation between Canada and the United States on matters relating to the Arctic until the Americans were prepared to recognize Canada's claim, and in 1986 legislation was introduced to extend Canada's jurisdiction in civil- and criminal-law matters over the disputed area.

The fate of all four initiatives is highly instructive. The "straight baseline" case was never taken to the World Court for a ruling, and hence has no legal force. The 1989 federal budget cancelled the submarines and the icebreaker project for lack of funds. The 1986 legislation never moved passed first reading and died on the order paper with the 1988 election. Reintroduced only in October 1989, it still had not been debated over a year later.

Clark's declaration that no other agreements would be concluded until the Americans acknowledged the Canadian claims was forgotten by 1988, when the Mulroney government announced an agreement on the narrow issue of foreign vessels in those waters. The "agreement" merely required the Americans to ask for Canadian consent before their icebreakers travelled in the Northwest Passage. No mention was made of submarines or private vessels, such as oil tankers, and the document expressly stated that sovereignty claims were not affected by the deal.

After the 1991 budget, when further restraint and defence cutbacks were announced in the name of deficit reduction, the Defence minister was publicly musing that the Americans and/ or NATO might have to defend Canada's northern security and sovereignty interests because the country was unable to afford to do so itself.

By then the *Polar Sea* incident had long since faded from public memory, but the image of a government reluctant to criticize American actions had not. Indeed, it had been reinforced by its deviation from the traditional relationship between Canada and the United States. In areas where U.S. interests were well known — East-West relations, Latin America, the Middle East, or international finance — Canadian policy initiatives were either non-existent or virtually identical to those of the Americans. In areas where Canadian and U.S. interests clashed — Arctic sovereignty, Central America, acid rain, and sustainable development, for example — Canadian initiatives were largely rhetorical or limited to agreements that avoided a direct challenge to the overall U.S. position.

As the following analysis demonstrates, only in those areas where American interests were minimal, such as South Africa or Third World aid, did the Canadian government attempt to take a leadership role consistent with its middle-power image.

Examples abound of the Conservatives' unwillingness to pursue a leadership role in foreign-policy areas where U.S. interests were dominant. Improved bilateral relations with the Soviet Union and the provision of aid to the emerging democracies of Eastern Europe, the lifting of a ban on official contacts with the PLO, and the withdrawal of diplomatic recognition for the Cambodian opposition forces dominated by the genocidal Khmer Rouge were all initiatives that previous Canadian governments might well have taken on their own. Instead they occurred only after the United States took similar action.

Among the more striking examples of this decline in independent Canadian foreign-policy making was the swift and fulsome support for the American invasion of Panama in December 1989. The prime minister's statement the following morning echoed Bush's in tone and rhetoric, even going so far as to repeat Bush's description of Noriega as a "thug," a fact that did not go unnoticed by the media. Similarly, Saddam Hussein was described by Mulroney as a "criminal of historic proportions," echoing Bush's comparison of Saddam to Hitler.

Canadian support for the unprecedented American incursion in Panama came only two months after Mulroney had announced Canada would become a member of the Organization of American States (OAS), a body many critics consider to be totally dominated by the United States. For the previous seventeen years, Canada had held observer status at the OAS; the unwillingness of earlier governments to commit to Canada's becoming a full-fledged member had always been based on the belief that such membership would compromise the independence of national foreign-policy decisions.

But the initiative that cemented the image of the Mulroney government as a mere appendage of American foreign policy was the Persian Gulf War. From beginning to end, both Mulroney and Clark echoed precisely the official lines coming from Washington. Canada was among the first to support the decision to end the sanctions period and proceed to the use of force, and among the most ardent supporters of the semantic fiction that the U.S.-led multinational forces represented the United Nations.

At least one poll taken during this period addressed the question of Mulroney's role squarely; the results suggested that the prime minister's motives were questioned by many Canadians. A significant number expressed the concern that his decision was based on an opportunistic desire to increase his popularity, while more than 60 percent expressed the view that his decision, although the correct one, had been unduly influenced by his close relationship with the American president.

The irony is that Mulroney's determined efforts to maintain and strengthen this alleged "special relationship" cost him personal popularity while achieving little for the country. For the reality is that the special relationship does not exist.

Unlike previous prime ministers, Mulroney seems unable to recognize that an American president will act in the best interests of his country. Mulroney apparently believed that the personal empathy and public-relations success of an event like the Shamrock Summit of 1986 would cement his relationship with Ronald Reagan. As veteran journalist Claire Hoy pointed out, this simply was not the case. "Reagan has never hesitated to hit Canada in what he sees as the American interest, whether Mulroney is happy about it or not" — hence the various American countervail incidents (such as shakes and shingles) throughout the negotiations on the Free Trade Agreement and Reagan's refusal to commit the United States to more than a "study" of the possible effects of acid rain.[1]

Other experienced journalists and broadcasters, who had covered events during the Trudeau era and since covered Mulroney during his American visits, also commented on this phenomenon. The Washington-based correspondent for the *Toronto Star*, Bob Hepburn, once declared that Mulroney's "telephone diplomacy" simply "doesn't exist." In spite of Mulroney's public statements that he could pick up the telephone and speak to Reagan at will, Hepburn concluded that the two men spoke no more than once or twice a year and that "Mulroney is banking on his 'friendship' to help him out, but Reagan doesn't look at it that way." This sentiment was shared by Quebec broadcaster Michel Guenard, who decried the fact that Mulroney "wants to reinvent the wheel in his relationship with the Americans." More importantly, Guenard expressed amazement that, after several years in power, Mulroney still "doesn't seem to understand that in politics you have no friends, just interests." He concluded, as did the opposition parties and most Canadians, that Mulroney's attempts to curry favour could actually weaken Canada's bargaining position in important negotiations. The Free Trade Agreement itself, and the American government's subsequent decision to appeal retroactively a case involving Canadian pork producers, seemed to confirm their worst fears.[2]

Other areas of foreign policy were taking a back seat to the defence-policy initiatives of the neoconservative element of the cabinet.

Following on a solid year of controversy over Perrin Beatty's recommendation to purchase nuclear submarines, the Defence White Paper promised in the Throne Speech and finally released in June 1987 ploughed ahead with a series of recommendations to drastically increase the size of Canada's armed forces.

That this was taking place at the same time as the dramatic evolution of *perestroika* and *glasnost* appeared to escape members of the cabinet committee involved. In 1983, some 50 percent of Canadians had opposed both the American Star Wars initiative and the use of Canadian airspace for the testing of cruise missiles. Their concern was directly related to the perceived danger of nuclear war.

By 1987, one year after the second Reagan–Gorbachev Summit in Reykjavik, over 42 percent of Canadians surveyed indicated they believed this danger was lessening; 72 percent believed the changes in Eastern Europe would be real and lasting. Small wonder, then, that the Conservatives were perceived to be locked in a time-warp with their Cold War rhetoric and concern for a greatly enhanced defence capability. Support for increased military spending dropped from 47 percent in 1983 to 37 percent in 1987. By 1989, it had fallen still further, to barely 29 percent. In December 1989, Decima found that Canadians believed, by a margin of two to one, that monies spent on military equipment and technology should instead be used to finance non-military technology development — the so-called peace dividend.

In the end, however, the defence-spending proposals failed, not because of the public's concern with the allocation of the peace dividend, but at the hands of another neoconservative objective, deficit reduction. By 1989, fresh from an election victory in which he had assured Canadians that he had made no costly campaign promises, only "pre-existing program commitments" for which he had already budgeted, Finance minister Michael Wilson discovered the national coffers were empty. Not only was there no new money for nuclear submarines, icebreakers, or frigates, but a number of bases would have to be closed, primarily in Atlantic Canada and/ or Liberal-held ridings.

If defence policy had been of some importance to the Tories during their first term, the same could not be said of development assistance. This had long been a traditional area of interest to

Canadian governments in their pursuit of Canada's role as a middle power, but no pretence had been made since the 1984 election campaign about the low level of importance attributed to it by the Mulroney Conservatives. On the contrary, development assistance had been among the first areas targeted in the deficit-reduction drive. Instead of reaching the 0.7 percent goal by 1990, as Mulroney had rashly promised before his election, the first budget pushed that target back to 1995. In 1987, it was delayed even further, to the year 2000. In the 1991 budget Finance minister Wilson indicated that the government's new target for 1995 would be 0.47 percent, up from 0.43 percent in the current year, but two percentage points lower than the level of funding in place when they assumed power in 1984.

Unfortunately many non-governmental agencies involved in Third World development are dependent in large measure on government funding, and must use such projections to plan ongoing projects. The continual backtracking on funding and objectives meant that several agencies were constantly on the verge of collapse, and one, the internationally respected World University Services (WUSC), was forced to declare bankruptcy in February 1991 when the federal government refused to advance funds to make up for a shortfall caused primarily by the cutbacks.

Joe Clark, who had threatened in the past to resign if Overseas Development Aid (ODA) support was reduced any further, was unable to prevent a $262 million cut in funding for the 1991–92 fiscal year and a $1.6 billion reduction in promised funding through to 1995. The cuts led many experts to speculate that WUSC would not be an isolated incident, and that Clark would have to rethink his threat.

More important still was the government's apparent disregard for Canada's international reputation, which was clearly damaged by the WUSC failure. Similarly, a set of new creative accounting measures, designed to give the appearance of greater direct spending on aid, failed to impress either domestic or international observers and led to further questioning of Canadian sincerity. These measures redefined official development assistance to include both low-interest loans and export credits forgiven by the Export Development Corporation, items which had never before been considered part of the ODA budget.

As an editorial in the *Ottawa Citizen* of March 9, 1991, concluded, while neither of these measures would aid the most needy people in developing countries, it was clear that "the Mulroney government is determined to mix business with charity."

This narrow approach to development aid had already been demonstrated on a number of occasions, most notably by the government's outright rejection in 1987 of its own parliamentary committee's report, *For Whose Benefit?*, which recommended reducing the percentage of "tied" aid — funding that must be used to purchase goods and services provided by the donor.

In 1991, Clark was still extolling the virtues of tied aid, pointing out that sixty-five cents out of every aid dollar is spent on Canadian goods and services. Another parliamentary committee report, on the problems of Third World debt, received similar short shrift from the government. (This is not surprising in light of the fact that one of its principal recommendations was for Canada to forgive its Third World loans.)

In short, as the gap between the government's original rhetoric and later actions in foreign policy has grown over time, a consistent pattern of behaviour has emerged. The problem here is essentially the same as in social policy, in that the neoconservative element of the Mulroney government simply does not support the concept of development assistance, and the minister in charge has been unwilling or unable to convince them of its merits.

This pattern of rhetoric versus actions can also be found in the government's approach to the newly emerging area of international environmental security. In the face of near-universal acclaim for the 1987 United Nations–sponsored Brundtland Report on sustainable development, the Mulroney government recognized the political benefits of jumping on the environmental bandwagon at home and abroad. But, once again, the government tripped over its neoconservative philosophy of non-intervention in the marketplace. The implementation of sustainable development policies requires considerable government intervention, usually through regulation and sanctions — concepts that are anathema to neoconservatives.

As a result, the Mulroney government's record on environmental matters at home and abroad has been one of grand promises and few actions, despite some apparently well-intentioned efforts by individual ministers responsible. Like Margaret Thatcher and Ronald Reagan, Brian Mulroney has given numerous supportive international speeches meant to lead nowhere.

Moreover, given the reluctance of the government to challenge or contradict American foreign policy, early Canadian efforts to develop an international leadership role failed. Such was the case in the wake of the 1987 Montreal Protocol on ozone protection and the 1988 World Conference on Climate Change held in Toronto. By the time follow-up conferences occurred in Bergen and Geneva, the government was unprepared to support the targets or timetables it had initially endorsed because they were not approved by the Americans.

Nor was it prepared to play anything more than a passive role in negotiations, agreeing with the majority but not attempting to lead the pack. A leaked internal American memo at the Geneva conference caused considerable consternation in Canada and abroad when it suggested that the Canadian participants had agreed in advance to support the American position.

Indeed, the only area of traditional Canadian involvement internationally that has been relatively unaffected by the Mulroney era is human rights. This appears to be due in no small measure to the personal interest taken in the subject by the minister for most of this period, Joe Clark, as well as the fact that few, if any, expenditures were required to further the aims of this foreign-policy objective.

Apart from the use of economic sanctions, notably in the case of South Africa, the international human-rights agenda has been of little interest to the Americans. As a result Clark's spadework and determination, especially in the context of the Commonwealth, where Canada has traditionally taken a leadership role, have allowed both Mulroney and Canada to achieve a measure of respect and several modest successes in this area.

Mulroney's relatively unflinching opposition to apartheid in particular, even at the expense of alienating Margaret Thatcher during Commonwealth meetings on at least two separate occasions, has won him a considerable measure of support among Third World leaders. Indeed, Brian Mulroney's reputation in the Caribbean and in many parts of Africa is undoubtedly far better than it is at home.

However, the Mulroney government's failure to live up to its commitments on development assistance and its inability to stake a claim to leadership on the vital issue of environmental security outweigh these few successes. More importantly, the loss of Canada's reputation for independent policy positions has caused most Canadians to view his government's foreign policy as a mere appendage of that of the Americans, a situation they find both unacceptable and incompatible with their self-image.

Perhaps most revealing of Mulroney's attitude towards international affairs was his aborted bid for the position of secretary general of the United Nations. His stern speech on human-rights abuses at the Commonwealth Conference in Lusaka, held only days before voting for the prestigious post began, was obviously an audition piece. As several External Affairs officials in Ottawa admitted, Mulroney's rhetoric about tying aid to human-rights records had been just that — rhetoric. There was no specific plan to implement such an approach, which would be difficult, in any event, to justify in light of ongoing trade negotiations with Mexico, a known rights violator. Canadians, however, were unequivocal in their support for Mulroney's U.N. candidacy, with more than one respondent to polls on the subject suggesting it would be the best thing for Canada, if not the world.

The legacy of the Mulroney government in foreign policy is almost non-existent. Compared to other policy areas, in which the neoconservative agenda has wreaked havoc in a concrete fashion, the apparent lack of interest in foreign policy on Mulroney's part and the inability of his long-time External Affairs minister, Joe Clark, to impose his will on the cabinet in more than a few areas of concern, has meant the Conservative record is most notable for its absence and omissions.

It is, if anything, a record of missed opportunities and a lack of understanding of the role that Canada could logically play on the world stage. With the neoconservative element of the cabinet not committed philosophically to either development aid or the newly emerging area of sustainable development, the government failed to show leadership on either, despite the fact that the majority of Canadians would have been supportive. In the end, the Mulroney government's foreign-policy record must be seen as an insignificant footnote to the text authored by their American counterparts.

NOTES

1. C. Hoy, *Friends in High Places*, p. 175.
2. Ibid, pp. 159–61.

9. Breaking the Pattern
Returning to the Liberal Vision of Canada

To govern is to make choices.
— Duc de Lévis, *Maximes de Politiques* (xix)

There are enough reasons for Canadians to be legitimately disappointed in me as a political leader. I don't want them taking their disappointments out on Canada. If they want to take it out on Brian Mulroney, it's easy. You throw him out of office.
— Brian Mulroney, *Maclean's*, January 6, 1992

W hen Canadians put their faith in Brian Mulroney in 1984, they expected him to govern, to lead, and to inspire. They expected his government to identify the national interest and make decisions that furthered its objectives. They hoped he would show them a vision of the future that built on their past and expanded their horizons. They knew the world was changing, and they wanted their government to help them adapt to these changes by laying out options and making tough choices.

It was some time before Canadians realized that the man who was their prime minister did not understand their hopes, their fears, or their expectations. Nor did he share their values and their image of the country. Most galling, however, was the realization that Brian Mulroney and his government did not appreciate the trust Canadians had placed in them. Politics was a game, and winning was everything. Holding on to power and rewarding friends and allies were valid ends in their own right. Intent on preserving their position, Mulroney's government was prepared to mislead, manipulate, and malign. Their misuse of public office for their personal and partisan ends, to say nothing of their blatant disregard for parliamentary democracy and the standard "rules of the game," led Canadians to distrust not only politicians, but the political system itself. Their lack of vision and failure to identify the national interest over the competing claims of special interests has led Canadians to lose sight of their historical ability to compromise. The Mulroney approach has produced disunity, diminished all Canadians by playing to the lowest common denominator, and encouraged selfishness rather than tolerance and generosity.

There can be little doubt that Brian Mulroney and his government have made many choices over the past seven years, choices that have had a profound impact on the country. But their choices do not reflect the promises they made to Canadians in two election campaigns. Most Canadians view their constitutional, trade, and tax "initiatives" as unmitigated disasters rather than achievements. Yet, unwilling to accept responsibility for these choices, the Mulroney Conservatives have blamed everyone but themselves for the situation in which Canadians now find their country.

And the country is in very serious difficulty. Canadians, struggling to recover from the economic vicissitudes of a recession more severe than that of 1981–82, are now being asked by their government — a government that has failed to deliver on any of the four "pillars" of its platform: economic recovery, social justice, national reconciliation, and constructive internationalism — to put aside their personal concerns and make further sacrifices in the name of global competitiveness and long-term prosperity.

The same government is asking them to forgive and forget the débâcle that was Meech Lake and once again put their trust in it to resolve the constitutional issue it created. Worse still, given his desperate need to resolve the problem before the next election, Brian Mulroney is promoting a package less acceptable to many Canadians than Meech Lake, all the while claiming it is a reasonable compromise. And once again he is attempting to blackmail the public and opposition parties by arguing they would reject it at the country's peril.

Grim predictions abound concerning the future of the country. National unity is believed by many to be a mirage, fast disappearing on the horizon. Each new poll indicates growing public discontent, inflexibility, and, more dangerous still, apathy. Survey after survey reveals that basic tenets of our political culture are in danger — from bilingualism and multiculturalism to universal social programs and health care, there is increasing concern that the programs once considered important elements of the Canadian identity are not working. Traditional values are being destroyed by the national government's disinformation campaigns and continued failure to show commitment to them.

One economic report after another outlines our declining competitiveness, the devastation of the manufacturing sector, the permanent loss of hundreds of thousands of jobs, and the monstrous size of the national debt.

The Canadian people have lost confidence in their elected representatives; in some polls, the largest group of respondents choose "none of the above" when asked to indicate their preferred political leader. A growing number are expressing their displeasure by shifting their support to the Reform Party or the Bloc Québécois, leading political analysts such as Robert Jackson of Carleton University to conclude that Canada is imminently facing the "Italianization" of the political system; he fears a fragmentation of the national vote in which no party receives enough support to form a government, and no party is truly national.

Faced with such doom and gloom, it is hardly surprising that Canadians expressed less confidence in their own future and the future of their country than did any other nation surveyed by Gallup in early 1991. From citizens of the "supremely confident and self-sufficient" country Peter Newman described in 1984, Canadians have become among the most pessimistic and fatalistic in the world.

What is so painful about this negative litany of events is that the situation was largely avoidable. As we have seen, many of the crises of the past seven years, real though they may be now, were artificially created by this government, often because it failed to understand the implications of what it was doing. Certainly it was not inevitable that the Progressive Conservative party, by comparison with its Republican counterpart a more moderate entity, closer to the centre of the political spectrum, would be captured by a right-wing neoconservative faction unrepresentative of the mainstream of the party and the population, and lacking any understanding of or sympathy for the Canadian political culture.

Nor was it inevitable in 1984 that Canada's economy would decline so quickly or so severely. Many of the structural problems in the economy had been identified well before 1984. The massive transformation brought about by the globalization of markets would have occurred regardless of the party in power in Ottawa, but the devastation suffered by the Canadian economy in adapting to these changes was caused to a great extent by the government's failure to respond.

Given Canada's history, it is remarkable how little the present government did to remedy these structural problems or moderate the effects of the transformation. Instead, it reversed the course being taken by previous governments to address the issue and then, trusting in the "corrective effects" of the marketplace, largely ignored it. It was not until May 1991 that the Mulroney government began to speak of the remedial action necessary to place Canada on a competitive footing. Yet their actions demonstrate they continue to be enamoured of a reliance on market forces that simply does not work. Indeed, the laissez-faire marketplace the neoconservatives yearn for no longer exists internationally, and never really existed in Canada.

Similarly, on the constitutional front, it was hardly inevitable, only two years after a substantial package of reforms had been implemented with considerable public support, that a new government would launch a further round of negotiations. Nor was it inevitable that such a government would follow a completely different process and, even more astonishing, attack the previous consensus rather than attempt to build on it. It was not to be expected that a national government would fail to consider nation-building its prime objective.

Clearly, the Mulroney Conservatives are not to blame for every single misfortune that has befallen the country since they came to power. Yet there are few areas that remain unaffected by the neoconservative agenda and incompetence of this government. From economic policy, national unity, and social justice to the negative image of politicians, political institutions, and the political process itself, virtually all of the fundamental elements of the political system have lost credibility with ordinary Canadians.

Indeed, the Mulroney government could hardly have done more damage if it had deliberately set out to do so. The eminent British parliamentary authority K.C. Wheare describes the essential role of the legislature, and by extension the government, to legislate, legitimate, and educate. The Mulroney Conservatives have only legislated, and, as the events outlined in a previous chapter confirmed, they have often been abusive and incompetent in doing so. Their abuse of the legislative process, in turn, has led to decreased legitimacy, while their deliberate attempts to obfuscate and mislead rather than educate have led to public confusion and distrust.

The spectacle of Joe Clark defending Brian Mulroney's partisan jibes at the NDP government in Ontario just days after the Throne Speech had waxed eloquent on the need for a less partisan approach to government; of Mulroney defending Clark's "community of communities" philosophy of federalism, having trashed those same views at the 1983 leadership convention; or of Michael Wilson being described as the economic saviour of the nation, despite his introducing the most regressive and unpopular measures in generations — all speak volumes about the lack of credibility and honesty surrounding the Mulroney government.

Given the unpopularity of this government over most of its mandate, one might wonder why the decision to "stay the course" came so easily to Michael Wilson and other prominent neoconservatives in the cabinet, and why they were repeatedly able to convince Brian Mulroney to support them. A large part of the answer would seem to be that their viewpoint, while still an aberration in Canada, was receiving considerable reinforcement abroad, most notably from the Americans. The importance of the "neoconservative sweep" of the 1980s, epitomized by the rise of Margaret Thatcher and Ronald Reagan, cannot be underestimated in terms of its influence on like-minded Canadian politicians.

The Mulroney government's legacy, therefore, closely parallels that of Britain, Japan, and the United States. These three countries, dominated for more than a decade by like-minded right-wing regimes, are, like Canada, suffering the negative economic and social consequences of neoconservative initiatives.

For example, the Mulroney government's record has much in common with the Thatcher/Major, Nakasone, and Reagan/Bush regimes in terms of wealth distribution: the policies of all four administrations led to a dramatic increase in the gap between rich and poor and to the decline of the middle class.

The U.S. government's own data reveal that the decade of the 1980s witnessed the wealth share of the top 1 percent of Americans increase from 27 to 36 percent, while their incomes rose by an incredible 74.2 percent. The after-tax income of the top 10 percent of the population climbed from 29 to 33 percent, and the incomes of the bottom 10 percent dropped 10.5 percent. By 1986, the trend was already sufficiently clear for economist Lester Thurow to declare, "We're in the midst of a real surge toward inequality, the economic equivalent of tectonic plate movements."

In Britain and Japan, similar patterns emerged. By 1985, after Margaret Thatcher had had six years in power, her policies had left the average Briton poorer than the average Italian, according to the International Monetary Fund. The lowest 10 percent of the British population had seen real incomes drop nearly 10 percent in that period, while the top 20 percent enjoyed real gains of 22 percent.

In Japan, meanwhile, a super-rich class of landowning multi-millionaires was created by the uneven boom that left the average middle-class Japanese wage earner living in a tiny apartment and fantasizing about owning a bicycle.

What brought about these results, of course, was the neoconservative economic agenda. It should hardly be surprising, then, to see that the Mulroney government's economic program, based on the same laissez-faire approach to the marketplace adopted by these three countries, also mirrors their initiatives, and has had similar consequences.

Economists conclude the upward redistribution of wealth resulted from three specific types of economic policies — privatization, deregulation, and tax-bracket reductions and exemptions. All three measures have been vigorously pursued by the Mulroney government over the past seven years.

But, while many of the policies of the Mulroney government and their consequences have mirrored the experience of other contemporary right-wing regimes, the degree of political upheaval currently taking place in Canada cannot be found elsewhere. Moreover, the current national-unity crisis, which encompasses not only the constitutional issue, but the loss of faith in political institutions and politicians, is a uniquely Canadian development.

As Part One of this book illustrated, the balance of the explanation for the current malaise would seem to rest with the personality of the prime minister, the incompetence of his government, and his brokerage approach to governing. In particular, the tendency to equivocate and to avoid responsibility for their actions led the Mulroney government to blame the system for many of their own failings.

The very existence of a constitutional "issue" is a unique Canadian phenomenon. That federalism and the constitutional issues arising from it have been a central focus of Canadian political discourse in one way or another since 1867 is mystifying to other countries.

In the past twenty years, however, Canadians were in no doubt as to the rules of the game and the appropriate position of their national government in the seemingly unending struggle with the provinces. They agreed with Pierre Trudeau that provinces should speak for their citizens, and a national government should speak for all Canadians. They expected to see negotiations in which both sides compromised, not ones in which the federal government acquiesced to the provinces in all areas and gave away the store.

The arrival of the Mulroney Conservatives, with their antithetical view of federalism, removed those basic ground rules. That the national-unity issue became a crisis, then, is primarily the result of the Mulroney government's underlying approach to federalism and to the role of government.

The Meech Lake Accord was doomed to failure from the beginning, not only because of the severely flawed process by which it was achieved, but also because the government failed to recognize most Canadians do not share its commitment to the decentralized version of federalism the accord represented. As the Nixon Republicans were identified with a "states' rights" federalism that was seen as a thinly disguised attempt to pass financial responsibility to the states, loosen regulatory measures, and diminish the protection of rights, so the Conservatives' "community of communities" approach is viewed by many Canadians as a fatal move towards fewer national standards, diminished guarantees of rights, and decreased protection of less-advantaged regions.

The numerous polls since the demise of Meech Lake indicating overwhelming support for the Trudeau vision of federalism, *even within Quebec*, should have provided the Mulroney government with sufficient incentive to alter its approach in the next round. However, the appointment of Joe Clark as minister responsible for National Unity signalled that the concept of strong central government may be intolerable to the elements of Mulroney's Quebec–West coalition, regardless of the consequences.

Meanwhile, the public's loss of faith in the political system itself, and in the elected officials running it, is a separate but related phenomenon. In the end, it may actually present a *greater* threat to national unity in the sense that no future constitutional deal, regardless of its content, will be considered legitimate unless the process by which it is struck is perceived to be credible. The current debate over constituent assemblies and a national referendum reflects the difficulty politicians will have in devising an acceptable mechanism. And all of this will inevitably hinge on the credibility of the politicians involved.

Both Reagan and Thatcher were forthright about their beliefs and policies before they were elected, and remained committed to those views once in office. Both leaders were able to articulate persuasively their neoconservative vision, and to demonstrate impressive leadership skills in office.

Brian Mulroney, however, never told Canadians what he really believed or what he planned to do once he won. Admittedly, he failed to do so largely because he did not know. But his lack of a clear vision, equivocating on matters of principle, and subsequent adoption of a largely neoconservative agenda *while steadfastly denying this was the case* are unacceptable behaviour for a national leader.

It could be argued that Mulroney and his colleagues might have prevented much of the damage to their credibility and that of the political system if only they had stated their objectives clearly, rather than trying to deny and obfuscate. Instead, any remotely controversial policy initiative was denied, even while being put in place, rather than justified as necessary.

On the other hand, a more forthright approach to the neo-conservative agenda would not likely have lessened the negative public reaction to the agenda itself. Indeed, if they had accurately portrayed their real objectives in 1984, the Mulroney Conservatives would not have been elected.

It is highly instructive to note that, ultimately, after the negative effects of Thatcher and Reagan's right-wing agendas became better known and were questioned, the party in power and its leadership were forced to adapt. Margaret Thatcher was replaced by the more moderate John Major, Nakasone by Kaifu, and Ronald Reagan by George Bush, who was obliged to campaign on a "kinder, gentler America" and nevertheless lost seats in both the House and the Senate.

Although Brian Mulroney indicated in 1991 that he expected to be around to fight the next campaign, the electoral success of his government is likely to require more than a change of leadership. There is no evidence that the Canadian public has moved significantly to the right despite seven years of the neoconservative agenda. The public was extremely reluctant to support the Mulroney Conservatives in 1988, when evidence of their agenda was mounting, and this resistance was overcome only in the last few weeks of the campaign, primarily because of the lack of credible opposition and the government's empty rhetoric extolling the virtues of childcare, women's rights, and universal social programs in order to reassure a sceptical public.

Moreover, the many polls and surveys that indicate widespread despair over the fate of the country also provide compelling evidence of the lack of significant shift in positioning on the political spectrum. These polls indicate a decline in support for certain policies or programs, such as universality or bilingualism; yet, it is important to note how high the starting point was and how small the decline has been, despite trying circumstances. Some 58 percent of Canadians, for example, still support bilingualism, despite the fact they also believe it is not working well at the moment. However, believing something is not working, and not wanting it to work, are two entirely different things.

Even former supporters of the Mulroney government have come to recognize that it simply is not in step with the Canadian public. Columnist Jeffrey Simpson, a frequent apologist for the government during much of its first term in office, has become increasingly critical, not only of its ineptness, but of its political agenda.

Expressing astonishment in a *Globe and Mail* column of October 30, 1990, that the Tories still did not recognize the degree to which the Canadian public is liberal-minded, Simpson argued against their proposed privatization of Petro-Canada primarily because of the political damage he believed it would do. Having stated in the beginning that "many are the reasons for the unpopularity of this government," he went on to say: "But the core problem is quite simple. This is the most right-wing government . . . since the early 1930s." He concluded that the Conservatives were attempting to impose far too many "changes in behaviour which the political culture has traditionally resisted."

Unfortunately, the government does not appear to have been paying attention. Many members of Mulroney's cabinet still do not understand that Canadians are essentially liberal in their values and outlook, while they themselves are not. Others in the neo-conservative camp are more realistic, recognizing that cloaking their agenda in liberal rhetoric would make it more appealing to a stubborn public with antithetical, if misguided, views.

Even so, the Mulroney government did not expect the outcry that developed over the CBC, Via Rail, Rafferty-Alameda, or Oka. Its response in these instances has changed little over seven years — astonishment and anger are followed by an attempt to describe the individuals or groups who criticize as misled, unrepresentative, marginal, or unpatriotic.

Of course, the contention that Canadians remain essentially liberal raises the question of why both mainstream opposition parties, traditionally supportive of liberal values, have failed to obtain a greater degree of public support.

In part the answer would seem to be that liberals everywhere have had difficulty coming to grips with the use of their vocabulary by the neoconservatives. Mulroney & Company on numerous occasions declared themselves to be in favour of traditional liberal policies and programs — social security, universality, childcare, environmental assessment programs — and so it often has been hard for the public to see them for what they are.

This problem has been confronted by American Democrats in the past with varying degrees of success. F.D. Roosevelt's well-known lines from an earlier confrontation — "Let us not be deluded that overnight these Republicans have become the friend of the average man and woman. Can the Old Guard pass itself off as the New Deal? I think not!" — were more successful, for example, than Ted Kennedy's attempt to revive them in 1980.

Despite developing his "They are no friends of labour, of seniors, of the environment . . ." theme at length in his closing speech to the Democratic Convention, Kennedy was forced to admit it would take longer than he had hoped for the right-wing agenda to become well known. As he bitterly concluded, "The Republican Convention was awash in crocodile tears, but it is by their long record and not their recent words that you shall know them."

However the neoconservative agenda has now been unmasked in all three countries from which the Mulroney government drew comfort. Overwhelmingly favourable response to criticism of the Republican agenda by a former high-ranking supporter, Kevin Phillips, and strong support for the theme of "resurgent" liberalism as expressed by Lester Thurow and Robert Reich, suggest the American people are more than ready for a return to the politics of community over the politics of greed and selfishness. As John Kenneth Galbraith wrote in the foreword to *The Resurgent Liberal*, "Liberalism is, I think, resurgent. One reason is that people are becoming so painfully aware of the alternative."

In Canada, where these semantic problems are also becoming less relevant as the consequences of the Mulroney government's policies become evident, several obstacles still remain if liberals are to translate the public's philosophical support for their values into electoral success. These hurdles involve both the content of the liberal message and the way it is expressed. The problem, simply put, is the perceived lack of credible spokespersons for the liberal alternative.

In 1988, despite majority opposition to the free-trade agreement, the federal Liberal Party was not able to convince Canadians that it had either a coherent alternative agenda or a competent team to manage it. The NDP attempted to present itself as the "real" liberal alternative and downplay its socialist leanings, but failed to accomplish either.

The next election, most observers agree, will see a massive rejection of Brian Mulroney and his Conservative government. But few analysts are prepared to make predictions about the nature of the government that will replace them. While the Bloc Québécois and the Reform Party pose a serious threat to the Conservatives, who will most certainly lose seats to them in both Quebec and the West, the current fragmentation of party support along regional lines means that neither the Liberals — who will likely dominate in Atlantic Canada and split the vote with the Bloc in Quebec and the NDP in Ontario — nor the NDP — who will gain seats in the West — can be assured of forming a government.

Unless one or both mainstream parties attempting to embody the liberal message demonstrates the capacity to overcome these hurdles, the next election may once again leave the vast majority of liberal-minded Canadians underrepresented and the country deprived of a strong national government.

Until very recently, the conventional wisdom in Canada attributed "core" levels of support to the three major national parties, levels below which they could not fall in public-opinion polls because of hard-core support from a certain percentage of the population. In all three cases, this core level of support was not sufficient for a party to form a government. Therefore, past federal elections were won by the Liberal Party by combining their traditional core vote — at roughly 33 to 35 percent, the highest of the three parties — with a percentage of the uncommitted or "swing" voters. The size of Liberal victories was determined by the percentage of the swing vote they could attract, given that the swing vote was more likely to turn to them than to the other parties.

Although somewhat oversimplified, the 1984 and 1988 Conservative victories can be explained by that party's unprecedented ability to build on its core support, not only by attracting a larger share than usual of the swing vote (especially in Quebec), but also by attracting first-time support from traditional Liberals.

Polls measuring voter preference during the past two years suggest that this conventional wisdom about core support may need to be re-examined. Moreover, they clearly indicate the Canadian public's support for liberalism is not yet being translated into electoral support for either mainstream opposition party, even though the Liberals have been jockeying with the NDP for first place for most of that time.

For most of the past year and a half, the Conservatives have consistently fallen well below their traditional core level of support, forcing analysts to conclude that even some of the party's most ardent supporters have been alienated, at least temporarily. As a result, the party finds itself in third place, just ahead of the Reform Party. However, the important question still to be resolved is where the discontented Conservative vote will finally position itself. At present, the difference between the party's actual level of support and its traditional core level is virtually identical to the level of support being identified with the Reform Party. While it is unclear whether the present level of support for Reform is reflective of the well-known interelection "parking" phenomenon, or whether it is indeed a solid trend, it is evident that no disenchanted Conservative core votes have been directed towards the other two mainstream parties, nor are they likely to be.

Meanwhile, for most of this same period, after short-lived and predictable increases in support related to the publicity of their leadership campaigns, both the Liberals and the New Democrats have remained at or slightly below traditional core levels of support on a national basis. The importance of this finding cannot be overestimated. Despite the fact these two parties find themselves in first and second place, respectively, in the polls, they are far from having achieved a sufficient level of support to form a government, particularly as the three-party system traditionally works to their disadvantage.

In other words, despite the unprecedented unpopularity of the current government, neither of the two mainstream parties has been able to capitalize on voter disenchantment and build significantly on its traditional base. Indeed, in some surveys, they have barely held on to that base. Not surprisingly, the level of undecided voters in many polls has been well over the traditional 20 to 25 percent; by late 1991, it had reached an unheard-of 37 percent and showed little sign of abating, suggesting that a significant proportion of potential liberal-minded supporters were parking their vote to register their displeasure with the current alternatives.

At the same time, the "volatility index" of the Canadian electorate (a measure of the willingness of voters to change their party allegiance over time), always high in Canada compared to other Western democracies, has increased significantly. In short, voter attachment to political parties is weak and easily shifted.

In addition, evidence from the last two federal elections and various provincial elections suggests that the conventional wisdom concerning traditional sources of support for the mainstream parties may also need to be revisited. Ethnic groups in particular appear to be diversifying their partisan attachment, especially intergenerationally, while women and youth appear to be decreasing their attachment to any party.

This evident dissatisfaction with the opposition mainstream political parties has been manifested not only in the number of undecided voters and the increased support for fringe parties, but also in the growing trend towards citizen involvement in advocacy groups and single-issue movements. As a number of recent studies have documented, on issues ranging from the environment to abortion, an increasing number of Canadians have chosen to work outside of the structure of traditional political parties to achieve their objectives, in large measure because they have concluded these parties cannot adequately represent their interests, despite the fact many of their positions are supported by party platforms.

The explanation for this continued failure of liberal proponents to capture voter support lies partly with the content of their message and partly with their failure to update their vocabulary and methods of communication.

Survival, as Darwin demonstrated, is primarily a matter of successful adaptation to changing circumstances. In Canada, both mainstream political parties and politicians appear to be having difficulty coming to grips with this fundamental truth, either because they have failed to identify correctly the changes taking place or because they have failed to devise an appropriate response to these changes that is, nevertheless, consistent with their traditional values and principles.

The way political parties attempt to increase their popular support and forge or renew coalitions will be vital to their success or failure. Part of the legacy of the Mulroney years has clearly been an increasingly sceptical, cynical, and disenchanted electorate. If any lesson was learned from the Meech Lake débâcle, it was that the Canadian public expects not only more consultation on important issues than the government was prepared to entertain, but meaningful consultation, not a public-relations exercise to legitimize decisions already taken. Political parties, it would appear, must give the appearance of openness, both in terms of grass-roots support and internal decision making.

After enduring seven years of dishonesty and deception at the highest levels, Canadians are demanding that politicians representing a party, and the processes by which a party selects its candidates, must be above reproach. Although the attempt by the Reform Party to weed out "undesirable" candidates through a formal screening process was a ludicrous overreaction to this concern, it nevertheless indicates an awareness of the importance of the issue that the mainstream parties have yet to demonstrate.

As they consider reform of their internal constitutional and electoral processes, the two mainstream opposition parties will need to respond to this new reality carefully. This is particularly true in light of the numerous and highly publicized imbroglios that bedevilled the Liberals' 1988 candidate-nomination processes and subsequent delegate selection for leadership conventions, ominous signs of which are again emerging in Metro Toronto.

Canadians have also become thoroughly tired of equivocation, and expect politicians to offer forthright positions on the issues. The consistency of their message and their continued commitment to those positions over time would appear to be almost as important as the nature of the positions themselves. Attempts by the Liberals and NDP in the recent past to cover the waterfront on the constitutional issue, and the apparent reneging of Jean Chrétien on the GST position he had taken throughout the leadership campaign, suggest this lesson has not yet been learned.

In sum, all of these new political realities must be addressed by mainstream opposition parties and their leaders. However, attention to process alone will not ensure a return to liberal government in Canada. Canadians know the world is changing. They know Canada has a number of deep-seated structural problems that must be addressed in order for this country to meet the challenges of the twenty-first century. They know hard choices must be made, and they want to see a frank discussion of the options. They also know that neither the Mulroney Conservatives nor their neoconservative philosophy are up to the challenge. The problem is that Canadians are not convinced that the proponents of liberalism have the answers either.

Liberal-minded politicians fail to inspire confidence in Canadian voters primarily because, even when they have articulated specific policy proposals or initiatives, they have seemed unable, in recent years, to place these disparate measures within the context of an overarching philosophical framework that speaks to contemporary values and problems. Liberalism, in brief, currently appears to many observers in Canada and elsewhere to lack the vision and the vocabulary necessary to demonstrate relevance.

By contrast, neoconservatives everywhere have been extremely successful at rewriting history, particularly in terms of the liberal record. More importantly, they have created and gained acceptance for what Robert Reich terms the "parables" of liberalism and conservatism — simplistic explanations of reality — because they tell a story that is comforting and easy to understand.

Liberalism, according to neoconservatives, failed because it was too permissive in its approach to social policy and too lax and undisciplined in its handling of the economy. At the core of this parable are "the perils of liberal indulgence and permissiveness" that led to "social excess and public irresponsibility." The solution, of course, is simply to impose discipline and order on the chaos left behind by these profligate liberals. If strong measures are taken, everything will be all right, and the world will return to the way it was.

This punitive approach obviously holds considerable appeal. Once citizens "pay" for the sins of the past, the rewards will more than justify the temporary costs and short-term pain. Not surprisingly, the parable is also dependent on a paternalistic scenario in which supporters are the "we" who will do the imposing, and everyone else — workers, the poor, unions, and Third World countries — are the "they" who must pay the price and be punished.

In the past, one of the great strengths of liberalism was its ability to modify its message and adapt its policies to changing circumstances without losing sight of its fundamental values and principles. A succession of liberal spokespersons was able to articulate a new vision that inspired citizens and gave them a sense of communal purpose and identity — Macdonald's "National Policy," Pearson's "Middle Power Role," and Trudeau's "Just Society." This "mission statement" provided the overall explanation for the policies and the role of government necessary to accomplish this objective.

The failure of contemporary liberals to meet this challenge was addressed by New York governor Mario Cuomo in his keynote address to the Democratic Convention in San Francisco in 1984. Having delivered a blistering attack on the Republican record, and anticipating another Democratic defeat, Cuomo urged his fellow liberals to begin immediately the task of articulating the new liberal public philosophy. Correctly surmising that such a process would be difficult but essential if the party were to make gains in 1988, he concluded: "For 50 years we Democrats created a better future for our children, using traditional Democratic principles as a fixed beacon, giving us direction and purpose, but constantly innovating and adapting to new realities. . . . It is our job to do this again. We must make Americans remember how futures are built."

Today, Canadian liberals are still attempting to distinguish themselves from the government by criticism rather than proactive policies, clinging perversely to the notion that party platforms should be released during election campaigns and not before.

Despite overwhelming evidence that Canadian voters are searching in vain for a meaningful alternative, Canadian liberals have given little evidence of their readiness to assume the task of governing.

To do so, they will need to resolve a number of internal conflicts about the direction of contemporary liberalism. The appropriate degree of government intervention in the economy, the proper balance of federal and provincial responsibilities, the definition of social-policy objectives as springboard or safety net, and the redefinition of Canada's role in the global context — all of these issues require urgent attention if the underlying public philosophy of liberalism is to be made meaningful and coherent.

The need to redefine the liberal message is particulary significant in a period of economic restraint. In the past, liberalism has been perceived to be successful in periods of strong economic growth, when it could implement its social and cultural agenda without undue concern for the cost. As the Canadian and global economies retrench, liberalism must respond to the public's concern that it is only interested in the redistribution of wealth. Liberals, in short, must prove that they are able to create wealth as well as to allocate it.

In addition, the return to a liberal vision of government — one that is not all-pervasive but as interventionist as necessary to achieve liberal objectives — will need to be supported by a more sophisticated and realistic alternative to the conservative parable. Given the neoconservative legacy of individualism — epitomized by the denial of private and governmental responsibility for the less fortunate and the pursuit of an alleged "meritocracy" regardless of the social costs — one such theme may be that of *interdependence*, both globally and domestically. Another may be *responsible government*. Both would allow the concepts of equal sharing, sacrifice, and obligation to be melded with the more traditional liberal values of tolerance, equal opportunity, and individual rights. Most importantly, the new liberal parable must demonstrate two things: first, that it is aware of current problems and prepared to solve rather than ignore them; and, second, that agreement on the problems does not mean agreement on the solutions. There must be a clear liberal alternative to the neoconservative approach to such issues as declining competitiveness and increasing social-program costs.

As this study has demonstrated, the retreat from governance has been no less extreme in Canada than in the United States. The lengthy delay in recognizing this reality has been in considerable measure attributable to the lack of a forceful liberal alternative. Canadian liberals, for example, might profitably focus on objectives such as "fair and equitable" economic growth, keeping in mind the liberal view of wealth creation as a means to achieve social well-being, rather than as an end in itself. An emphasis on investment in human resources and expanding choices for workers; on a new "partnership" between government, business, and labour; and on a renewed emphasis on creativity and innovation to produce a knowledge-based economy in which higher-value products, rather than lower wages and benefits, are the key to increased productivity and competitiveness, would seem to offer great promise.

Needless to say, this approach requires an integration of social and economic policy objectives, in which childcare, retraining, pension reform, a clean environment, incentives for research and development, and the elimination of internal trade barriers must be considered integrally related tools to achieve these objectives. Similarly, foreign-policy objectives will need to be framed in terms of the integration of development, peace and security, and environmental concerns in order to provide a meaningful alternative to the neoconservative vision of the new world order.

The message is clear. The political system and its institutions are essentially sound. Canadians are neither cranky nor difficult. Rather, they are disillusioned and dismayed by the behaviour and the legacy of the Mulroney government. They are not demanding, but discriminating. During the experience of the last seven years, Canadians have been forced to lower their expectations, but their standards have remained high.

Those who suggest that voters' expectations have become unreasonable, or that they are sending mixed messages through public-opinion polls, have missed the point. Canadians do not want their country run like a business. Nor do they want the people in charge to ignore the wishes and the values of the people who have elected them. They have indicated very clearly their support for strong leadership, but it must be based on liberal principles and an acceptable, comprehensive national vision. It is not Canada or its political system, but Brian Mulroney and his government who have been found wanting.

Nor do Canadians believe the situation is hopeless. Rather, they believe it can be salvaged by the right party with the right leader. They are only unsure as to who represents the right choice. Proponents of liberalism, languishing in disfavour in the wilderness for the past seven years, have never had a better opportunity to redefine the liberal message and win the enthusiastic support of voters for their efforts, but it is no sure thing. The next election is theirs and the country's to win.

Bibliography

Aucoin, P. "The Machinery of Government." In D. Taras and L. Pal, eds., *Prime Ministers and Premiers: Political Leadership and Public Policy in Canada*, pp. 50–68. Toronto: Prentice-Hall, 1988.

Bain, G. "The Form Chart Still Favours a Tory Ascendancy." *Report on Business*, September 1986, pp. 21–23.

Beauchesne, E. "Federal cuts threaten medicare, provinces say." *Ottawa Citizen*, June 11, 1991.

Behiels, M. *The Meech Lake Primer*. Ottawa: University of Ottawa Press, 1989.

Bercuson, D., J. Granatstein, and W.R. Young. *Sacred Trust?* Toronto: Doubleday, 1986.

Campbell, C. "Mulroney's Broker Politics: The Ultimate in Politicized Incompetence." In Gollner and Salee, eds., *Canada Under Mulroney: An End of Term Report*, pp. 309–35. Montreal: Véhicule Press, 1988.

Canadian Centre for Policy Alternatives. *Canada Under the Tory Government*. September 1988.

Caplan, G., M. Kirby, and H. Segal. *Election*. Scarborough, ON: Prentice-Hall, 1989.

Carleton School of Public Administration. *How Ottawa Spends*. Annual. Ottawa: 1984–91.

Citizens' Forum on Canada's Future. *Report*. July 1991.

Clarke, H., J. Jenson, L. Leduc and J. Pammett. *Absent Mandate*. Toronto: Gage Educational Publishing Company, 1991.

Cohen, A. *A Deal Undone*. Vancouver/Toronto: Douglas and McIntyre, 1990.

Courchesne, T. "Decentralization a Central Effect of Trade Deal." Address to All-European Canadian Studies Conference, the Hague, January 1991.

d'Aquino, T. "The Canada–U.S.–Mexico Consultations on Free Trade." Speech delivered to World Forum on Mexico, Mexico City, November 28, 1990.

Department of Finance. *Budget Papers*. Annual. Ottawa: 1985–91.

Doerr, A. *The Machinery of Government in Canada*. Toronto: Methuen, 1981.

Dungan, P., and S. Murphy. "Outlook for the Canadian Economy Through 2002." Institute for Policy Analysis, University of Toronto, January 1991.

Economic Council of Canada. *Good Jobs, Bad Jobs*. Annual Report, 1990; *Legacies*, Annual Report, 1989.

External Affairs and International Trade Canada. *Statement by the Secretary of State for External Affairs*, December 20, 1989.

Fagan, D. "Tax Man Goes Soft on Companies." *Globe and Mail*, June 1, 1991.

Fleming, R. *Canadian Legislatures*. Hull: Les Editions Marquis, 1988.

Forbes, H.D. "Hartz-Horowitz at Twenty." *Canadian Journal of Political Science*, December 1988: 795–812.

Fraser, G. *Playing for Keeps*. Toronto: McClelland and Stewart, 1989.

_____. "Tories' Good News Agenda Falls Prey to Confusion." *Globe and Mail*, June 3, 1991.

French, R. *How Ottawa Decides*. Toronto: James Lorimer, 1984.

Frizzell, A., J. Pammett, and A. Westell. *The Canadian General Election of 1988*. Ottawa: Carleton University Press, 1989.

Gessell, P. "Joe Clark's Community of Communities." *Ottawa Citizen*, April 20, 1991.

Global Economics Ltd. "The Federal 1989 Budget: An Analysis of its Distributional Impact." May 1989.

Goar, C. "A Year After Meech: The Malady Lingers On." *Toronto Star*, June 15, 1991.

_____. "The Blueing of Canada." *Toronto Star*, December 31, 1987.

A. Gollner and D. Salée. *Canada Under Mulroney*. Hull: Les Editions Marquis, 1988.

Grady, P. "Taking Stock of Tory Tax Reform." Paper presented to the 25th annual meeting of the Canadian Economic Association, June 2, 1991.

Gratton, Michel. *So, What Are the Boys Saying?* Toronto: McGraw-Hill Ryerson, 1987.

Gregg, A., and M. Posner. *The Big Picture*. Toronto: Macfarlane Walter and Ross, 1990.

Hiebert, J. *Summary of Findings*. Royal Commission on Electoral Reform, 1991.

Horowitz, G. "Conservatism, Liberalism and Socialism in Canada: An Interpretation." *Canadian Journal of Political Science*, May 1966.

House of Commons. *Debates*: April 8, 1991, pp. 19139–56; April 11, 1991, pp. 19341–46; June 17, 1991, pp. 1892–94.

_____. Legislative Committee on Bill C-40. *Proceedings*, Issue 2, January 31, 1989.

_____. Standing Committee on Foreign Affairs and Defence. *For Whose Benefit?* 1986.

_____. Standing Committee on Justice and the Solicitor General. *Proceedings* 21 (December 12, 1989): 23–25.

Howard, R. "Defence Spending Rises as Foreign Aid Slashed." *Globe and Mail*, February 27, 1991.

Hoy, Claire. *Friends in High Places*. Toronto: Key Porter Books, 1987.

Kymlica, W. *Liberalism, Community and Culture*. Oxford: Clarendon Press, 1989.

Liberal Caucus Research Bureau. *Honesty and Integrity in Government: The Mulroney Record*. Ottawa: July 1988.

Library of Parliament. Information and Technical Services Branch. "Closure in the Canadian House of Commons," Doc. No. 31e, April 1991.

_____. "Vacancies in the House of Commons Since June 25, 1968," Doc. No. 63.

_____. "Ministerial Resignations, April 20, 1968–June, 1984," Doc. No. 61.

_____. Research Branch.

"The Canada Assistance Plan," MR-54E, February 1990.

"Canada-U.S. FTA: Major Issues," BP 182-E, December 1988.

"Canada-U.S. Trade Disputes," CIR 91-1E, January 1991.

"Child Care in Canada," CIR 87-11E, March 1991.

"Conflict of Interest Rules for Federal Legislators," CIR 79-3E, April 1991.

"Federal Deficit and Debt," BP 176-E, April 1988.

"Federal Spending: Changing Trends," CIR 87-2E, March 1991.

"Federal-Provincial Fiscal Arrangements," CIR 86-23E, February 1991.

"Homelessness in Canada," CIR 89-8E, January 1991.

"Housing: Current Issues," BP 229-E, April 1990.

"The Meech Lake Accord: A Constitutional Conundrum," BP 186-E, January 1989.

"The 1991 Federal Budget," BP 251-E, February 1991.

"Official Bilingualism in Canada," CIR 86-11E, February 1991.

"OPEC and Canada's Oil Industry," MR 65-E, September 1990.

"The Persian Gulf Conflict: Implications for Canadian Defence Policy," MR-86E, March 1991.

"Reforming the House of Commons," BP 117-E, November 1984.

"Regional Development in Canada," CIR 88-13E, January 1991.

"Research and Development in Canada," BP 213-E, July 1989.

"South Africa," CIR 87-12E, February 1991.

"The Standing Orders of the House of Commons: Highlights of the 1991 Amendments," BP 265-E, June 1991.

"Tax Expenditures and Public Policy," MR-27E, December 1988.

Lipset, S.M. *Continental Divide. The Values and Institutions of the U.S. and Canada.* New York: Routledge, 1990.

Love, A. "Multiculturalism Can Spur National Unity." *Policy Options*, February 1991: 21–24.

MacGregor, R. "Frustration Makes Us Think of Impeachment." *Ottawa Citizen*, February 15, 1991.

Maclean's. Special Election Edition. November 14, 1988.

_____. "The Rising Fury over Bilingualism," April 22, 1991, pp. 16–20.

Martin, P., A. Gregg, and G. Perlin. *Contenders: The Tory Quest for Power*. Scarborough, ON: Prentice-Hall, 1983.

Maser, P. "Rebuild Nation, Disillusioned Canadians Say." *Ottawa Citizen*, June 1, 1991.

Morton, D. "Mulroney Courts Disaster If He Heeds Right-wing Lobby." *Toronto Star*, December 11, 1989.

_____. "Decentralization Bid Doesn't Match Country's Mood." *Ottawa Citizen*, June 27, 1991.

Mulroney. B. *Where I Stand*. Toronto: McClelland and Stewart, 1983.

National Council of Welfare. "The GST and the Poor." January 1990.

———. "The Canada Assistance Plan: No Time for Cuts." Winter 1991.

Ottawa Citizen. "Foreign Aid Cuts: Still More Lowering of Goals" (editorial), March 9, 1991.

Pammett, J., and J.-L. Pepin. *Political Education in Canada.* Ottawa: Institute for Research on Public Policy, 1988.

Pammett, J., and M.S. Whittington. *Foundations of Political Culture.* Toronto: Macmillan, 1976.

Phillips, K. *The Politics of Rich and Poor.* Toronto: Harper Collins, 1990.

Prime Minister's Office. "Notes for a Statement by the Prime Minister in the House of Commons." September 9, 1985.

Reich, R. *The Resurgent Liberal.* Toronto: Random House, 1989.

Ritchie, G. "A Canada–Mexico–U.S. Free Trade Agreement: Watch Out!" *Business Quarterly* 55/22 (Winter 1991): 18–19.

Sears, V. "CBC About to Lose its Power to Promote National Unity." *Toronto Star,* June 12, 1990.

The Senate. Standing Committee on Social Affairs, Science and Technology. *Children in Poverty.* January 1991.

Shiffrin, L. "Tories Trying to Bolster Sensitive, Caring Image." *Ottawa Citizen,* August 14, 1986.

Simpson, J. *Spoils of Power: The Politics of Patronage.* Toronto: Collins, 1988.

Speech from the Throne. 33rd Parliament, 1st Session. September 1984; 2nd Session, 34th Parliament, April 3, 1989; 3rd Session, 34th Parliament, May 13, 1991.

Stasiulis, D.K. "The Symbolic Mosaic Reaffirmed: Multiculturalism Policy." In *How Ottawa Spends* (Ottawa: Carleton School of Public Administration, 1988–89).

Statistics Canada. *Canadian Economic Observer: Historical Supplement, 1988–89.*

———. "Children and Poverty," Fact Sheets #1-5 in *Poverty in Profile, 1988.*

Stevenson, M. "Ideology and Unstable Party Identification in Canada: Limited Rationality in a Brokerage Party System." *Canadian Journal of Political Science,* December 1987: 813–49.

Toronto Dominion Bank, Dept. of Economic Research. *Report on the 1991 Federal Budget.* February 1991.

United Nations Development Programme. *Annual Report* (1991).

Walkom, T. "Deficit Hype Hides Lean, Mean Tory Agenda." *Toronto Star,* March 25, 1991.

Wallace, B. "Political Breakdown." *Maclean's,* April 22, 1991, pp. 12–13.

Whyte, J. "The Future of Canada's Constitutional Reform Process." In J.C. Courtney and D. Smith, eds., *After Meech Lake,* pp. 237–50. Saskatoon: Fifth House Publications, 1991.

Wilson-Smith, A. "A Call to Arms: Canadians Debate their Battle Role." *Maclean's,* January 28, 1991, pp. 34–37.

———. "The Private P.M." *Maclean's,* June 10, 1991, pp. 14–22.

Young, C. "Shifting Blame Won't Help Save Confederation." *Ottawa Citizen,* December 4, 1990.

Index